# France, humanitarian intervention and the responsibility to protect

MANCHESTER
1824

Manchester University Press

# France, humanitarian intervention and the responsibility to protect

Eglantine Staunton

Manchester University Press

Published byManchester University Press
Oxford Road, Manchester M13 9PL

www.manchesteruniversitypress.co.uk

British Library Cataloguing-in-Publication Data
A catalogue record for this book is available from the British Library

ISBN 978 1 5261 4240 5 hardback
ISBN 978 1 5261 6702 6 paperback

First published 2020
Paperback published 2022

Typeset
by Toppan Best-set Premedia Limited

*To Michael and Juliette, my two sunshines*

# Contents

# List of figures, graphs and tables

**Figures**

**Graphs**

## Tables

# Preface

France has been a central actor in human protection, yet the existing literature has too often focused on Anglo-Saxon states or states that are wary of its development. In order to address this gap, this book provides an original and much-needed account of France's relationship to human protection since the 1980s. It analyses a tale of two norms using an innovative theoretical framework. The first is 'France's domestic norm of human protection', and the second is the dominant international principle or norm of human protection at the time (chiefly humanitarian intervention in the 1990s and the responsibility to protect (R2P) in the 2000s). Through this tale of two norms, and also thanks to elite interviews with key actors such as Gareth Evans and Bernard Kouchner and an analysis of fourteen case studies, the book reshapes our understanding of the development and influence of key principles and norms of human protection. It also corrects prevailing assumptions about France's foreign policy and allows us to anticipate its future foreign policy more accurately. Last but not least, by showing how important it is to pay more attention to the interplay between domestic and international norms and building an innovative framework that can be used beyond the analysis of France and human protection, the book makes a key contribution to the literature on norms and International Relations theory more generally. The book is therefore an essential read for anyone interested in human protection, peace and conflict studies, France, foreign policy analysis, International Relations and norm diffusion.

# Acknowledgements

I would first like to thank my colleagues for their invaluable feedback and support. I am particularly grateful to Tim Dunne and Richard Devetak for their instrumental guidance throughout this project, and also for their mentoring over the years. I am also grateful to Luke Glanville, Adrian Gallagher, Chris Reus-Smit, Alex Bellamy, Phil Orchard, Jason Ralph, Jack Holland, Graeme Davies and the anonymous reviewers for their valuable input and support. Additionally, I am indebted to the Hon. Gareth Evans, Dr Bernard Kouchner, Professor Mario Bettati and Roland Dumas for taking the time to meet me and answer my questions. Special thanks also go to Tony Mason and Manchester University Press for believing in this book. This research was partly funded by the University of Queensland and the Australian Government: I am grateful to both. I am also grateful to SAGE Publications Ltd, under their Green Open Access Sharing and Archiving Policy, for permission to reproduce sections of Eglantine Staunton, "France and the responsibility to protect: a tale of two norms", *International Relations* 32/3 (2018), 366–387 (copyright © 2018 The Author(s), DOI: 10.1177/0047117818773857) in the book, in particular in Chapter 1. Similarly, I thank Taylor and Francis Ltd for permission (4517530699360) to reproduce sections of Eglantine Staunton, "Two decades later: understanding the French response to the Rwandan genocide", *Modern & Contemporary France* 24/3 (2016), 299–315 (copyright © 2016 Association for the Study of Modern & Contemporary France, DOI: 10.1080/09639489.2016.1180508) in Chapter 3.

From a more personal point of view, I thank my family for supporting me throughout this exciting yet challenging process but more generally for always being there for me. In particular, I want to thank my patient, kind, funny and caring husband Michael. There are not enough words to express how grateful I am to him for helping me – and being there – every step of the way. Michael's beautiful soul, his constant positivity and his

unwavering faith in me have not only allowed me to undertake this project; they have made my work infinitely better. Thank you also to our wonderful daughter Juliette, who brings me so much joy and inspires me to always aim higher while reminding me of what matters.

# Abbreviations

| | |
|---|---|
| BRICS | Brazil, Russia, India, China and South Africa |
| CAR | Central African Republic |
| CSDP | Common Security and Defence Policy |
| DRC | Democratic Republic of the Congo |
| EC | European Communities |
| ECOWAS | Economic Community of West African States |
| EU | European Union |
| EUFOR | European Force |
| EUROFOR | European Rapid Operational Force |
| EUTM | European Union Training Mission |
| FOMUC | Force Multinationale en Centrafrique / Multinational Force in the Central African Republic |
| FRY | Federal Republic of Yugoslavia |
| ICISS | International Commission on Intervention and State Sovereignty |
| ICRtoP | International Coalition for the Responsibility to Protect |
| IICK | Independent International Commission on Kosovo |
| IISS | International Institute for Strategic Studies |
| ISAF | International Security Assistance Force |
| ISIL | Islamic State of Iraq and the Levant |
| KFOR | Kosovo Force |
| MICOPAX | Mission de Consolidation de la Paix en Centrafrique / Mission for the Consolidation of Peace in Central African Republic |
| MINURCAT | United Nations Mission in the Central African Republic and Chad |
| MINURSO | United Nations Mission for the Referendum in Western Sahara |

| | |
|---|---|
| MINUSCA | United Nations Multidimensional Integrated Stabilization Mission in the Central African Republic |
| MISCA | International Support Mission to the Central African Republic |
| MONUC | United Nations Organization Mission in the Democratic Republic of the Congo |
| MONUSCO | United Nations Organization Stabilization Mission in the Democratic Republic of the Congo |
| NATO | North Atlantic Treaty Organization |
| NGO | non-governmental organisation |
| OSCE | Organization for Security and Co-operation in Europe |
| P3 | France, the United States and the United Kingdom |
| P5 | France, the United Kingdom, the United States, China and Russia |
| RECAMP | Renforcement des Capacités Africaines de Maintien de la Paix / Reinforcement of African Peacekeeping Capacities |
| RPF | Rwandan Patriotic Front |
| RRF | Rapid Reaction Force |
| R2P | responsibility to protect |
| SFOR | Stabilisation Force |
| UN | United Nations |
| UNAMIC | United Nations Advance Mission in Cambodia |
| UNAMID | United Nations–African Union Mission in Darfur |
| UNAMIR | United Nations Assistance Mission for Rwanda |
| UNIFIL | United Nations Interim Force in Lebanon |
| UNIKOM | United Nations Iraq–Kuwait Observation Mission |
| UNMEE | United Nations Mission in Ethiopia and Eritrea |
| UNMIBH | United Nations Mission in Bosnia Herzegovina |
| UNMIK | United Nations Interim Administration Mission in Kosovo |
| UNMIL | United Nations Mission in Liberia |
| UNMIS | United Nations Mission in Sudan |
| UNOCI | United Nations Operation in Côte d'Ivoire |
| UNOSOM | United Nations Operation in Somalia |
| UNPROFOR | United Nations Protection Force |
| UNTAC | United Nations Transitional Authority in Cambodia |
| UNTSO | United Nations Truce Supervision Organisation |

# Introduction

Since the end of the Cold War, the international community has increasingly made human protection a priority. France has been at the forefront of these efforts: it helped to kick off the debates on human protection at the United Nations (UN) in the 1980s; has spent years involving itself in a variety of complex human protection efforts worldwide; stood firmly against the Iraq War; leads the way on the responsibility of the permanent members of the UN Security Council not to veto resolutions on mass atrocity situations, even though it is one of the five permanent members which holds such a veto; and is the current penholder for the situations in Burundi,[1] the Central African Republic (CAR), Côte d'Ivoire, the Democratic Republic of the Congo (DRC), Lebanon, Mali and, to a certain extent, Syria and Bosnia and Herzegovina.

Yet when President François Hollande announced in 2015 that France would intervene for humanitarian purposes in Mali and the CAR, some international commentators were quick to argue that the world was witnessing the emergence of a "Hollande doctrine" (Tisdall 2013). By associating France's will to protect with the French President at the time and underestimating the role it had played in human protection in the previous decades, these narratives considerably overlook the commitment to human protection that has informed French foreign policy since the end of the Cold War.

They also hint at a broader gap in the existing literature: when it comes to human protection, the focus is too often on Anglo-Saxon states or states that are wary of its development (in particular, Brazil, Russia, India, China and South Africa – more commonly known as the BRICS) (see for example Vaughn and Dunne 2015; Ziegler 2016). As a result, even when studies stop to look at France, it is to focus on particular interventions, in specific geographical domains and historical moments. For instance, when it comes to analysing the emergence and development of humanitarian intervention during the 1990s, authors such as Allen and Styan (2000), Kroslak (2007) and Zic (2000) help us better understand France's involvement in specific humanitarian crises such as those in Rwanda and former Yugoslavia or during specific periods of the 1990s. Yet they do not analyse France's overall role in the emergence and development of humanitarian intervention – and the rationale behind it – throughout the decade. A review of the literature available on the 2000s and the 2010s demonstrates that this shortfall is not confined to the 1990s, but is in fact both widespread and ongoing.

These oversights are problematic for two main reasons. First, they prevent us from fully understanding the development of key international principles and norms such as humanitarian intervention and the responsibility to protect (R2P) by overlooking the role played by France over the years. Additionally, they preclude us from fully analysing France's past and current foreign policy since they lead us to underestimate the role played both by France's commitment to human protection, and the growing influence that international principles and norms have had on France's conception and practice of human protection. This book thus tells the much-needed story of France and human protection in order to address these shortfalls.

It should be clear that its focus is on the use of force (consensual or not) for humanitarian purposes. The year 1987 is used as a starting point since it corresponds to the emergence of what this book describes as France's domestic norm of human protection and to the beginning of France's efforts – normatively, diplomatically and militarily – to facilitate the authorisation and undertaking of military interventions for humanitarian purposes by the international community. Additionally, from an international point of view and as discussed in more depth in the section "Humanitarian intervention" below, the late 1980s and early 1990s correspond to when the UN Security Council began consistently authorising the use of force for humanitarian purposes by broadening what constitutes a threat to international peace and security.

Rather than focusing on France in general, this book mainly concentrates on the various French executives – defined as the President at the time, his key advisors and his ministerial office-holders. This focus can be explained by the fact that throughout the Fifth Republic (which has been in place since 1958), the President has been in charge of foreign affairs, to the point that foreign policy is often referred to as *domaine réservé* (reserved domain) of the President.[2] Yet, in view of the fact that the government (understood as the ministerial office-holders and their advisors) was also allocated some power by the Constitution in terms of foreign policy and that this became particularly important during *cohabitations*,[3] the focus of the book is on the executive as a whole.

It should however be clear that the idea here is not to use 'executive' as an umbrella term that would suggest that it has been a static and uniform entity throughout time. It is expected that different executives will have diverse agendas and priorities. Even within each executive, it is common for members to disagree on specific issues because of competing goals or even personal beliefs. Additionally, ministerial office-holders and advisors change throughout each presidency: for instance, as shown in more detail in the Appendix, François Mitterrand had seven different prime ministers and four ministers of foreign affairs; Jacques Chirac had four prime ministers and five ministers of foreign affairs; Nicolas Sarkozy had one prime minister and three ministers of foreign affairs; and Hollande had two prime ministers and two ministers of foreign affairs. Each minister came with their own advisors. Consequently, this book specifies as far as possible which members of the executive it is referring to and pays particular attention to the President, the Minister of Foreign Affairs and the Permanent Representative to the UN because they are central actors of human protection. When the term 'executive' (or even 'France') is used, it refers to the official position put forward at the time to the UN and the international community more generally by these key members on behalf of France. The use of the term 'executives' in its plural form is used to emphasise that despite the changes, the official position promoted remained unchanged.

## Human protection

Before going further, it is necessary to clarify what is meant by 'human protection'. To borrow the words of the former UN Secretary General Ban Ki-Moon, human protection is "a subset of the more encompassing concept of human security ... [which] addresses more immediate threats to the survival of individuals and groups" (2011). The use of such terminology in this book can appear surprising since many practitioners and academics consider the expression to be too vague, and thus favour more specific terms – such as protection of civilians, R2P or atrocity prevention – in order to showcase the actual focus of their work.

While it is essential to distinguish key concepts such as those above, the expression 'human protection' remains the one best suited for this analysis for two reasons. First, it reflects the fact that the various French executives in power since the 1980s have used a similar broad approach. As this book shows, rather than talking specifically about the protection of civilians, R2P or atrocity prevention, they mainly refer to the importance of promoting human rights – in particular, the right to life – and the associated duty and right to intervene to protect endangered populations. Second, this terminology allows the analysis of France's relationship to various domestic and international principles and norms that emerged before – or in parallel with – each other and which aim, or aimed, to protect populations under immediate threats to survival. Therefore this book conceptualises human protection as a regime "comprising principles, norms, rules, and decision-making procedures" (Bellamy 2016, 113), and within this regime, it focuses on humanitarian intervention, R2P and what it refers to as France's domestic norm of human protection.

### Humanitarian intervention

Humanitarian intervention has always generated controversy and probably always will. In this book, it is defined as an international principle rather than a concept or a norm.[4] This can be explained by the fact that it faced international contestation in the second half of the 1990s, which prevented it from reaching the status of international norm. Yet it was more than a concept, for it began to create an 'oughtness' to react to human suffering and influenced perpetrators, for instance by forcing them to attempt to cover up their actions.

Some progress in terms of the promotion of human rights had already been achieved in the era following the Second World War and made the emergence of humanitarian intervention during the 1990s possible (see Dunne and Staunton 2016). However, it can be argued that humanitarian intervention as we know it emerged at the beginning of the 1990s, when the UN Security Council became willing to authorise the use of force on the grounds that the human suffering created by humanitarian crises within states constituted a threat to international peace and security.

In contrast to the existing literature, which often focuses on interventions that take place without the host state's consent (see for instance Holzgrefe 2003, 18; Nardin and Williams 2006, 1; Weiss 2012a, 7), this book also covers consensual interventions. This choice can be explained by the fact that from the end of the Cold War, an increasing number of interventions authorised by the UN had very strong humanitarian components, while benefiting from at least the partial or coerced consent of the parties. Excluding such interventions would thus considerably limit the scope of this analysis.

### The responsibility to protect

In light of the criticism of humanitarian intervention by the end of the 1990s, R2P was developed in the 2001 report of the International Commission on Intervention and State Sovereignty (ICISS) and was unanimously endorsed at the 2005 World Summit. It has been used in eighty-one UN Security Council resolutions and has been the subject of ten annual reports from the UN secretaries general.[5] Put simply, it means that states have a responsibility to protect their own populations – not just their citizens – from genocide, war crimes, crimes against humanity and ethnic cleansing, while the international community has a responsibility to assist them and to react in a "timely and decisive manner" if they fail to do so (see Articles 138–139 in UN General Assembly 2005). In order to facilitate its implementation, UN Secretary General Ban outlined a three-pillar strategy in his 2009 report: "Pillar one is the enduring responsibility of the State to protect its populations. ... Pillar two is the commitment of the international community to assist States in meeting those obligations. ... Pillar three is the responsibility of Member States to respond collectively in a timely and decisive manner when a State is manifestly failing to provide such protection" (Ban 2009, 8–9). R2P involves much more than reacting to mass atrocity situations through military interventions, since a strong emphasis is put on prevention, while the use of force is seen as a last resort. However, in light of the focus of this book on military interventions, special attention is given to pillar three and, more specifically, to the use of force under pillar three.

R2P is defined as a concept between its emergence in 2001 and 2004; as an international principle between 2005 and 2011; and as an international norm thereafter. The choice of this terminology and dates does not aim to create controversy around the key stages of the development of R2P, since this is not the focus of this book. Instead, it aims to provide a clear framework of analysis to study France's relationship to R2P as it evolved. As Bellamy argues, the shift from concept to principle in 2005 reflects "the fact that governments ha[d] indeed agreed on its content [at the 2005 World Summit] and ha[d] pledged to act in accordance with it" (2009a, 7).

R2P then reached the status of international social norm from 2011 onwards, when states like the United States were "moved by a felt imperative to act to protect Libyan civilians" (Glanville 2016, 185). Additionally, since 2011, even though it has faced contestation, it has created an 'oughtness' for states and the international community to protect populations and has defined "standards of appropriate behavior for actors" (Sikkink 1998, 518). Even though the international community has failed to protect civilians in several cases, and more efforts are needed to make 'never again' a reality, we can still detect the influence of the norm in several ways. For instance, Glanville argues that in the case of Syria, we can see the impact of the norm "in the acceptance of the international community that ... they are bound to respond; in the efforts of states to justify the significance of the actions they have taken to protect the vulnerable and to provide excuses when they have refused to act; and in the willingness of states to condemn those, particularly Russia and China, who they claim are standing in the way of the international community discharging its [R2P]" (2016, 185).

## France's domestic norm of human protection

Finally, this book argues that there is a domestic norm of human protection which contends that France has a special role to play in human protection in light of its history, values and rank. It is a norm rather than an influential concept or principle because it has driven – or at the very least, strongly influenced – the various executives' commitment to human protection over time, and it has provided clear expectations of how to act in humanitarian crises and, in particular, promoted an 'oughtness' to intervene to protect when it is deemed necessary and beneficial.

As explained in more depth in Chapters 1 and 2, the norm emerged at the end of the 1980s,[6] thanks to the domestic norm entrepreneurs Bernard Kouchner and Mario Bettati and the endorsement of key members of the executive at the time, in particular President Mitterrand and his Prime Minister, Chirac (see also Staunton 2018, 372–374). This endorsement and the rapid development of France's domestic norm of human protection can partly be explained by the fact that the latter is directly linked to two key components of France's identity. As explained in more depth throughout the book, the first is the idea that France is the 'homeland of human rights' and as such has a special duty to promote them, particularly the right to life. The second is the notion of *rang* (rank), or prestige and grandeur, that has influenced – or rather, obsessed – French leaders such as Louis XIV, Napoleon and Charles de Gaulle for centuries.

Because norms evolve, different degrees of attention have been given to France's history, values and rank, depending on the composition of the French executive at the time and the context. Similarly, the way the norm has been implemented has evolved over the years, and so has the terminology used (in particular, from Chirac's presidency onwards, the expression *devoir d'ingérence*, used under Mitterrand, was replaced by less controversial terminology such as 'responsibility to act').[7] However, as this book shows, the claim that France has a special role to play in human protection because it is the 'homeland of human rights' and 'a state that matters' remained influential throughout the presidencies of Mitterrand (1981–95), Chirac (1995–2007), Sarkozy (2007–12) and Hollande (2012–17).

As Chapter 1 explains in more depth, it is interesting to note that the executives' obsession with France's rank played a double role: as mentioned previously, it was part of the reason why France was involved in human protection, but increasingly, it also strongly influenced how France practised human protection. There was indeed a need to make sure that implementing France's perceived responsibilities as a major power and the 'homeland of human rights' did not threaten France's image and status, for instance by making it appear unable to handle a specific crisis.

In addition to influencing why the various French executives were committed to human protection since the 1980s, France's domestic norm helped define how they conceptualised human protection. First, it meant that France promoted the creation of a right to intervene in the domestic affairs of a state only in order to fulfil a perceived duty to protect. Additionally, the norm led to a broad understanding of human protection. It was not limited to specific emergencies or populations, but rather included any situations where suffering was taking place. Similarly, the tools available to address the emergency were not restricted. Prevention was favoured, but coercive military intervention was often deemed necessary.

## A tale of two norms

The first work of its kind to tell the much-needed story of France and human protection, this book uses an innovative theoretical framework. It argues that the best way to study France's relationship to human protection is to analyse 'a tale of two norms'. The first norm is France's domestic norm of human protection, and the second is the dominant international principle or norm of human protection at the time: humanitarian intervention during the 1990s and R2P since the 2000s. It should be clear that even though the idea is compelling, this book does not argue that humanitarian intervention and R2P are two historical versions of the same norm: as Chapter 4 explains in more depth, the two differ on many points. Instead, it argues that humanitarian intervention was the leading principle of human protection in the 1990s while R2P has been the leading norm of human protection since the 2000s, and that to fully understand their emergence and development, their respective relationships with France's domestic norm of human protection need to be analysed. Indeed, the domestic and international principle and norm each have their own trajectory, yet they are also interconnected and have influenced each other as they evolved. Analysing the complexity of this relationship thus reveals much more about norm development and the actual emergence of humanitarian intervention and R2P than any other models (see for instance Pape 2012) that mistakenly reduce their development to a simple linear story (Staunton 2018, 367).

As explained in more depth in Chapter 1, the book builds on the norm diffusion literature – and more specifically, on the respective work of Finnemore and Sikkink (1998) and Acharya (2004; 2011; 2013; 2015) – and offers a theoretical framework defined by four key stages for studying the complex historical interplay of the two norms: entrepreneurship, localisation, subsidiarity and internalisation. Because norms are not static, these stages are likely to recur as the international context evolves and/or new forms of contestation emerge, and the framework can be used to analyse these developments (see also Staunton 2018, 368–372).

The analysis is based on in-depth qualitative research grounded in process tracing and complemented by counterfactual analysis (Betts and Orchard 2014, 19). It relies on the rigorous discourse analysis of speeches in both French and English made by key members of the various French executives (in particular, the French presidents, ministers of foreign affairs, ministers of defence and permanent representatives to the UN) on France's foreign policy, human protection and specific interventions; and UN draft resolutions submitted or sponsored by France. The book also draws on the data analysis of France's troop contributions to interventions undertaken for humanitarian purposes by the UN, the European Union (EU) and the North Atlantic Treaty Organization (NATO), and unilaterally, along with comparisons of France's contribution with other key states such as the United Kingdom, Germany and the United States.

Fourteen case studies were selected as focal points: Cambodia, Somalia, Bosnia and Herzegovina, Kosovo, Rwanda, the DRC, Myanmar/Burma, Iraq (1991 and 2003), Côte d'Ivoire, Libya, Syria, Mali and the CAR. The 'positive' cases (where an intervention took place) were selected using the following criteria: the claim made by the executive that the intervention was mainly undertaken for humanitarian purposes;[8] the importance of the troop contribution from France; the length of the intervention; the role the intervention played on France's conception of human protection; the institutional framework chosen to intervene; and the geographic area in which the intervention took place. The 'negative' cases (where an intervention did not take place) were selected for their significance either because France refused to intervene when it was expected to (as in Rwanda early on or Iraq in 2003), or because France was not able to intervene despite its will to do so (as in Myanmar/Burma in 2008). The book also analyses news articles and reports in order to explain the context at the time and how France's actions or lack of action were perceived.

Lastly, elite interviews of key personalities such as the Hon. Gareth Evans (Co-Chair of the ICISS), Kouchner (norm entrepreneur of France's domestic norm of human protection and former French Minister of Foreign Affairs), Bettati (distinguished international legal scholar and Kouchner's advisor) and Roland Dumas (former French Minister of Foreign Affairs) were also undertaken in order to fill the gaps.

With the exception of Chapter 1, which theorises the tale of two norms, this book is divided according to the key phases of the development of humanitarian intervention and R2P. Chapter 2 analyses the emergence of humanitarian intervention as we know it (1987–94), while Chapter 3 covers the period when it faced international contestation (1995–99). Chapter 4 studies the emergence of R2P (2000–04), while its transition from international principle to international norm between the 2005 World Summit and Libya is investigated in Chapter 5 (2005–11). Finally, Chapter 6 focuses on its development after Libya (2012–17).

Once again, the purpose of this timeline is not to generate controversy but rather to provide a clear framework of analysis to study the evolution of France's relationship to human protection as humanitarian intervention and R2P evolved. Additionally, this structure allows comparisons to be made with the French presidential history: whereas Mitterrand was in office during the emergence of humanitarian intervention, Chirac was President when it faced international contestation and when R2P emerged. Similarly, Sarkozy was in office when R2P gradually reached the status of international norm. Finally, Hollande was President when the international norm developed in the post-Libya era.

The book argues that, influenced by France's domestic norm of human protection, Mitterrand and key members of his various executives played a role of norm entrepreneur in the emergence of humanitarian intervention by promoting key resolutions to the UN General Assembly and the Security Council in the late 1980s and early 1990s. In addition to this normative and diplomatic role, both Mitterrand's and Chirac's executives helped shape the way the international community practised human protection throughout the decade through France's military contribution to international interventions undertaken for humanitarian purposes.

In contrast, France played no role in the emergence of R2P during Chirac's presidency because it was excluded from the ICISS. This can be explained by the fact that by the end of the 1990s, France's conception of human protection was deemed to be controversial and outdated by key actors of the international community, because throughout the 1990s, France appeared to be promoting only a right – rather than a duty and a right – to intervene to protect, actively took part in coercive interventions and also undertook the controversial *Opération Turquoise* in Rwanda.

In the early 2000s, however, it demonstrated that its voice still mattered by opposing the Iraq War and continued to intervene for humanitarian purposes. Additionally, despite its lack of norm entrepreneurship, France became a norm consolidator of R2P by actively supporting it normatively, diplomatically and militarily from 2006. This active support was, however, not always beneficial for the development of the international norm. In particular, Sarkozy and his executives promoted a broad and rather unique understanding of R2P and ended up – at times – endangering the emerging norm instead of promoting it. In view of the influence of France's domestic norm of human protection since the 1980s and its will to remain more than a "middle sized power" (Chirac 1995a), and in light of the fact that R2P was broadly defined in the 2005 World Summit Outcome Document in order to increase its chances to be successfully localised by member states, the promotion by France of a broad understanding of R2P was not surprising. However, it showed how much impact a state like France could have during the development of the international norm, even if it was not involved in its emergence.

After Libya, Hollande and his executives began to stop encouraging such a broad interpretation of R2P, making France a more traditional promoter of the international norm. This shift can partly be explained by the executives' will to not endanger France's status as a key actor of human protection and by the changing domestic and international contexts, but it can also be argued that the international norm – as understood by the majority of the international community – was beginning to be internalised in France.

The recent influence of R2P on France's conception and practice of human protection has shown that a new dynamic in France's relationship to human protection is beginning to emerge. During the 1990s and early 2000s, while France's domestic norm of human protection was very influential on the various executives, the same cannot be said about humanitarian intervention and R2P. This lack of influence on France is not surprising, for the impact of an international principle or norm on a state like France is expected to be only proportional to its strength, especially when a related domestic norm exists and is influential. Yet, as mentioned previously and as explained in more depth in the book, humanitarian intervention was a relatively weak international principle in the 1990s, and R2P was only a concept in the early 2000s.

Things began to change, however, when R2P started gaining international traction. It began to have restrictive effects on where and how France could respond to mass atrocities during Sarkozy's presidency, and its influence progressively strengthened throughout Hollande's mandate. Once again, this was to be expected: as explained in more depth in Chapter 1, while a state like France can play a strong role in the emergence and development of an international norm like R2P, its influence progressively reduces as the international norm becomes stronger. In contrast, while an international norm can have a limited impact on a state like France during the early stages of its development – especially if that state has a related domestic norm – its influence will strengthen as it develops, at least until the international context evolves and/or new forms of contestation emerge. However, the beginning of the internalisation of R2P did not mean that France's domestic norm became obsolete, as its influence remained visible in many ways even during Hollande's presidency and in particular, continued to lead France to promote a wide understanding of the international norm's scope.

In addition to the evolution of this relationship between the domestic and the international principle and norm, a shift in how France practised human protection throughout the decades can also be noticed. At the beginning of the 1990s, Mitterrand and his executives favoured intervening worldwide, via the UN, using a humanitarian approach. In the second half of the 1990s, in light of the change of domestic and international contexts and in order to fulfil France's perceived duty to intervene to protect without endangering its rank, Chirac's executives focused on Europe, favoured intervening via NATO and the European Union and used a more coercive approach.

The 2000s witnessed some continuity with the second half of the 1990s: a strong focus on Europe, the favouring of intervention via NATO rather than the UN and the determination to build the European Union's capacity to intervene. Yet the executives also resumed their interventions for humanitarian purposes in the Middle East and Africa, at times using unilateral operations to support – yet not be limited by – UN interventions. Hollande's presidency was more unusual in that France's military interventions for humanitarian purposes were then predominantly in Africa, and the French executives at the time did not hesitate to rely on unilateral interventions. However, this shift can mainly be explained by the domestic and international contexts at the time rather than by a will to resume *Françafrique* practices or to withdraw from multilateralism.[9] It is important to note that these trends were not unique to France, but they contributed to reinforcing how the international community practised human protection.

As explained in more depth in the Conclusion, as the first work of its kind to tell the much-needed story of France and human protection, this book brings together human protection, France's foreign policy and International Relations theory and makes key contributions to each field. By investigating France's relationship to human protection, it helps us to better understand how key principles and norms of human protection have emerged and developed, and the growing influence they have had on states like France as they have evolved. It also suggests that expanding the focus of the literature to other non-Anglo-Saxon states that are supportive of human protection is a necessity if we are to ever gain a full understanding of human protection. Next the book corrects prevailing assumptions about France's foreign policy and allows us not only to better comprehend its past and present foreign policy, but also to anticipate that of the future. Last but not least, because its innovative framework can also be used to study the interplay of other domestic and international norms, it makes a broader contribution to the literature on norm diffusion and International Relations theory more generally.

## Notes

1 Penholders take the leading role in convening UN Security Council meetings and drafting resolutions on a specific issue.
2 The French expression for 'reserved domain' was invented by Jacques Chaban-Delmas in 1959 to refer to areas of national policy – usually foreign policy and national defence – where the President is seen as being personally in charge.
3 A *cohabitation* is a period when the President and the government are from different political parties as the result of the legislative elections. During the Fifth Republic there have been three *cohabitation*s: two during François Mitterrand's presidency (1986–88 and 1993–95) and one during Jacques Chirac's (1997–2002).
4 The distinction between concept, principle and norm is best explained by Bellamy, who argues that a concept is "an 'idea' – a thought or suggestion about a possible norm or course of action" and that a principle "implies that it has acquired a status of shared understanding and that there is sufficient consensus to allow it to function as a foundation for action", while a norm "is best understood as 'collective understandings of the proper behaviour of actors'" (2009a, 5–6).
5 As of 4 September 2019.
6 Even though France had undertaken some *missions civilisatrices* (civilising missions) in the past, these interventions were strongly tied to its colonial endeavours and therefore have to be distinguished from human protection. Similarly, France's *interventions d'humanité* (interventions of humanity) such as those undertaken by France in Lebanon and Syria in 1860 remained isolated events rather than a concrete strategy to protect endangered populations.
7 The term *devoir d'ingérence* is often translated as duty or responsibility to intervene or interfere, but because none of these English expressions fully captures the concept, the French term is used throughout the book.
8 This nominalist approach does not mean that a state simply has to claim that an intervention is humanitarian to be humanitarian, but it allows us to not get caught up in the evaluation of interventions from a purported objective standpoint, and to analyse the range of normative claims made by the executives to explain and justify an intervention.
9 The expression *Françafrique* is often used in a pejorative way to criticise the 'neo-colonial' strategy of France in Africa.

# Theorising the tale of two norms

As explained in the Introduction, investigating France's relationship to human protection over time requires analysing a tale of two norms where the first is France's domestic norm of human protection, and the second is the dominant international principle or norm of human protection at the time – humanitarian intervention during the 1990s and R2P since the 2000s. Although fascinating, this task is quite challenging from a theoretical and methodological point of view for two reasons. First, it calls for a framework that allows the investigation of the emergence and influence of both domestic and international principles or norms rather than focusing on the development of one international norm in two different contexts (the domestic and the international). Second, it requires theorising the evolving historical relationship between these interconnected yet distinct principles or norms as they evolved.

In order to do this, this book builds on the respective work of Finnemore and Sikkink (1998) and Acharya (2004; 2011; 2013; 2015) to develop an innovative framework defined by four key stages: entrepreneurship, localisation, subsidiarity and internalisation. Because norms are not static, these stages are likely to recur as the international context evolves and/or new forms of contestation emerge, but the framework put forward can be used to analyse these developments. Before exploring it in more depth, this chapter first investigates some of the key factors that have influenced France's conception of, and contribution to, human protection over the years.

## Making sense of France's conception of, and contribution to, human protection

Identifying what influences a specific aspect of a state's foreign policy is not an easy task, because many factors are at play. Nevertheless, when it comes to France's conception of, and contribution to, human protection over time, four factors are particularly important: the international normative context, France's domestic norm of human protection and its link to key components of its identity, the obsession of the various executives with France's rank, and how the executive at the time perceived the international and domestic contexts. It would be mistaken to argue that only these four factors have influenced France's conception and practice of human protection over the years. For instance, as mentioned in the Introduction, the composition of the French executive at the time has been particularly important. However, it is essential to emphasise the importance of these specific factors because they have played a central role over the years, regardless of the composition of the executive at the time.

### The international normative context

First, France's conception of, and contribution to, human protection cannot be fully analysed without taking into account the international normative context. The section "Theorising the tale of two norms" below investigates the process by which international principles and norms can impact a state like France, but before this, it is important to discuss the extent of the impact these international principles and norms can have. Human rights norms provide a valuable example.

The rationalist literature sees norms and international institutions as "the bargain forged between (powerful) states" (Barnett 2010, 6). For instance, Mearsheimer argues that "realists maintain that institutions are basically a reflection of the distribution of power in the world. They are based on the self-interested calculations of the great powers, and they have no independent effect on state behaviour" (1994, 7). In regard to human rights and humanitarian intervention, this understanding of norms and institutions has led Krasner to argue that "the content of human rights issues … reflected the concerns of those states which possessed a preponderance of economic and military power" (1995, 166). Similarly, Pape puts forward the concept of "pragmatic humanitarian intervention" to explain that a state should intervene when the risk of casualties is close to nil since it maximises the benefits received from intervening (2012, 43).

Even though this literature is useful for explaining some of the opportunities and constraints experienced by states, it overlooks the constitutive attribute of norms. Norms indeed influence identity and interests by being "standards of appropriate behavior for actors with a given identity" (Sikkink 1998, 518). As Finnemore explains, "the international system can change what states want. It is constitutive and generative, creating new interests and values for actors. It changes state action, not by constraining states with a given set of preferences from acting, but by changing their preferences" (1996b, 5–6).

Risse and Sikkink (1999, 17–35) provide a good example of the constitutive power of norms with their 'spiral model', which deepens our understanding of how human rights norms have become internalised – or 'taken for granted'[1] – in the domestic affairs of states. They identify five phases in order to show how political leaders end up internalising and implementing norms even though they originally did not plan to do so: (1) repression and activation of network, (2) denial, (3) tactical concessions, (4) prescriptive status and (5) rule-consistent behaviour. They argue that this outcome can be explained by the fact that the opposition – with the support of the international community – has means (such as shaming) to either make sure that the leader of a country implements the norm, or is replaced by a new leader who will. Additionally, the internalisation process takes place by linking the state's identity to human rights since they are "part of the yardstick used to define who is in and who is outside of the club of liberal states" (Sikkink 1998, 520). This is not to say that there will no longer be violations of human rights, but rather that it becomes harder for new administrations to not promote them.

As illustrated by the spiral model and as explained in more depth in the section "Theorising the tale of two norms" below, the more robust an international norm becomes, the stronger its impact will be. Consequently, it is essential to take into account the influence of the international normative context and more specifically, in light of this book's objective, the impact of both humanitarian intervention and R2P – at the various stages of their development – on France.

*The domestic normative context*

Even though it is necessary to take into account the influence of the international normative context, this is not enough. The domestic normative context also needs to be analysed. More specifically, and as demonstrated throughout this book, France's domestic norm of human protection has had a strong impact on the various French executives over the years and is key to making sense of France's conception of, and contribution to, human protection. The norm contends that France has a special role to play in human protection in light of its history, values and rank.

This book argues that the domestic norm emerged in the late 1980s thanks to the work of the norm entrepreneurs Bernard Kouchner and Mario Bettati,[2] and to the endorsement of key members of the executive at the time (see also Staunton 2018, 372–374). As mentioned in the Introduction, this endorsement and the rapid development of France's domestic norm of human protection can partly be explained by the fact that it is directly linked to key components of France's identity, which have remained fairly stable over the years.[3] The importance of these ideational factors is not surprising since, as argued by the constructivist literature, identity informs interests, which in turn informs action (Hopf 1998, 175).

The first component is the idea that France is the 'homeland of human rights' and as such has a special duty to promote them (in particular, the right to life). This aspect of France's identity has often been traced back to the French Revolution and has been promoted by French leaders over many decades, regardless of their political affiliation (see Macleod and Voyer-Legér 2004, 80; Treacher 2000, 23). For instance, Charles de Gaulle declared, "the vocation of France is human, to serve the cause of the human being, the cause of freedom, the cause of the dignity of the human being" (in El Moustaoui 2011, 291).[4] As the following chapters show, the presidencies of François Mitterrand, Jacques Chirac, Nicolas Sarkozy and François Hollande were no exceptions. As explained in more depth in the next section, the second influential ideational factor is the notion of *rang* (rank), or prestige and grandeur.

*France's rank*

While the will to promote France's rank is an important part of the domestic norm of human protection and, consequently, of the reasons why France has been involved in human protection, it also deserves to be discussed as a single factor because it has influenced – or rather, obsessed – French leaders such as Louis XIV, Napoleon III or de Gaulle for centuries. As Grosser argues, "elsewhere, prestige is considered as a tool allowing to better reach political or economic ends. For [France], prestige constitutes an end in itself" (1995, 64). Similarly, Smouts talks about a "worship of 'rank'" and explains that "France, 'because it is France', claims to have a global vocation. It must express itself on, and intervene in, world affairs. The worst criticism the French can make of their leaders' foreign policy is not that it is expensive and hazardous, but that it is flat and lacking in style" (Smouts 1998, 7; see also Bozo 2012, 7; Macleod 2004; Treacher 2000, 23–24).

While the reasons put forward to promote France's rank have evolved slightly according to the domestic and international contexts at the time, four symbols have been consistently used to promote France's rank over the years: its permanent seat at the UN Security Council; the fact that it is a nuclear power; its cultural influence (in particular through francophone Africa and its overseas territories and departments); [5] and last but not least, the idea that it is the 'homeland of human rights'. It is interesting to note that even though the idea that France is the 'homeland of human rights' is a specific component of France's identity, it has also often been associated with France's rank. The various French executives have indeed argued that the values France fought for during the French Revolution were part of what makes it a state that matters. In light of this continuity, and as illustrated throughout the book, the idea that France is 'more than a middle sized power' has remained uncontested during the presidencies of Mitterrand, Chirac, Sarkozy and Hollande.

It is important to note that as well as contributing to France's central role in human protection (because it was seen as needing to play an active role in human protection in light of its rank), the various executives' obsession with France's rank also influenced how they intervened for humanitarian purposes. More specifically, France's practice of human protection evolved over time in terms of the breadth of its interventions, the institutional framework chosen to intervene and the strategy used in the field. It was indeed one thing to intervene to fulfil France's perceived responsibilities as a major power and the 'homeland of human rights', but it was another to allow these interventions to threaten France's image and status. Therefore, in order to prevent situations where promoting human protection and promoting France's rank constituted conflicting goals, the various executives adjusted the way France practised human protection in order to reconcile these goals.

### The perception of the domestic and international contexts

A last factor that needs to be taken into account is context. Here again, the rationalist literature offers key tools of analysis to explain the motivations of a state like France and the opportunities and constraints it has to take into account when designing its foreign policy. As Finnemore and Sikkink argue, "the current tendency to oppose norms against rationality or rational choice is not helpful in explaining many of the most politically salient processes we see in empirical research – processes we call 'strategic social construction', in which actors strategize rationally to reconfigure preferences, identities, or social context" (1998, 888).

In particular, neo-realism constitutes a good starting point for analysing a state's foreign policy since it focuses on the role played by states' interests, while taking into account the influence of the international realm. Like classical realists, neo-realists argue that the security dilemma, which is caused by the lack of an international 'Leviathan' or "the absence of any legitimate hierarchical source of authority" (Krasner 2001, 229), guides states' actions. The anarchical international system is seen as leading states to promote their national interest which is "defined as power" (Morgenthau and Thompson 1985, 5). Power, in turn, is defined in material terms in order to include geostrategic, political and economic interests. States are seen as rational actors that "aim to maximise their relative power position over other states" (Mearsheimer 1994, 11) because they have to "be more concerned with relative strength than with absolute advantage" (Waltz 1979, 106).

While this book shares with neo-realists the idea that the national interest matters, it borrows from Weldes's work (1996), and more particularly from her emphasis on the importance of perception and interpretation for studying how it matters. Weldes argues that the national interest is important because it "forms the basis for state action. Second, it functions as a rhetorical device through which the legitimacy of and political support for state action is generated" (1996, 276). Nevertheless, she argues, what matters is not necessarily the national interest or the constraints and opportunities faced by the executive per se, but rather the way they are perceived and interpreted, since "determining what the particular situation faced by the state is, what if any threat a state faces, and what the 'correct' national interest with respect to that situation or threat is, always require interpretation" (1996, 279). The idea here is not to argue that domestic and international contexts are necessarily understood differently by different people. Rather, the aim is to emphasise the idea that perception and interpretation play a key role in the way decision makers see the world, and therefore, this perception needs to be explored in order to define – at the very least – the kind of foreign policy the decision makers thought was available to them.

This analysis is particularly important in the study of French foreign policy, which is seen as a *domaine réservé* of the executive power, and in particular of the President. Consequently, it is directly impacted by how a handful of people interpret the domestic and international contexts. For instance, when studying France's practice of humanitarian intervention in Africa during Mitterrand's presidency, this book builds on comments made by Prunier (1997) and others and argues that the Fashoda syndrome influenced France's foreign policy in the continent,[6] even though the fact that the Anglo-Saxons had hegemonic claims in the region has been contested.[7] The book therefore also takes into account the role played by the various executives' perception of the domestic and international contexts at the time.

### Theorising the tale of two norms

With the factors that have influenced France's conception and practice of human protection over time clarified, it is important to focus on how to study the historical interplay between France's domestic norm of human protection on the one hand and the international principle and norm of human protection (humanitarian intervention and R2P) as they evolved on the other. In order to do so, this book synthesises and builds on the respective work of the International Relations theorists Finnemore and Sikkink (1998) and Acharya (2004; 2011; 2013; 2015) to develop a framing capable of analysing the two-level relationship between domestic and international norms.

Finnemore and Sikkink explain through their concept of the "norm life cycle" that "norm influence may be understood as a three-stage process. … [T]he first stage is 'norm emergence'; the second stage involves broad norm acceptance, which we term, … a 'norm cascade'; and the third stage involves internalisation" (1998, 895). Acharya also investigates norm diffusion through his "norm circulation" model, but "pays greater attention to agency and feedback in norm dynamics" (2013, 466) by arguing that it is "a two-way process" (2013, 469). More precisely, he explains that "global norms offered by transnational moral actors are contested and localized to fit the cognitive priors of local actors (localization), while this local feedback is repatriated back to the wider global context along with other locally constructed norms and help to modify and possibly defend and strengthen the global norm in question (subsidiarity)" (2013, 469).

Both models are invaluable contributions to the literature on norms, yet they both have limitations when it comes to achieving the objectives of this book. For instance, while they acknowledge that "domestic norms … are deeply entwined with the workings of international norms [because] many international norms began as domestic norms and become international through the efforts of entrepreneurs of various kinds" (Finnemore and Sikkink 1998, 893), the role played by domestic norms – and in particular, by individual norms – is not explored enough in Finnemore and Sikkink's 'life cycle' framework, and neither is the interconnection between domestic and international norms during the emergence and development of these international norms. Additionally, in contrast to this book, the model promotes a rather static view of norms (Wiener 2014).

Acharya's 'norm circulation' model emphasises the dynamism of norms and pays greater attention to agency, but argues that "norm circulation occurs when the less powerful actors feel marginalised in the norm creation process or feel betrayed by the abuse of the norm by the more powerful actors in the implementation stage" (2013, 469), which, as this book shows, is not always the case. Additionally, even though it acknowledges the role domestic or even regional norms can have in the emergence and development of international norms (Acharya 2011; 2013), the model is not designed to analyse the role played by one specific domestic norm. Finally, while it is important to stress that norms are not static (Acharya 2013, 466) – a claim shared by this book – the concept of 'norm circulation' does not emphasise enough how the relationship between domestic and international norms evolves once the international norm becomes stronger.[8]

Despite these limitations and even though these authors conceptualise the way norms emerge and develop in very different ways, this book argues that – combined together – the tools of analysis they put forward can be used to study the interplay over time between France's domestic norm, and humanitarian intervention and R2P (see also Staunton 2018, 369–372). More specifically, and as illustrated by Figure 1, it explains that four key stages can be defined to study the relationship between the norms as they evolved: (1) entrepreneurship, (2) localisation, (3) subsidiarity and (4) internalisation. It borrows the concepts of entrepreneurship and internalisation from Finnemore and Sikkink's "norm life cycle" model, and the concepts of localisation and subsidiarity from Acharya's "norm circulation"

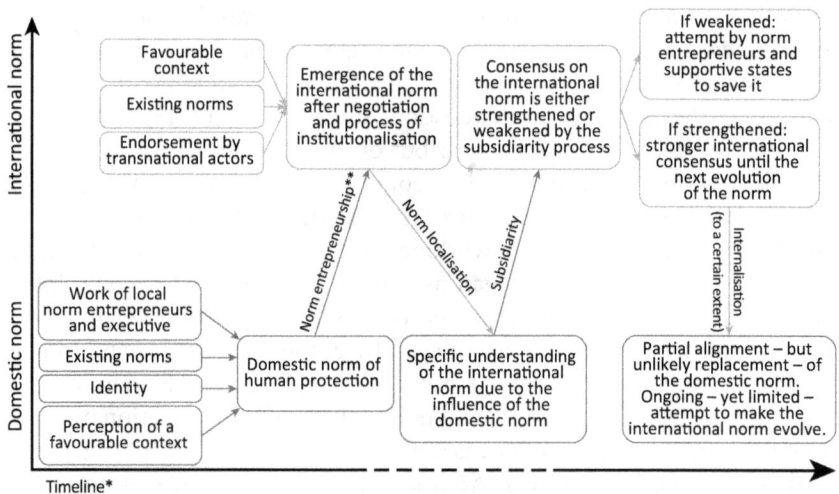

\* Because norms are not static, this overall process is likely to continue to occur over time. The dotted line on the timeline also reflects the idea that the localisation and subsidiarity processes can occur several times while the global consensus on the international norm is being negotiated.

\*\* The concepts of norm entrepreneurship and internalisation are borrowed from Finnemore and Sikkink (1998), while the concepts of norm localisation and subsidiarity come from Acharya's work (2004, 2011 and 2013).

Note: A previous version of this figure was developed in Staunton (2018, 370). However, the figure above has been adjusted in order to reflect more explicitly the fact that it is likely that both norms will keep existing in parallel of one another, and at times, will continue to clash with one another, even after the internalisation phase. As a consequence, France will keep trying to influence the international norm, even though its impact is likely to be more limited and/or will require extensive collaborations with other members of the international community (see the section 'Internalisation').

**Figure 1** Theorising the tale of two norms

model. The following sections explain each stage in more detail, but first it is important to emphasise that because norms are not static but are rather in constant evolution, these stages should not be seen as a unidirectional representation of the development of norms, but instead as a collection of individual segments or stages that will be repeated as the international context evolves and/or new forms of contestation emerge.

*Norm entrepreneurship*

The first step – norm entrepreneurship – aims to allow the investigation of the specific role an actor like France can play in the early stages of the emergence of an international principle or norm like humanitarian intervention and R2P. Some social theorists would argue that states are passive norm takers and play a modest – if any – role in the emergence and development of international principles or norms. However, this approach is problematic because, as Chapter 2 illustrates in depth, states can play a central role in the early stages of the emergence of a principle or norm. It is thus necessary to draw upon the literature that studies the role played by agency to better understand how this is possible (Staunton 2018, 370–371).

The aim is not to argue that one actor can alone lead to the emergence of a principle or norm such as humanitarian intervention or R2P, since, to borrow Acharya's words, "the creation of international norms is never a one-source, one-way, or a one-step process. Nor is it carried out by a single agent" (2015, 77). Several factors such as a favourable context, the cooperation of "transnational moral agents" (Acharya 2015, 75) and the existence of complementary norms do indeed need to be present for the international principle or norm to emerge. However, we need to be able to analyse the specific role played by states like France to reduce the level of "controversy, competition over ownership, mistrust and even rejection" around the international principle or norm (Acharya 2013, 468). Finnemore and Sikkink's work helps us achieve this goal (Staunton 2018, 370–371).

Finnemore and Sikkink define the concept of norm entrepreneurship as "the purposive efforts of individuals and groups to change social understandings" (2001, 400), in particular through the process of framing, as norm entrepreneurs use "language that names, interprets, and dramatizes" specific issues in order to gain public traction (1998, 897). Given that not all norms are equal and thus many will not be successfully internalised and internationalised, Sikkink argues that "networks of nongovernmental organisations eventually need to secure the support of powerful state actors who endorse the norms and make normative socialisation a part of their agenda" (1998, 519). Once this process has taken place, states become norm entrepreneurs at the international level. They then need to secure the support of key international organisations, which Finnemore and Sikkink refer to as the institutionalisation of the emergent norm (1998, 900) and define as "the way norms become embedded in international organisations and institutions" (Finnemore 1996a, 161).

The existing literature has explored the emergence of specific international norms and principles of human protection, and although the role played by France specifically has not been addressed in depth,[9] the work done on the emergence of human rights, humanitarian intervention and R2P is particularly relevant to this book. First, in regard to human rights, after reminding us of the favourable changes of context both internationally and domestically,[10] the literature highlights the central role played by key norm entrepreneurs after the Second World War as they encouraged policymakers "to question the principled idea that a country's internal human rights practices are not a legitimate topic of foreign policy and the causal assumption that national interests are furthered by support of repressive regimes that violate the human rights of their citizens" (Sikkink 1993, 140).

For instance, Sikkink emphasises Raphael Lemkin's role in the emergence of the Genocide Convention; Alejandro Alvarez, Andre Mandelstam and Antoine Frangulis's contribution to the emergence of "norms for the international protection of human rights"; and Herbert George Wells's involvement in reinserting human rights "into the war-time debate over war aims" (1998, 518). She also highlights the role played by nongovernmental organisations (NGOs), for instance in "the early campaigns that were the precursors of the current human rights policies, especially in the Geneva Convention and the campaign for the abolition of slavery; in the inclusion of human rights language in the UN Charter; and in the linkage of human rights to the process of the unification of Europe" (1993, 170).

However, while these individuals and NGOs played a central role by pressuring their government to take action, Sikkink reminds us that the emergence of human rights norms would not have been possible without the endorsement of key states and the fact that human rights relate to their identity as liberal states (1998, 520). This support allowed the emerging norms to be promoted internationally and institutionalised by key international organisations, eventually leading to their internalisation by other states.

Similarly, the research undertaken by key authors such as Bellamy, Finnemore, Barnett, Wheeler and Weiss helps us understand how humanitarian intervention emerged and evolved over the years.[11] Although the full extent of their contributions cannot be addressed in detail here, they offer a strong understanding of why states began to intervene in other states' affairs for humanitarian purposes by not restricting their analysis to geostrategic and economic reasoning. For instance, they emphasise the importance of having a favourable normative context and the role played by decolonisation and self-determination, since by allowing a redefinition of humanity for Europeans, these norms changed state behaviour and allowed non-Christians to beneficiate from humanitarian intervention (Finnemore 1996a, 160–161, 184). They also explore why from 1992, the UN Security Council became willing to enlarge its definition of what constitutes a threat to international peace and security, thus allowing more interventions to take place (Bellamy 2009b, 237; Wheeler 2003, 32–33).[12] However, the role played by specific norm entrepreneurs like France remains under-investigated.

With regard to R2P, Acharya provides a good overview of its emergence by arguing that it has several sources ("the work of the ICISS, the idea of humanitarian intervention (the 'right to intervene'), human rights promotion, the just war tradition and the idea of responsible sovereignty developed in the context of Africa and IDPs"); contexts ("the Middle East, the Balkans and, above all, Africa"); and norm entrepreneurs ("Canadians, Australians, Africans and others") (2015, 76). His work is complemented by authors such as Bellamy and Glanville. In particular, they emphasise the importance of the shock created by the NATO intervention in Kosovo by arguing that it increased the debate and contestation around humanitarian intervention that had begun with the failures to stop mass atrocities in Rwanda and Srebrenica (Bellamy 2010, 38; Glanville 2012, 10).

Scholars have also investigated how R2P's meaning and content were negotiated through "a process of norm contestation and diffusion that took place between 2001 and 2005" (Bellamy 2011, 9). For instance, Bellamy emphasises the compromises that had to be made for the concept to be endorsed at the 2005 World Summit: "the 'responsibility to rebuild' after an intervention was dropped in its entirety; proposed limits to the use of the veto by the UN Security Council were dropped; criteria to guide decision making about armed intervention were dropped; and the idea that absent Security Council authorisation, intervention for humanitarian purposes might be legitimised by the General Assembly or regional organisations was rejected" (2011, 9).

Last but not least, they also underline the role played by norm entrepreneurs such as Francis Deng, Roberta Cohen and Kofi Annan, who contributed to creating R2P by reframing the meaning of sovereignty (Glanville 2010, 233–234; 2012, 9–10; Bellamy 2011, 10–11). Even though the idea that sovereignty entails responsibility emerged centuries ago (see Glanville 2010), the norm of non-intervention remained predominant during the Cold War and the 1990s and meant that interventions – even if they were for humanitarian purposes – were seen as a violation of state sovereignty (see Dunne and Staunton 2016). Nevertheless, with the concept of "sovereignty as responsibility", actors such as Deng, Cohen and Annan helped reconcile sovereignty and human rights. The work of norm entrepreneurs remained important even after R2P was adopted at the 2005 World Summit. As Bellamy argues, the UN Security Council had to wait for the election of new non-permanent members to use the concept, and norm entrepreneurs such as Ban Ki-Moon had to keep working on the promotion of the emerging norm in order for it to gain international traction (Bellamy 2011, 28–32).

In light of these contributions, this book draws upon the existing literature on human rights, humanitarian intervention and R2P and borrows tools of analysis from Finnemore and Sikkink to study the emergence of humanitarian intervention and R2P and, more specifically, the extent of the role played specifically by France, since this has not been investigated in enough depth. Because an international norm cannot emerge without the support of various transnational actors and factors, it can be challenging to isolate the specific role played by one actor. This challenge can nevertheless be overcome by identifying what could have been expected to happen without France's effort and by analysing how the French proposals were received by, and impacted, the international community.

As explained in more depth in Chapters 2 and 4, the book argues that, influenced by France's domestic norm of human protection, the French executive at the time played a role as norm entrepreneur in the emergence of humanitarian intervention. Yet, after being associated by the international community with the limits of humanitarian intervention, France was excluded from the discussions on R2P and therefore did not play a role in its emergence.

*Norm localisation*

The institutionalisation process generates debates, contestations and negotiations on what the emerging international norm actually consists of, often leading to the appearance of key differences between the norm entrepreneurs' original vision and the emerging international consensus. This is facilitated by the fact that the emerging norm is often not clearly defined, in order to "provide opportunities for localisation" (Acharya 2004, 241) and maximise the chances it has to be globally adopted. For instance, while the international community settled on a definition of R2P in the 2005 World Summit Outcome Document, it was very brief and open to interpretation. As a consequence, even ten years on from the World Summit, the expression 'manifest failing' of paragraph 139 still sparked "a large amount of ambiguity and inconsistency" (Gallagher 2014, 428).

In light of these different interpretations, we need to be able to determine the properties of the international principle or norm that are being taken on or ignored by specific actors like France over time. To borrow Vaughn and Dunne's metaphor, "all norms have an identifiable 'DNA' that can be observed in different institutional domains – we [need to] examine how far the patterning of the norm's code can be identified in the domestic political realm" (2015, 30). Acharya's concept of norm 'localisation' – which he defines as "a complex process and outcome by which norm-takers build congruence between transnational norms (including norms previously institutionalised in a region) and local beliefs and practices" (2004, 241) – helps us achieve this goal (Staunton 2018, 371). By encouraging us to look at states' "preconstructed normative beliefs and practices", the concept helps us understand how key members of the executive "perform[ed] acts of selection, borrowing, and modification in accordance with a pre-existing normative framework to build congruence ... [with the] emerging global norms" (Acharya 2004, 269).

Even though this concept of localisation has been designed for the study of different understandings of the same norm at the domestic and international scales, it can be used for studying the relationship of complementary yet distinct principles or norms such as France's domestic norm of human protection on the one hand and humanitarian intervention and R2P on the other. The only foreseeable difference is that, in light of France's specific and pre-existing domestic norm of human protection, we can expect that the localisation process will take longer to occur and may lead to bigger differences of interpretation of the international norm between the French executives and the international community.

This is confirmed by the following chapters – in particular, Chapters 2 and 5 – which show that the influence of France's domestic norm on the various executives meant that France promoted a broad definition of human protection: it was not limited to specific emergencies or populations, and the use of coercive force was often deemed necessary. This led to a broad understanding of humanitarian intervention and R2P, which at times clashed with the consensus reached by the international community.

### Subsidiarity

Once a state like France has adjusted its understanding of the emerging international principle or norm to its domestic context, the literature suggests that it will then attempt to promote this slightly different understanding to the international community. This is where Acharya's concept of "subsidiarity" becomes helpful (Staunton 2018, 371). He argues that it is "a *process whereby local actors create rules with a view to preserve their autonomy from dominance, neglect, violation, or abuse by more powerful central actors*" (2011, 95, emphasis in original). Although the concept was mainly designed to analyse "the normative behavior of Third World countries" (Acharya 2011, 96), it can be used to examine the relationship between a domestic and an international norm, no matter what the origin of the domestic norm is. For this purpose, this book uses the more recent – and broader – definition put forward by Acharya, which argues that subsidiarity is the process through which the domestic feedback which emerged from the process of localisation "is repatriated back to the wider global context ... and help to modify ... the global norm in question" (2015, 73).

Acharya argues that the localisation process is more likely to take place when less powerful actors feel "marginalised" or "betrayed" during the implementation phase (2015, 73). Even though it does not apply to France, the concept remains useful for an understanding of how it can impact the global consensus on the emerging international norm by promoting its own understanding of that norm during the subsidiary phase. As mentioned previously, in light of the strong influence of France's domestic norm of human protection, the various French executives have promoted a very specific understanding of humanitarian intervention and R2P which differed – and at times, clashed – with the international consensus. In particular, as Chapter 5 explains, France's conception of the origins and scope of R2P strongly differed from the consensus reached by the international community and led the French executive at the time to adopt and promote a unique position on the emerging norm.

Two outcomes can be expected from this subsidiarity process (Staunton 2018, 372). First, it can lead to the weakening or the endangering of the emerging international norm, especially since the consensus around the norm remains fragile during the early stages of its development. If this is the case, it can be expected that the norm entrepreneurs and the actors who have begun to internalise it will attempt to propose changes in order to promote its survival. If they are successful, the emerging international norm will evolve and continue to develop, while if they fail, it will disappear. The regime change orchestrated by NATO's 2011 intervention in Libya – in which France was a key actor – can be seen as a good illustration of how an emerging norm can be threatened by a subsidiarity process that pushes for a broader understanding of the international norm, and this case is investigated in Chapter 5.

The second scenario is that the fragile consensus around the emerging international norm will actually be strengthened by the subsidiarity process. This can first happen if the suggestions made are supported by the international community. For instance, at the time of its proposal,

Brazil's concept of 'Responsibility While Protecting' was well received by a majority of states (Acharya 2013, 478). In contrast, the strengthening of the norm may take place if the changes suggested are contested by a majority of the international community and contribute to the emergence of common ground between sceptics and enthusiasts of the emerging norm. As Chapter 5 shows, this was the case in 2008 when France referred to R2P when Cyclone Nargis hit Myanmar/Burma.

Before moving on to the last phase, it is important to emphasise that the localisation and subsidiarity processes can take place several times while the international norm emerges and progressively develops, especially if the subsidiarity process has led to a weakening of the emerging international norm and the norm is being reshaped. Additionally, these processes are likely to continue to occur, as norms are not static and thus are constantly the object of discussions and contestation. As Finnemore and Sikkink argue, though, one thing is to be expected: "these domestic influences are strongest at the early stage of a norm's development, and domestic influences lessen significantly once a norm has become institutionalised in the international system" (1998, 893).

*Norm internalisation*

Once an international norm gains sufficient traction, Finnemore and Sikkink argue that it eventually becomes internalised by the majority of the international community, meaning that it "achieve[s] a 'taken-for-granted' quality that makes conformance with the norm almost automatic" (1998, 904). This process does not always happen, as not all norms gain enough international traction, but they suggest three main reasons why states internalise new norms: to reinforce their international legitimation; "prominence" – due either to the quality of the norm or the quality of the states promoting it; and the "intrinsic characteristics of the norm", in terms of either its clarity or its content (1998, 906).

Finnemore and Sikkink's concept does not reflect sufficiently the fact that the international norm is not simply transferred into the domestic sphere as the consequence of a top-down process. This would lead us to assume that the domestic norm would gradually be replaced by the international one, which, as this book suggests, is an option but may not necessarily be the case. However, the concept remains useful for analysing this tale of two norms.

During this phase, it can be assumed that the international community shares a strong, basic understanding of the international norm, and promotes and implements it most of the time, or at the very least feels compelled to justify why it is not implementing it. As a consequence, the impact an individual state like France can have on its development becomes more limited, and it can be expected that the domestic norm will, to a certain extent, align on the international consensus, at least until the international norm evolves again or becomes contested (Staunton 2018, 372).

The extent of this alignment will, however, vary, depending on the strength of both the domestic norm and the international norm at the time. If the domestic norm remains strong, it can be assumed that, instead of being replaced by the international norm, they will both survive in parallel with one another, and at times will continue to clash with one another. The ongoing influence of the domestic norm also means that states like France will continue to attempt to influence the international norm, even if an impact will be more difficult to achieve and will require extensive collaborations with other members of the international community.

As explained by Finnemore and Sikkink, the key challenge when studying this phase of the tale of two norms lies in the fact that "because they are not controversial, ... these norms are often not the centerpiece of political debate" (1998, 904). Therefore it can become harder to study how specific actors like France define and implement the international norms, and whether or not their conception and approach match the global consensus. Nevertheless, this challenge can be overcome thanks to the analysis of the debates that regularly take place both internationally and domestically on human protection and specific crises, key domestic policies and guidelines, and France's response – or lack of response – to various humanitarian crises.

Because humanitarian intervention has never become a norm, it has never reached the stage of internalisation. However, as Chapters 5 and 6 argue, the influence of R2P on France's conception of, and contribution to, human protection has increased as the norm has strengthened, to the point that it can be argued that it began to be internalised – to a certain extent – during Hollande's presidency. However, it would be mistaken to assume that the domestic norm became redundant and irrelevant as the result of this process, as the norm remained influential during Hollande's presidency and led France to promote a broad understanding of the scope of R2P.

## Conclusion

This chapter, and the book more generally, emphasise the importance of taking into account the interplay between related, yet distinct, domestic and international principles and norms and show how this can be achieved by putting forward an innovative theoretical framework. The latter overcomes some of the weaknesses of the norm life cycle and the norm circulation models, which prevent them from being used to analyse this tale of two norms.

In particular, this framework brings together the local and the international, but in contrast to others, it allows the analysis of the interplay of two specific domestic and international norms. Furthermore, it makes it possible to take into account the fact that norms are not static and can be used to analyse these developments by emphasising that the various stages of the framework are likely to recur as the international context evolves and/or new forms of contestation emerge. That being said, the framework also takes into account the increasing influence that international norms can have – as they strengthen (at least until their next evolution) – on related domestic norms, and in turn, the reduced influence that domestic norms can have as the international norms become more established. Finally, instead of focusing on a case in which an international norm is interacting with a state that is resistant to, or wary of, the norm, the framework is designed to examine a case in which the state was often leading the debates, and it thus provides a different and valuable view of how norms develop and interact.

Consequently, the framework allows a better understanding of the emergence and development of key international principles and norms such as humanitarian intervention and R2P by allowing us to take into account the role played by specific states like France. It also helps us understand the way these states are influenced by these international normative developments as they strengthen. Even though it was designed specifically for the study of France's relationship to human protection over time, it can be used to study the interplay of other domestic and international norms. Therefore it not only advances our understanding of human protection norms and France's foreign policy, but also makes a broader contribution to the literature on norms and International Relations theory more generally.

## Notes

1 A more in-depth definition of internalisation is discussed in the section "Theorising the tale of two norms".
2 Bernard Kouchner is the co-founder of Médecins Sans Frontières (Doctors Without Borders) and Médecins du Monde (World Doctors). Mario Bettati was a distinguished international legal scholar and administrator of the Faculty of South-Paris.
3 Given that identity is a social construction based on intersubjectivity (Finnemore and Sikkink 2001, 391; Adler 1997, 327), change can occur. Identity can indeed change from the inside, for instance after a change in domestic politics; from the outside, for instance after an 'external shock' which fundamentally challenges the identity by going "to the heart of the self-understanding

of a state, and its core norms" (Steans 2010, 197); or through the influence of the normative context in which states are embedded, since it is both regulative and constitutive. Despite this possibility for change, this book sees identity as inherently stable. This is not to say that identity never evolves or alters, but simply that it is considered to be sticky or hard to change. As the book shows, the two components of France's identity under scrutiny here have remained particularly stable over time.

4 Translations are my own except where otherwise stated.

5 It should be noted that this book aims to stay away from neo-colonial rhetoric. Although useful, the neo-colonial account is too restrictive as it mainly focuses on Africa and has a tendency to oversimplify France's actions. Instead, the book argues that one of the central drivers of France's foreign policy worldwide has been the executive's obsession with France's rank, since this account allows a better understanding by providing a more multi-dimensional framework.

6 The syndrome can be defined as the fear of the spread of the presence of the Anglo-Saxons in Africa.

7 See for instance the Quilès report made to the General Assembly, where Herman Cohen argues that the United States "did not have a real geographic strategy in the region" (1998, 32).

8 Acharya does acknowledge that the localisation process can eventually lead to 'norm displacement' (2004, 253). However, this idea is not reflected enough in the actual 'norm circulation' model and does not explore alternatives in enough depth.

9 As mentioned in the Introduction, the existing literature on France and human protection focuses too much on particular interventions in specific geographical domains and historical moments.

10 These changes consisted in particular of external shocks, such as the atrocities committed during the Second World War (Schmitz and Sikkink 2002, 522); international changes, such as the end of the Cold War (Forsythe 1991, 55); and domestic factors, such as the civil rights movement in the case of the United States (Sikkink 1993, 170).

11 See for instance Barnett (2005; 2010; 2011); Barnett and Weiss (2008); Bellamy (2004; 2009b); Bellamy and Wheeler (2011); Finnemore (1996a); Weiss (2012a); and Wheeler (2000, 2003).

12 See in particular Resolution 794 on Somalia.

# 2

# France, a norm entrepreneur of humanitarian intervention (1987–1993)

This chapter investigates France's conception of, and contribution to, human protection from 1987 to 1993. This period is particularly interesting because on the one hand, it corresponds to the emergence of France's domestic norm of human protection during François Mitterrand's presidency (1981–95), and on the other, it witnessed the emergence of the international principle that was humanitarian intervention.[1] Consequently, it allows the analysis of both processes and their interplay in order to make sense of France's conception of, and contribution to, human protection during that period.

The chapter is organised in three main sections. The first discusses the emergence of France's domestic norm of human protection. The second analyses the extent of the role played by France in the emergence of humanitarian intervention and argues that France was a norm entrepreneur between 1987 and 1991 before helping, through its practice, to consolidate the international principle from 1992. The third main section is dedicated to a case study of French involvement in Bosnia and Herzegovina – France's main intervention at the time – in order to illustrate the evolution of France's conception of, and contribution to, human protection during that period.

## France's domestic norm of human protection

At the heart of France's domestic norm of human protection lies the concept of *devoir d'ingérence* (Staunton 2018, 372). Jean-François Revel coined the expression in June 1979, when he published an article condemning the acts of two African despots: Jean-Bédel Bokassa in the CAR and Idi Amin Dada in Uganda.[2] He argued that "the *non-ingérence* principle is applicable only to democracies; regarding other regimes, it is a synonym for non-assistance to a person in danger" (1979). This principle of non-assistance, which consists of punishing any person who would not assist a person in danger, is taken very seriously in France and can lead to five years' imprisonment and a 75,000 euro fine under Article 223-6 of the Penal Code. It is often used to justify the *devoir d'ingérence* (see for instance Kouchner 2002).

### *Where it began: the debate on the* devoir d'ingérence

Although Revel came up with the expression *devoir d'ingérence*, it was Bernard Kouchner, co-founder of Médecins Sans Frontières (Doctors Without Borders) and Médecins Du Monde (World Doctors), who became its promoter and practitioner (Staunton 2018, 373).[3] His will to promote the concept was sparked by the fact that the staff of the humanitarian NGOs he created had to constantly risk their lives and break international law in order to provide humanitarian relief (Kouchner in Colombani and Simon 1991).[4] Kouchner considered that this situation was unacceptable since the humanitarian workers would enter foreign states only to answer calls for help from victims: "we intervene after a call, on demand, never by transgression. And in order to protect the most vulnerable, the victims" (1991a). Therefore, in his view, the real crime did not exist in the violation of states' sovereignty by the NGO workers, but rather in the *non-ingérence*, since "to undermine this [call for assistance] amounts ... to non-assistance to a person in danger" (2002).

In January 1987 Kouchner and Professor Mario Bettati organised an International Conference on Humanitarian Law and Ethics in Paris to debate and promote the concept coined by Revel (Allen and Styan 2000, 835; Guillot 1994, 31; Staunton 2018, 373).[5] Kouchner opened the conference by asking, "can we let them die simply because a frontier separates us from the danger they are in?" (1987, 11). Kouchner and Bettati then argued that victims of a humanitarian crisis had a right to receive assistance: *un droit à l'assistance humanitaire* or 'right to humanitarian assistance', which was defined as a "new human right" (Kouchner 1987, 22; Bettati 1987, 24). To honour this human right, they argued, a *devoir d'ingérence* needed to be acknowledged, along with a subsequent *droit d'ingérence* (a right to intervene or interfere) in order to allow states to fulfil this duty and honour victims' right to life and assistance.

Even though some commentators consider that Kouchner used the expressions *droit* and *devoir d'ingérence* as if they were interchangeable, this is misleading,[6] and in fact it prevents us from understanding the French conception of human protection: the need to create an international right to intervene emerged only as a way to fulfil a duty to assist endangered populations and to implement victims' right to life and humanitarian assistance. Consequently, from the beginning, the rights of victims and the responsibility of states to intervene to enforce these rights were emphasised.

The source of the emergency was broadly defined in order to promote an extensive understanding of human protection. As Bettati explained, this was a necessity, since "the breadth of some violence or some domestic or international armed conflicts produces critical situations liable to create numerous victims whose survival and help depend on efficient and rapid humanitarian assistance. Some natural, industrial or nuclear catastrophes risk engendering similar consequences" (1987, 26). At the end of the conference, the participants passed a resolution that called for the recognition "in a single international document signed by all the states members of the international community, of both the right of victims to humanitarian assistance and the obligation of the states to contribute to this assistance" (Bettati and Kouchner 1987, 292).

*Endorsement of the French executive*

Some might argue that the impact of conferences often remains limited beyond the realm of the participants or the wider academic community. However, this conference was different. It not only managed to gather key speakers such as the UN High Commissioner for refugees Jean-Pierre Hocke and the Nobel Peace Prize holder Lech Walesa, but was also opened and concluded by President Mitterrand and his Prime Minister Jacques Chirac respectively, thereby obtaining a lot of public attention (Staunton 2018, 373).

Mitterrand declared, "the first human right, you will agree, is the right to life, and the first duty is the assistance to a person in danger, to a population threatened by perils. All of those who hold means of action are bound by this duty" (1987, 33). He added that "international law, as it has started to do, needs to recognise more and more the rights of the human beings, the rights of individuals and that the rights of individuals cannot be denied in everyday life, in everyday practice, or by the rights of states" (1987, 35). Similarly, Chirac argued that such a conference could not have taken place anywhere but France and explained that "my first reaction is of course unreserved support for everything that constitutes 'humanitarian morality' ... which consists of rushing quickly and everywhere as soon as human suffering sends a call for help. ... It is obvious that this morality is at the heart of our French traditions" (1987, 279–280).

Mitterrand was aware that promoting a *devoir d'ingérence* and creating a subsequent *droit d'ingérence* in international law would be challenging in view of the extent of the changes this would require and the time it usually takes for the international community to agree upon and implement controversial principles (Mitterrand 1987, 32). Nevertheless, he wanted France to attempt to achieve this goal (Mitterrand 1987, 32), and on 5 October 1987 he affirmed that "the *devoir d'ingérence* [would] one day appear in the Declaration of Human Rights" (in Védrine 1996, 543).

Consequently, in addition to diplomatically supporting the efforts of Kouchner and Bettati, the French President and Prime Minister invited the local norm entrepreneurs to be part of the government (Jeangène Vilmer 2012, 83; Guillot 1994, 32; Staunton 2018, 373). Kouchner was appointed Secretary of State for Humanitarian Action in 1988, and he remained in the post for four years before becoming Minister of Public Health and Humanitarian Action from 1992 to 1993, while Bettati became his legal advisor. The two rapidly received the support of Roland Dumas, Minister of Foreign Affairs from June 1988 to April 1992.[7] This commitment to promote the concept was essential given that, as argued in Chapter 1, for a norm to develop, both domestically and internationally, it has to be institutionalised by key actors. In this case, not only were the norm entrepreneurs supported by the executive, but they became part of it and immediately began to work towards the transformation of this recognised domestic 'duty' into an international 'right'.

Because the idea of *ingérence* was framed as a duty rather than simply a right, and in moral rather than legal terms, the support of French public opinion rapidly became strong.[8] In particular, the French population became supportive of any intervention that was presented as humanitarian. Smouts explains that "the debate [indeed] built up a very strong sentiment of moral obligation in public opinion that there was a duty, if not a right, to bring assistance to victims of famine, war, and catastrophes of all kind throughout the world. The climate was thus favourable for the unprecedented linking of military and humanitarian action" (1998, 36). This can be seen in a poll carried out in France by SIRPA (Service d'Informations et de Relations Publiques des Armées, or Service of Information and Public Relations of the Armies): "when asked if they approved or disapproved of the use of French armed forces, ... to bring assistance to populations in distress (famine and civil war)", the positive replies were "73 per cent in 1990, 79 per cent in 1991, [and] 81 per cent in 1992 and 1993" (in Smouts 1998, 34).

The executive's willingness to support Kouchner and Bettati's proposal, and to make the promotion of a *devoir d'ingérence* a priority of France's foreign policy, cannot be understood without taking into account the influence of two key ideational factors (Staunton 2018, 373–374). The first is the idea that France is the 'homeland of human rights' and as such, has a

special role to play in protecting and promoting these rights (in particular, the right to life). As mentioned in Chapter 1, this aspect of France's
identity has often been traced back to the French Revolution and is deeply
embedded in public opinion and among policymakers (see Macleod
2004, 80).

Mitterrand was no exception. For instance, only a few months after his
election, he referred to himself and the French population as "the sons of
the French Revolution" and explained that France was the "champion of
the rights of the citizen", before declaring that "in international law, the
non-assistance to populations in danger is not a crime yet. But it is a moral
and political failure that has already cost too many lives and too much
harm to too many abandoned populations" (1981). Chirac, although he
was from a different political party than Mitterrand,[9] also referred to
France as "the nation of human rights, architect of the Universal Declaration, champion of freedom and the dignity of human beings, everywhere
where it is endangered, land of hope for the oppressed, land of asylum for
thousands of refugees" (1987, 280). This conviction was also shared by
public opinion, facilitated by the fact that France had been described as
the 'homeland of human rights' in every aspect of public life (be it in
schools, political events or commemorations). Therefore France was seen
as having a central "role to play in this international fight": the promotion
of victims' *droit à l'assistance humanitaire* (Mitterrand 1987, 32), in order
to be "worthy of its past and its traditions" (Chirac 1987, 285).

As mentioned in Chapter 1, the second component of France's identity
that must be taken into account when trying to make sense of its contribution to human protection is France's rank. This has obsessed French leaders
for centuries to the point that it constitutes "an end in itself" (Grosser 1995,
64; see also Macleod and Voyer-Léger 2004). France is seen as 'more than
a middle sized power' thanks to its history,[10] cultural influence, nuclear
capacity and permanent seat at the UN Security Council, and as such,
believes that it ought to be involved in human protection.

When it comes to Mitterrand's presidency specifically, promoting
human protection had the advantage of helping France maintain its rank
in what was perceived to be a challenging changing world order (Boniface
2008, 57; Treacher 2000, 25; Zuqian 2002, 113–114). In other words,
playing a central role in human protection was seen as both a responsibility
in light of France's history, values and rank, and an opportunity to maintain
France's status and image. The gradual end of the Cold War and the subsequent reunification and empowerment of Germany were indeed seen as
an alteration of the balance of power in Europe that could considerably
damage France's status. As Macleod explains, during the Cold War,

Mitterrand had worked towards an "implicit power-sharing [with Germany], with France taking on the political and military leadership which was denied Germany, and Germany assuming leadership in economic and monetary matters" (1997, 247). Consequently, since the signing of the 1957 Rome Treaty, it had "buil[t] a Europe in its image" since "the Common Agricultural Policy, the common tariff policy, a powerful but unelected European Commission, and an elected but weak European Parliament served the French interests" (Zuqian 2002, 114).

The end of the Cold War, however, altered the balance of power, and Mitterrand's various executives became fearful that Germany would no longer be satisfied with the status quo and would endanger France's position by opening up to Eastern Europe.[11] Macleod argues that "at the time, these fears seemed justified when the German chancellor, Helmut Kohl, imposed his own plan for unification without consulting his allies, delayed recognition of the Oder-Neisse line as the eastern border of the new Germany, and pursued a policy of opening toward the East, based on Germany's economic and commercial power" (1997, 247). This shift was problematic for Mitterrand and his executives because they relied on France's status as European leader to promote its influence and power in the world. As Mitterrand's diplomatic advisor Hubert Védrine recalls, in 1985 "the President [was] even more determined to move forward [with the European construction] ... since none of the traditional portfolios of French diplomacy [was] otherwise very promising" (1996, 393). Consequently, Mitterrand's executives rapidly felt pressured to affirm France's status in order for it to not be overshadowed.

Mitterrand was also concerned by the perceived spread of the Anglo-Saxon presence in Africa. After the decolonisation process ended, France kept very close relations with its old colonies and francophone Africa in order to promote French interests in the region (see Domergue 1998; Gregory 2000b; Hansen 2008, 118; Renou 2002, 6–8).[12] As Gregory explains, in francophone Africa, "France found strategic resources, ... and a ready market for French goods, French culture and French ideas. With *Francophone* Africa, France was always more than a middle-size European state" (2000b, 436). Mitterrand thus believed that "France would no longer be entirely itself in the eyes of the world if it renounced its presence in Africa" (in Treacher 2000, 40).

Consequently, the perceived growing presence of Anglo-Saxons (especially Americans) in the continent – and more specifically in francophone Africa – was a concern for the French President. This fear of an Anglo-Saxon threat is often described as the "Fashoda syndrome", which can be defined as "the French complex concerning British/US influence in the African continent" (Kroslak 2007, 111). The syndrome takes its name from the French humiliation created by the Fashoda incident in 1898: the French and British colonial expeditions met in Fashoda (today Kodok in Sudan) when the French were trying to go from the west to the east of the continent (from Dakar to Djibouti), and the British from the north to the south (from Cairo to Cape Town). Following an ultimatum from the British and a tense diplomatic crisis, France withdrew without gaining any major concessions from the British. This incident is remembered and taught as a moment of great humiliation in French history (Staunton 2016, 308). The fear of the British influence in Africa extended to the Americans in the 1960s, when an "intense rivalry between Kennedy and Charles de Gaulle in Africa" developed (Muehlenbeck 2012, 155).

As Chapter 3 shows, whether the threat from the Americans was real or not in the 1990s remains contested. For instance, Renou argues that "the demand for democratisation in the early 1990s in *Francophone* Africa gave an opportunity to the USA, whose volume of trade with Africa (and therefore political interests) [was] bigger than with Eastern Europe, to try to undermine the French influence in its own sphere" (2002, 14). On the other hand, the Quilès report prepared for the French General Assembly strongly questioned the veracity of this claim (1998, 33).

What is not contested is the influence that the Fashoda syndrome had on Mitterrand. This concern was not new in the President's mind. For instance, the Quilès report explains that in 1957, when Mitterrand was Minister of Justice, he blamed the British for the troubles linked to the decolonisation of France's African colonies (1998, 31). The influence of the syndrome intensified towards the end of the Cold War and during the 1990s: according to Jean-Louis Debré, "Mitterrand reckoned that the Americans had a hegemonic claim" (in Kroslak 2007, 112), and it was already a complex time for France because its interests were threatened by the instability of the franc zone (Zuqian 2002, 114). Even though it was mainly Mitterrand who was affected by this fear, rather than his entire executive,[13] in view of the central role of the President in foreign affairs – the infamous *domaine réservé* – this syndrome played an important part in the design of France's foreign policy at the time since it only intensified Mitterrand's will to promote France's status and presence internationally.

Last but not least, with the end of the Cold War and the subsequent re-empowerment of the UN Security Council, France felt pressured to justify its permanent membership at the UN Security Council (Guillot 1994, 34; Utley 2000, 187). In contrast to the Cold War era, especially under de Gaulle's presidency, presenting France as 'the third way' between the United States and the Soviet Union by adopting as much as possible an independent policy was no longer enough. Mitterrand's executives felt that they had to contribute more in order to justify France's permanent seat.

This pressure was accompanied by an opportunity, in that the re-empowerment of the Security Council meant that the UN became a potentially strong institutional framework within which to promote France's rank. As Mitterrand explained, the UN "[was] developing under our eyes and finally appear[ed] as a true judge who tells the law and seeks to apply it, if needs be by force, therefore fulfilling an essential mission assigned by the San Francisco Charter" (1995, 77). Consequently, the French President made France's place at the UN a priority. To borrow Tardy's words, "because it [became] a source of legitimacy and a central organ of the regulation system, the UN impose[d] itself on a France particularly concerned to keep its rank in the context of the 'disruption of the world'" (2002, 933).

Consequently, the idea that France is the 'homeland of human rights' and 'more than a middle sized power' facilitated the endorsement of Kouchner and Bettati's concept of *devoir d'ingérence* by the executive at the time, and led to the emergence of France's domestic norm of human protection, which has impacted its conception of, and contribution to, human protection ever since by arguing that in light of its history, values and rank, France has a special role to play in the promotion of human protection.

## France, a norm entrepreneur of humanitarian intervention

For Mitterrand, promoting human protection normatively, diplomatically and militarily was a way to fulfil France's perceived duty in light of its history, values and rank, while allowing France to offer a pragmatic response to the changing international order by helping to showcase its rank. The French executive thus began lobbying for the emergence of an internationally recognised *droit d'ingérence* to honour victims' *droit à l'assistance humanitaire* at the end of the 1980s, before implementing what it perceived to be its *devoir d'ingérence* by heavily participating in – and often leading – UN interventions undertaken for humanitarian purposes around the world (Staunton 2018, 374–375). In doing so, it contributed to shaping and legitimising the practice of humanitarian intervention by the international community.

Before exploring France's contribution in more depth, it is important to highlight that it would not have been possible without the emergence of a favourable international normative context. As Dunne and Staunton explain, some key shifts had already taken place during the Cold War (2016).[14] The end of the Cold War was also determinant in allowing a debate to take place on sovereignty and human rights since the UN Security Council was no longer paralysed by the vetoes of the Soviet Union and the United States, and "complex humanitarian emergencies" received public attention because the focus was no longer on the opposition between the two blocs (Barnett 2011, 2–3).

## The normative role played by France

In light of this positive context, the French executive at the time, and in particular Kouchner and Bettati, began promoting the need for the international community to recognise an international right to intervene in order to fulfil victims' rights to life and assistance and states' duty to react (Staunton 2018, 374). Their efforts began with the UN General Assembly, and as early as 8 December 1988, a key resolution was adopted: "A/RES/43/131 on humanitarian assistance to victims of natural disasters and similar emergency situations" (Gregory 2000a, 60; Guillot 1994, 32; Lombart 2007a; Torrelli 1992, 239; UN General Assembly 1988).

Under Kouchner's instructions, Bettati drafted the resolution and spent weeks with the French Permanent Representative to the UN, convincing member states to vote in its favour (Bettati 1993, 642, 644; 2014; Kouchner 2014). They were helped by President Mitterrand, who had begun to promote the core idea of the resolution during his speech at the UN General Assembly on 29 September 1988:

> Two centuries ago, France undertook a revolution, her revolution, which has marked the course of history. ... As we prepare to celebrate this bicentenary, let's defend human rights more than ever. ... It is right today, in the case of some emergency situations, of distress or extreme injustice, to affirm a *droit d'assistance humanitaire*. ... So many people are still denied their most basic rights and so many men, women and children have misery as their homeland and a lack of rights as their only horizon. Hasn't the moment come to realise that there are rights of humanity and to define them? (1988)

Bettati recalls that France had to push for the resolution to be passed because the French initiative generated a large amount of debate before being adopted: "sometimes condescending, sometimes really hostile, few UN members volunteered to be co-authors of the draft resolution ... . The consensus reached on the text of Resolution 43/131 was laboriously obtained" (1995, 270). Nevertheless, after extensive lobbying and some redrafting and compromising, it was passed. It stated that the UN General Assembly "reaffirms the importance of humanitarian assistance for the victims of natural disasters and similar emergency situations" and "urges states in proximity to areas of natural disasters and similar emergency situations ... to participate closely with the affected countries in international efforts" (UN General Assembly 1988, 2).

Two years later, on 14 December 1990, Resolution 45/100 on "humanitarian assistance to victims of natural disasters and similar emergency situations" was also passed (Lombart 2007a; Torrelli 1992, 239). It reasserted the core of Resolution 43/131 by "reaffirm[ing] the cardinal importance of humanitarian assistance for the victims of natural disasters and similar emergency situations", and it authorised the creation of humanitarian corridors. The resolution indeed "request[ed] the Secretary-General to pursue, within existing resources, the necessary consultations ... with a view to determining means of facilitating the delivery of appropriate humanitarian assistance to the victims of natural disasters or similar emergency situations, including the establishment of relief corridors" (UN General Assembly 1990).

Both the content of Resolution 45/100 and also its sponsors testified to the progress accomplished by the French in gaining international traction behind the idea of a right to intervene in order to fulfil a right to humanitarian assistance. The Soviet Union, which had been opposed to Resolution 43/131 two years earlier and wanted the terms "to the demand of the state" to be added after "free access to victims" (Bettati 2014), asked to sponsor the 1990 resolution with France. According to Kouchner and Bettati, this shift of position can mainly be explained by the fact that, at the Soviet Union's request, France had intervened in Armenia following the 1988 earthquake in order to provide humanitarian assistance. The intervention was rapid and purely humanitarian, and consequently it helped rally the support of the Soviet Union by reassuring it about the intents of the resolutions (Bettati 2014; Kouchner 2014). This shift testified to the progress made in just two years: as a norm entrepreneur, France was building key coalitions with other permanent members of the UN Security Council.

Resolutions 43/131 and 45/100 were seen by the French executive as significant milestones in the emergence of an international right to intervene to provide humanitarian assistance. Bettati referred to Resolution 43/131 as "this 'right of humanitarian *ingérence*' that the Organisation now holds" (1993, 643) and explained, "we, in 1987, proposed a norm designed to allow the humanitarian organisations to rescue beyond borders. The French doctors by their stubbornness in the field, the diplomats by their determination, UN organs by their availability, and political men and women by their support in the national and international arena have allowed it to emerge at the UN General Assembly" (1993, 644; see also Kouchner in Allen and Styan 2000, 831–832).

These declarations were nevertheless exaggerated in view of the fact that both resolutions focused on victims' right to humanitarian assistance rather than on states' right to provide it. Additionally, in order for the resolutions to pass, Bettati had to considerably modify his original draft and included what he called "cosmetic dispositions" (2014). The latter actually considerably changed the content of the resolution. For instance, they re-emphasised the importance of "the sovereignty, territorial integrity and national unity of States" (UN General Assembly 1988; 1990). Finally, the international community agreed on a much narrower understanding of human protection than what Kouchner and Bettati had hoped for. While they wanted the resolutions to include any type of humanitarian crisis – no matter what its cause was – the expression "other similar emergencies" was understood as narrowly as possible by many signatories.

However, even though the declarations made by the executive at the time gave too much weight to the shift created by the resolutions, it would be mistaken to underestimate their importance. They constituted a key milestone in the emergence of a global consensus on humanitarian inter-vention by allowing the UN General Assembly to debate the idea. They also led France to play a central role in the adoption of other resolutions such as UN General Assembly Resolution 46/182 on the "Strengthening of the coordination of humanitarian emergency assistance of the United Nations" passed on 19 December 1991 (Lombart 2007a). This resolution provided forty-two principles for increasing humanitarian assistance ranging from prevention to rehabilitation (UN General Assembly 1991).

The executive's will to promote a right to intervene to assist the victims of humanitarian emergencies did not stop at the UN General Assembly. Building on the successes achieved, France also pushed for resolutions at the UN Security Council, which, in contrast to the General Assembly, has the right to pass resolutions binding on all member states. A key resolution that deserves our attention is Resolution 688 on Iraq, passed by the UN Security Council in 1991 following a Franco-Belgian draft, and despite the opposition of Cuba, Yemen and Zimbabwe and the abstention of China and India (Allen and Styan 2000, 837; Gregory 2000a, 60; Lombart 2007a; UN Security Council 1991c).

On 3 April 1991, during the Council of Ministers on the situation in Iraq, Mitterrand declared: "the *droit d'ingérence* needs to be recognised. There is an international campaign to be undertaken; this right will not be admitted for a very long time. ... The frontier is hard to draw. Nevertheless, it would be an advance in civilisation progress, a reordering of international society" (in Védrine 1996, 543). The next day, despite the close ties between France and Iraq since 1972 (Saul 1995, 83, 90), Rochereau de la Sablière requested a meeting of the Security Council (UN Security Council 1991a). On 5 April 1991 a revised version of the draft submitted by France and Belgium became Resolution 688, which condemned violence and requested that "Iraq allow immediate access by international humanitarian organisa-tions to all those in need of assistance in all parts of Iraq and to make available all necessary facilities for their operations" (UN Security Council 1991c).

Mitterrand congratulated himself on the fact that "France ... took the initiative with this new right, quite extraordinary in the history of the world, which is a sort of *droit d'ingérence* inside a state when some of its population are victims of persecution" (in Lombart 2007a). Dumas affirmed that the resolution was "without historical precedent since it entail[ed] and allow[ed] a right to intervene in the domestic affairs of a state" (in Torrelli 1992, 239). Similarly, Kouchner stated that "unhappy and alone, threatened by death, the Kurds, ignored yesterday, have imposed the *droit d'ingérence!*" and talked about "an important threshold being crossed" (in Colombani and Simon 1991). He argued that by "using exactly the terms of the humanitarian resolutions that Serge Telle and Mario Bettati had, in our name, made the General Assembly vote for in 1988 and 1990 ... the international community thus affirmed a right to a humanitarian gaze inside states" (1991b, 266).[15] In other words, the executive considered this resolution a key milestone in the development of human protection by seeing it as a ruling of the Security Council on domestic affairs.

Nevertheless, once again, the global consensus on the resolution differed in significant ways from the French understanding. Even though France's intent was to focus on the situation within Iraq (see de la Sablière in UN Security Council 1991b, 53–54), the Council was able to pass Resolution 688 only because it was framed as an answer to the threat to regional stability created by the massacres perpetrated by the Iraqi government. This allowed the council to rule by justifying that there was a threat to international peace and security (Wheeler 2000, 144).[16] Additionally, Resolution 688 did not explicitly authorise or approve the use of force to stop these massacres (Malone 2006, 90).

However, despite these limitations, it would be mistaken to underestimate the importance of the resolution, for internal repression was part of what mobilised the international community (Nigel Rodley, in Wheeler 2000, 144). Additionally, even though the resolution only ambiguously linked the humanitarian crisis with the notion of threat to international peace and security, it constituted a key milestone in the emergence of humanitarian intervention by giving the opportunity to the Security Council to debate the broadening of the meaning of what constitutes a threat to international peace and security (Wheeler 2000, 146). Finally, while the resolution did not explicitly authorise the use of force, a coalition mainly led by the United States, the United Kingdom and France undertook a military intervention, Operation Provide Comfort, using the resolution as justification and contributed to showing that this kind of intervention was necessary at times. According to Bellamy, it indeed led the international community to begin to acknowledge that "there is a 'humanitarian exception' to the non-intervention rule" (2004, 218).

Consequently, in light of the influence of its domestic norm of human protection in a changing world order, France played a key normative role in the emergence of humanitarian intervention at the end of the 1980s. Gareth Evans offers a good account of the impact of the French contribution internationally. In particular, in regard to Kouchner, he argues that

> [He] did not invent the concept of, or even the expression, 'humanitarian intervention'. ... But what Kouchner did do was give it a new lease of life by inventing and popularising the expression *'droit d'ingérence,'* ... which had real resonance in the new circumstances of the post-cold war world. ... In the recurring debates of the 1990s, the banner call from those demanding forceful action in the face of catastrophe was invariably, echoing Kouchner, 'the right of humanitarian intervention', the right to intervene. In making the response to mass atrocities the single most debated foreign policy issue of the decade, rather than one that could comfortably be ignored by policymakers, his contribution was outstanding. (2008a, 32)

Therefore, even though Kouchner's view was somewhat exaggerated, he was not entirely wrong in saying that "the organisation of a *droit d'assistance* codified by the states" was emerging and that the French executive played a central role in this shift (Colombani and Simon 1991).

### *A strong military involvement for humanitarian purposes*

From 1992, the idea of a recognised need – if not right – to intervene to assist endangered populations was beginning to gain traction among the international community, and as a consequence, France's contribution shifted from a normative role to that of implementer. By actively taking part in interventions for humanitarian purposes, Mitterrand's various executives not only contributed to legitimising humanitarian intervention, but also considerably helped shape the way the international community implemented it.

### The UN, the institutional framework chosen to intervene

First, in terms of the institutional framework chosen to intervene, France selected the UN and thus heavily contributed to the interventions the international organisation undertook for humanitarian purposes. As Graph 1 shows, France's troop contribution considerably increased in 1992, making France the highest troop contributor of the UN from April 1992, with a peak of 9,379 troops in August 1993 (UN 1992; 1993). This

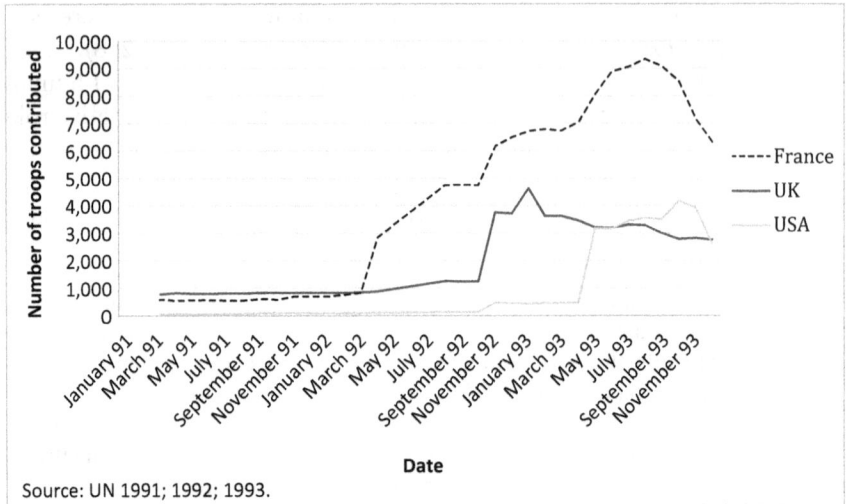

Source: UN 1991; 1992; 1993.

Note: Data not available before 1991 or for January–February 1991 and May–July 1992.

**Graph 1** Troop contributions to the UN by France, the United Kingdom and the United States, 1991–93

contribution was well above those made by the other P3 members (the United States and the United Kingdom). In addition to this concrete contribution, France was one of the first states to respond to the UN Secretary General Boutros Boutros-Ghali's 1992 Agenda for Peace. It offered "to place up to 1,000 French troops at the UN's disposal on 48 hours' notice" (Gregory 2000a, 61–62), and suggested that other member states should also identify national units that could rapidly be put at the disposal of the UN (Smouts 1998, 23).

Given that France had been promoting human protection at the UN since 1988, because the UN had the power to authorise humanitarian interventions and seemed increasingly willing to do so, and in light of the fact that France was eager to justify its permanent seat at the UN Security Council, this choice of institutional framework can appear logical in retrospect. However, it actually constituted a rupture in the relationship between France and the UN.

During the Cold War, France had complex relations with the UN. Tensions began when the United States undermined France's position by deciding to address the Korean War through the UN General Assembly rather than the Security Council in order to avoid a Soviet Union veto (Gregory 2000a, 58; Smouts 1997, 26–27). The Suez Crisis and the UN's promotion of decolonisation also made relations between France and the international institution more difficult (Gregory 2000a, 58; Smouts 1997, 25, 28–29). They became particularly tense during Charles de Gaulle's presidency (1959–69), as illustrated by the fact that he used to refer to the UN as a *machin*, which is a pejorative term for 'thing'. Although these relations began to normalise in the 1970s when France accepted the leadership of the United Nations Interim Force in Lebanon (UNIFIL), it was only at the beginning of the 1990s, when France promoted the idea that the UN was the institution best suited to undertake interventions for humanitarian purposes, that they improved (Gregory 2000a, 59).

A worldwide military commitment

Another important characteristic of France's contribution to human protection in the early 1990s consisted of the geographical location of its interventions for humanitarian purposes. As would be expected in view of the strong ties between France and Africa, France contributed troops to UN interventions taking place in the continent. However, as Graph 2 shows, it took part in most of the UN missions that occurred between 1990 and 1993, no matter where they were located, by participating in UNTSO (United Nations Truce Supervision Organisation), UNIFIL, UNIKOM (United Nations Iraq–Kuwait Observation Mission), MINURSO (United Nations Mission for the Referendum in Western Sahara), UNAMIC (United Nations Advance Mission in Cambodia), ONUSAL (United Nations Observer Mission in El Salvador), UNTAC (United Nations Transitional

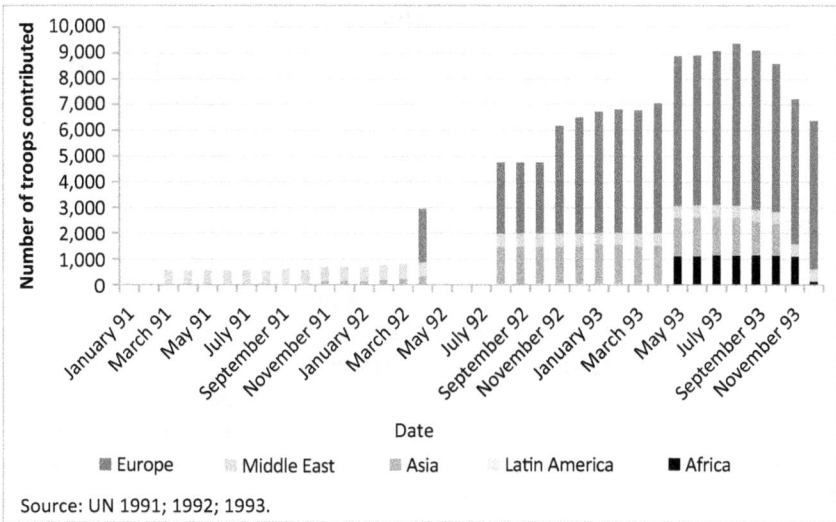

Source: UN 1991; 1992; 1993.

Note: Data not available before 1991 or for January–February 1991 and May–July 1992.

**Graph 2** France's troop contributions to UN humanitarian interventions by geographic area, 1991–93

Authority in Cambodia), UNPROFOR (United Nations Protection Force) and UNOSOM (United Nations Operation in Somalia) (UN 1990; 1991; 1992; 1993).

In fact, seven of these nine operations took place outside the African continent, and the only substantial intervention in which France took part in Africa was UNOSOM. The majority of the French troops were deployed in Europe to support UNPROFOR (in former Yugoslavia) and Asia to assist UNTAC. This meant that "for the first time since the end of the Indochina war, the sun ha[d] not set on the French army" (Guillot 1994, 34).

Therefore between 1988 and 1993, in addition to playing a normative role in the emergence of humanitarian intervention, France helped shape the way the international community implemented it by choosing the UN as the institutional framework to intervene and not limiting its interventions to its usual perceived zone of influence, Africa. In addition to allowing France to fulfil its perceived duty in light of its history, values and rank, Mitterrand's executives' commitment to human protection helped justify France's permanent seat at the Security Council while showing states such as the United States and Germany that it was still powerful both diplomatically and militarily. By showing that France was willing – and able – to intervene worldwide for humanitarian purposes, France indeed proved that "it [was] able to assume the political, military, financial and human costs" of the interventions (Tardy 1999, 80; see also Treacher 2000, 25).

## Bosnia and Herzegovina

France's commitment and contribution to human protection is best illustrated by its involvement in the conflict in former Yugoslavia and more specifically in Bosnia and Herzegovina. This intervention has the merit of allowing the study of the evolution of France's position and strategy over time, since it lasted several years (this section covers the beginning of the conflict up to 1993, while its resolution is discussed in Chapter 3). More importantly, the conflict is particularly relevant because it mobilised by far the most French troops deployed in any conflict at the time. Furthermore, it took place outside Africa, and consequently contributed to creating a rupture in France's tradition of intervention: as Rollet argues, since "the context of the intervention [was] no longer one of a post-colonial presence as was the case in Africa. Nor was it a Cold War configuration during which Western armies [were] getting ready to face the Soviet armies" (2006, 7). Finally, this conflict is important because both Mitterrand and Chirac (when he became President in 1995) were heavily involved in its resolution. It thus played a central role in their level of willingness and their strategy to intervene to address humanitarian emergencies throughout the decade.

## A strong involvement

The declarations of independence of Slovenia and Croatia in June 1991 triggered military attacks from the Serbs (under the leadership of Slobodan Milosevic), as they were determined to "preserve a unitary state that they would dominate" (Ramsbotham and Woodhouse 1999, 276). These attacks spread to Bosnia and Herzegovina in March and April 1992 following the declaration of independence proclaimed on 3 March 1992 (McQueen 2005, 55; Rollet 2006, 29).

As Védrine recalls, Mitterrand and his various executives had been involved in the resolution of the conflict in former Yugoslavia since its initial stage (1996, 609–610). In particular, in Croatia, France seemed determined to find a common strategy among the European Communities (EC) and was favourable to the creation of a Western European Union interposition force authorised by the Security Council (Védrine 1996, 609). However, France's involvement became particularly focused on Bosnia and Herzegovina as the conflict intensified. This involvement can first be explained by the fact that the various French executives felt compelled to act for humanitarian purposes, especially since the crisis was taking place in France's backyard (Soulet 2012; Treacher 2000, 30). Mitterrand declared on 27 June 1992 after the EC Summit in Lisbon that "there [was] what we could call a mandatory minimum, what we have called a *devoir d'assistance* and even a *droit d'ingérence*, which is an idea I personally supported at the United Nations platform, and this minimum must tend to enforce the right to life" (Mitterrand 1992). The French population's support of the *devoir d'ingérence* and the heavy mediatisation of the conflict also pressured and facilitated France's commitment (Soulet 2012).

Additionally, Mitterrand and his executives wanted to strengthen France's status by demonstrating to the world that it was a state that mattered and that, as a powerful state, it should and could play a central role in the resolution of a conflict which was threatening to destabilise the continent (Macleod 1997, 254; Soulet 2012; Treacher 2000, 30). They were also concerned about the perceived growing influence of Germany. As Zic explains, "it was believed to be only a matter of time before a reunified Germany outstripped France politically and militarily, as had already happened economically" (2000, 18). This fear was reinforced by the fact that Germany unilaterally recognised the independence of Slovenia and Croatia on 23 December 1991, without waiting for the official discussion and announcement of the EC on 15 January 1992 (Rollet 2006, 39). Additionally, the divisions among EC members on how to handle the conflict were problematic because what would become the Maastricht Treaty was being negotiated at the time (Dumas 2011, 420–421), and as mentioned previously, France relied on its status as European leader to promote its rank. However, the conflict also represented a key opportunity to counterbalance the influence of Germany while showing the United States that the EC – which France had always seen as "a counterweight to the international influence of the United States" (Macleod 1997, 245) – was capable of managing crises in its own backyard (McQueen 2005, 56).

Consequently, in light of France's history, values and rank, Mitterrand and his executives became heavily involved in the conflict, both diplomatically and militarily. France pushed for, and supported, Security Council resolutions on the situation in Bosnia and Herzegovina and the strengthening of the mandate of UNPROFOR, which had originally been created for Croatia but rapidly also became in charge of stabilising Bosnia and Herzegovina. More specifically, between 1992 and 1993, it co-drafted fifteen draft resolutions on the situation.[17]

Additionally, Jean-Bernard Mérimée, the French Permanent Representative to the UN, vowed in front of the UN Security Council that France would "do what it believe[d] to be its duty in order to tirelessly promote, within the framework of our Organisation, the chances for peace" (UN Security Council 1993b, 4). Consequently, France – along with other European powers – kept working towards a peace plan, to the point that, as Treacher argues, "French efforts to bring about a permanent resolution to the conflict were unmatched by any other country (2000, 30).[18] Finally, France drafted proposals for the creation of an international tribunal for the former Yugoslavia in February 1993 and pushed for its creation at the Security Council (UN Security Council 1993c, 8–9; 1993f, 10–12). This was a key initiative from the French executive at the time, since it was the first time the UN Security Council authorised the creation of an international criminal jurisdiction (Bettati 2014).

In addition to its diplomatic role, France also played a central role militarily. Mérimée explained that "the French Government ha[d] spared neither men nor resources" (UN Security Council 1993a, 19). For instance, despite the high level of casualties (François Léotard in Juppé 2001), France was the main troop contributor to UNPROFOR, with an average contribution of 4,589 troops between its deployment in April 1992 and December 1993 (it peaked in August 1993 when it reached 6,284 troops) (UN 1991; 1992; 1993). As illustrated by Graph 3, the level of this contribution was considerably higher than those made by other members of the Contact Group at the time (the United Kingdom, the United States and Germany) which was established to help find a solution to the conflict. Moreover, French generals were in charge of the operation from 1993 onwards (Ramsbotham and Woodhouse 1999, 278).[19]

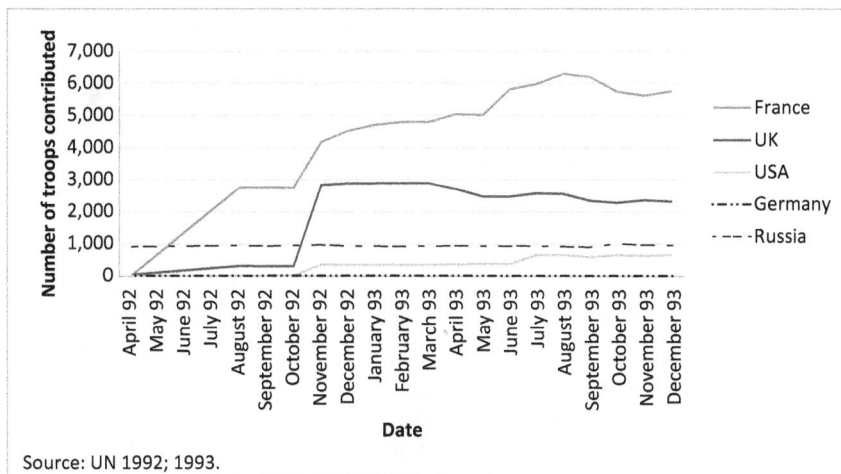

Source: UN 1992; 1993.

Note: Data not available for May–July 1992. The first troops were sent in April 1992.

**Graph 3** Comparison of troop contributions to UNPROFOR, 1992–93

The prominent role of France in the early stages of the conflict was facilitated by the fact that other key powers were reluctant to take the lead. Therefore, "taking advantage of the United States' indecisiveness over whether the war in Bosnia did or did not constitute a vital national interest, of Russian hesitation in the face of domestic problems, of British reluctance to engage in a conflict so far away, and of German reticence to repeat the painful experience of recognising the two dissident republics" (Macleod 1997, 254), France assumed the leading role in the early stages of the conflict and remained a central actor throughout its unfolding (Zic 2000, 20). Because the conflict could not disrupt the unity between the twelve members of the EC, especially since the EC needed to counterbalance the influence of the United States and was negotiating the Maastricht Treaty, Mitterrand and his executives made sure that they included Germany in the decision-making process, while at the same time controlling Germany's influence so that France would still assume the leading role (Macleod 1997, 248–249).

*Not always effective*

Even though France played a central role in the early stages of the conflict, its involvement was not always beneficial or effective. This can be explained by three main reasons. First, in the early stages of the conflict, Mitterrand and his executive at the time appeared reluctant to name and criticise the main perpetrators of the atrocities – the Serbs (Michel Marian, in Rollet 2006, 37). The rationale often put forward to explain this lack of explicit condemnation was that France was pro-Serb: as Alain Juppé, Minister of Foreign Affairs from 1993 to 1995, declared in a hearing to the French National Assembly, "at the origin, ... Germany was rather sensitive to the Croats' claims while France was more sensitive to the Serbian one" (Juppé 2001).

The reasons for this pro-Serb position have largely been attributed to Mitterrand's own appraisal of Serbia and the break-up of Yugoslavia. Sutton argues that "an avowed personal sympathy for the Serbs, partly on account of courage shown in the Second World War, was coupled to a tendency to equate Croatia with the Ustashi cause and to be sceptical about the political viability of an independent Bosnia" (2007, 296). This position would have led Mitterrand to declare to one of his advisors, Bernard Henry Lévy, "While I am alive, never, you hear me, never, will France wage war against Serbia" (L'Express 2005). Nevertheless, this claim has been contested by other advisors of the President. In particular, Védrine argued that Mitterrand's goal was not directly to support the Serbs, but rather to maintain a position of neutrality in order to not fuel the conflict and to facilitate an agreement (1996, 629–630).

Whatever the reason, Mitterrand's position meant that during the first months of the conflict, France did not define the main group responsible for the atrocities. As Marian explains, "the French President refuse[d] to distinguish the aggressor from the aggressed one" (in Rollet 2006, 37). Consequently, Mérimée declared on 30 May 1992 before the Security Council, "the situation is complex, and there are many shared wrongs and responsibilities ... The purpose of the resolution ... is not to punish or isolate certain parties" (in UN Security Council 1992b, 39, 41).

The French strategy appeared to be evolving when Mitterrand came to Sarajevo unannounced on 28 June 1992 – a particularly significant date because it was the anniversary of the assassination of Archduke Franz Ferdinand and, consequently, of the beginning of Franco-Serbian coopera- tion during the First World War (Le Guilledoux 1998). He declared that "what [was] happening [was] not acceptable. It [was] the line that should not be crossed" (in Le Guilledoux 1998). This visit was facilitated by the fact that "French public opinion, opposition parties, and even the Socialist party [became] more and more outraged by the news of concentration camps, stories of ethnic cleansing, and the implacable siege of Sarajevo, all of which were blamed on the Serbs" (Macleod 1997, 246). Nevertheless, the French President lightened his declaration by adding that "it [was] not about waging war against anyone. France is not the enemy of any of the republics in the region" (in Le Guilledoux 1998), thus showing that he had not completely changed his position.

As a consequence, it was only on 13 November 1992 that the French Permanent Representative to the UN openly criticised the actions of the Serbs in front of the Security Council: "The Council must tell the Serbian leaders of Bosnia and Herzegovina that the international community rejects two things. It rejects the taking of territory by force and wants to see the territorial integrity of Bosnia and Herzegovina strictly respected. ... The Council further rejects the forced displacement of populations and the shelling of cities under siege" (Mérimée in UN Security Council 1993a, 17–18). This change of position intensified during the second *cohabitation*, which began in March 1993.[20] In particular, on 31 March 1993 Mérimée declared, "it is essential that the Serbian side understand that a new stage in the conflict ravaging the Republic of Bosnia and Herzegovina has been reached, and that the Security Council has decided to have recourse to force to see that its decisions are respected" (in UN Security Council 1993d, 4). He also explicitly mentioned for the first time that the Serbs were responsible for ethnic cleansing (in UN Security Council 1993d, 4–5). After this, France continued to denounce the crimes committed by Milosevic's regime (see for instance UN Security Council 1993e, 7–9; 1993g, 12; 1993h, 7–8).

This reluctance to explicitly condemn the Serbs was accompanied by a strict humanitarian approach. As mentioned previously, Mitterrand was reluctant to "add war to war", and as a consequence, France's priorities were to focus on finding a diplomatic solution and providing humanitarian assistance (Rollet 2006, 41–42). This meant that even if UNPROFOR had the necessary Chapter VII mandate to use force to deliver humanitarian assistance,[21] France – which was the main troop contributor – "restricted [its] forces to a classic peacekeeping mission of only using force in self defence" (Wheeler 2000, 252). Additionally, France and other European Union states became strongly opposed to the 'lift and strike' strategy promoted by the United States, which suggested lifting the arms embargo to end the military dominance of the Serbs, and undertaking air strikes against them (McQueen 2005, 71). The United States' proposal was seen as unacceptable by the French executive at the time, who argued that the strikes would endanger the UN (and thus French) troops on the ground, would lead to retaliation and would escalate the conflict (McQueen 2005, 70; Wheeler 2000, 253; Zic 2000, 19).

This traditional peacekeeping approach – which was commonly adopted by the UN during its operations during the Cold War – rapidly proved to be ineffective, however. A peaceful resolution to the conflict seemed more and more unlikely, and the Serbs were becoming increasingly violent, making it hard for the French to deliver humanitarian aid without the use of force (Ramsbotham and Woodhouse 1999, 277–278). Additionally, the UN troops on the ground became the target of some of the attacks. These limitations led General Janvier, UNPROFOR's Commander from March 1995, to describe the strategy adopted by Mitterrand's executive as "a fundamental mistake" since it consisted in "having a peace force in a war zone" (in Rollet 2006, 43).

In 1993 France's strategy appeared to be evolving with the *cohabitation* which began in March. The new executive called for the creation of safe areas in April and May 1993 (Alain Juppé in Assemblée Nationale 1994, 682; Juppé 2001). General Philippe Morillon, UNPROFOR's Commander at the time, had forced the executive's and the international community's hand by unilaterally declaring in March 1993 that Srebrenica, a Muslim enclave under persecution, was now under the protection of the UN (McQueen 2005, 58). On 16 April 1993, Resolution 819 made Srebrenica the first safe area (UN Security Council 1993i), and the status was given to five additional towns on 6 May 1993 in Resolution 824: Sarajevo, Tuzla, Žepa, Goražde and Bihać (UN Security Council 1993j). On 13 May France shared a proposal with the United States, the United Kingdom and Russia to begin discussions on a concrete policy on how the safe areas would work (McQueen 2005, 72). These eventually influenced Resolution 836 on the extensive measures UNPROFOR could take to protect the areas (McQueen 2005, 72). However, even though France deployed an additional 800 troops, the number of troops required to protect the areas was not met by the international community, and as Chapter 3 explains in more depth, the areas were left unprotected (Tardy 1999, 233).

While the support for the safe areas suggests a turning point in France's strategy, it would be mistaken to overestimate the extent of this shift. As Mérimée explained, "the designation and protection of the safe areas [was] not an end in itself, but only a temporary measure: a step towards a just and lasting political solution" (in UN Security Council 1993g, 13). More specifically, in the eyes of the French executive at the time, this option had the advantage of shutting down the 'lift and strike' strategy promoted by the United States, while also not committing itself to a peace enforcement approach (Wheeler 2000, 253; McQueen 2005, 71–72). As Chapter 3 shows, the key turning point in France's transition from a humanitarian to a peace enforcement approach happened only in 1994–95 following the Markale market attack, the kidnapping of the blue helmets and the election of President Chirac (Macleod 1997, 244; Rollet 2006, 46).

Finally, the institutional framework in which Mitterrand and his executives chose to get involved was criticised. As mentioned previously, at the early stages of the conflict, even before it spread to Bosnia and Herzegovina, France was eager to show that the EC could handle the tensions in its own backyard. It was thus particularly eager to keep the United States and NATO away from the crisis (Pierre Beylau in Treacher 2000, 30). This option satisfied American President George H. W. Bush who did not want the United States to assume a leading role (McQueen 2005, 56). Nevertheless, the European diplomatic efforts did not manage to stop the conflict and its spread into Bosnia and Herzegovina (Rollet 2006, 29; Macleod 1997, 244). Additionally, some key European states were divided on how to handle the situation (as illustrated by Germany's early recognition of Croatia and Slovenia). Finally, the EC's capacity to put together an intervention was limited (Mitterrand 1992).

Consequently, France decided to turn to the UN for management of the conflict and promoted the role of key European states within the UN framework (Treacher 2000, 30). However, the institution was unable to find a solution to the conflict and to prevent the attacks against civilians, to the point that General Francis Briquemont, Belgian Commander of UNPROFOR's mission in Sarajevo at the time, declared, "at the United Nations, political figures create resolutions almost every day, and do not give us the means to fulfil our mission. So all these resolutions of the United Nations, I do not even read them any more, and with the troops at my disposal, I try to do what I can" (in Tardy 1999, 235).

France was not the only state responsible for these problematic decisions. For instance, the traditional peacekeeping approach supported by France at the beginning of the conflict was supported by the international community, which was eager to not become part of the conflict and to focus its efforts on a peaceful settlement and the delivery of humanitarian aid (McQueen 2005, 56–57). Similarly, France was criticised for being opposed to the 'lift and strike' approach supported by the United States, but it was not the only state to oppose it: as McQueen argues, "Clinton's policy was so disliked by the Europeans, it was often referred to derogatorily as 'lift and pray'" (2005, 70). When criticising France for promoting the involvement of the UN instead of NATO, it is also important to emphasise that at the beginning, the United States did not want the UN – or NATO – to get involved (McQueen 2005, 56). Consequently, even though it would be mistaken to undermine the limitations of France's involvement, it would be just as mistaken to downplay the significant role that France played in the conflict resolution – both diplomatically and militarily – during its early stages.

## Conclusion

By supporting key resolutions at the UN General Assembly and the Security Council in order to promote the creation of a right to intervene in the domestic affairs of a state so as to fulfil a perceived duty to protect, France played a role of norm entrepreneur between 1988 and 1991 before actively intervening militarily for humanitarian purposes. Thus it not only contributed to the emergence and legitimisation of humanitarian intervention by promoting the right of individuals to life over the right of states to *non-ingérence*; it also influenced how the international community implemented it, for instance by promoting intervention through the UN, without restrictions in terms of the origin of the emergency or the population endangered.

While it is not possible to isolate a single factor to explain France's commitment to human protection, this chapter has emphasised the role played by France's domestic norm of human protection which emerged at the end of the 1980s. The idea that in light of its history, values and rank, France has a special role to play in the promotion of human protection became rapidly institutionalised and internalised by Mitterrand's executives and public opinion. In addition to allowing France to fulfil its perceived duty, promoting human protection also helped Mitterrand's executives offer a pragmatic response to the changing international order by helping showcase France's rank. Thus the latter played a double role: it was part of the reason why Mitterrand's executives felt compelled to promote human protection and it was an incentive for France to have a strong role to showcase what it could do.

While France played a central role in the emergence of humanitarian intervention, the impact of the international principle on France during the early 1990s remained limited. At most, it allowed France to intervene for humanitarian purposes by creating a favourable international context, but did not drive France's conception of, and contribution to, human protection. This is not surprising, since France's domestic norm of human protection preceded the emergence of humanitarian intervention, and the latter remained a relatively new international principle at the time.

### Notes

1  As mentioned previously, humanitarian intervention is defined as an international principle because it never reached the status of international norm due to the international contestation it faced in the second half of the 1990s. Yet it is more than a concept since to a certain extent, it began to create an 'oughtness' to react to human suffering and influenced perpetrators by forcing them to attempt to cover up their actions.

2  After proclaiming himself Emperor of Central Africa in 1976, Bokassa was behind the massacre of a hundred school children in 1979. The dictator Idi Amin was known for his reign of terror in Uganda. In 1978 he sent troops into Tanzania in an effort to annex the 'Kagera Salient'. See Revel (1979).

3 Kouchner's work in Biafra was a turning point for him. He was appalled by the situation and the conditions doctors had to work in: "the miserable petrol steriliser couldn't produce and often we finished our late-night sessions bare-chested, wearing only a pair of gloves" (in Davey 2015, 30). But most importantly, he was strongly opposed to the fact that "Red Cross Volunteers were required to remain strictly neutral in all political and military disputes" (Berman 2005, 228). This led him to create Médecins Sans Frontières.

4 For example, humanitarian workers had to break international law during the conflicts in Afghanistan, Salvador and Cambodia.

5 Bettati was called on by Kouchner to help him make the *devoir d'ingérence* part of international law.

6 In Kouchner's book *Le malheur des autres* (1991b), this distinction becomes very clear: he distinguishes the *devoir d'ingérence*, the *droit d'assistance* and the *droit d'ingérence*.

7 For instance, in 1991 Dumas argued that France "believes that the right of humanity precedes the right of the states, that the former should always inspire the latter and that the *devoir d'assistance humanitaire*, which is increasingly an integral part of the modern universal conscience, needs to be part of international legislation in the shape of a humanitarian *droit d'ingérence*" (in Torrelli 1992, 239). See also Dumas (1991).

8 As Davey argues, several events in the 1960s and 1970s had already contributed to the endorsement of humanitarianism in France – if not by the state, by NGOs. She especially underlines the importance of the conflicts in Biafra in 1968 and in east Pakistan (soon to become Bangladesh) in 1970 (2015, 28–36).

9 The President and his Prime Minister did not belong to the same political party, since the left-wing (Mitterrand's party) lost the legislative elections in 1986 and consequently, between 1986 and 1988, Mitterrand had to have a Prime Minister from the (right-wing) opposition. This was the first of three *cohabitations* during the Fifth Republic, which has been in place since 1958.

10 Once again, it is interesting to note that even though it is a very specific component of France's identity, the fact that France is seen as the 'homeland of human rights' has also been directly associated with France's rank. As this book shows, the various executives have indeed argued over time that the values France fought for during the French Revolution were part of what makes it a state that matters.

11 The use of the term 'executives' in its plural form emphasises the fact that the President's ministerial office-holders and advisors changed during his presidency.

12 The expression 'francophone' refers to French-speaking states of Africa, usually but not necessarily former French colonies. For instance, as Chapter 3 discusses in depth, Rwanda used to be a Belgian colony but still had very strong relations with the Mitterrand regime owing to the fact that the Habyarimana regime was pro-French and French-speaking.

13 In an interview with Kroslak, his Defence Minister François Léotard "confirms that it was Mitterrand who defined 'the power struggle between the Anglo-Saxons and the French in this part of world'" (in Kroslak 2007, 112).

14 For instance, "there was a strong emerging consensus on the need to adapt the constitutive rules of international society to include the promotion and protection of human rights – even if it is also true that sovereign states could negotiate and compromise these norms given their primacy as actors. Second, the absence of supranational governance in relation to key human protection principles, such as the anti-genocide Convention, did not mean governments could ignore these principles without incurring reputational and other costs. Third, basic human rights continued to be integral not just to the decolonization struggles that were occurring after the end of empire, but were also consistently conjoined with the right to sovereignty and non-interference. Fourth, linked to this argument, is the increasing enmeshment of the UN in the civil and ethnic conflicts that accompanied the emergence of independent yet fragile states in Africa in particular – in this respect, international peace and security was increasingly being understood in ways that were only intelligible in relation to claims about the justice and protection of peoples" (Dunne and Staunton 2016, 48).

15 Serge Telle was diplomatic advisor to Kouchner from 1988 to 1992.

16 See Article 39 of the UN Charter (UN 1945).

17 S/23067 (25 September 1991); S/23927 (15 May 1992); S/24421 (13 August 1992); S/24422 (13 August 1992); S/24554 (14 September 1992); S/24618 (5 October 1992); S/24636 (8 October 1992); S/24808 (13 November 1992); S/25440 (31 March 1993); S/25558 (8 April 1993); S/25826 (25 May 1993); S/25870 (3 June 1993); S/25798 (9 June 1993); S/25966 (17 June 1993); S/26263 (9 August 1993).

18 See for instance the 'European Union's peace plan' of November 1993, which then became the foundation of the peace plan of the Contact Group (Macleod 1997, 248).

19 "Lt. Gen. Jean Cot (France), from June 1993 to March 1994; Gen. Bertrand de Lapresle (France), from March 1994 to March 1995; and Gen. Bertrand Janvier (France), who took up the post from March 1995" led the operation (Ramsbotham and Woodhouse 1999, 278).

20 During this *cohabitation*, Mitterrand was from the Socialist Party (left wing), while his government was led by Edouard Balladur from the Union for France (right wing).

21 See UN Security Council Resolution 770 passed on 13 August 1992.

# 3

# France and humanitarian intervention in a climate of contestation (1994–1999)

The period 1994–99 constituted a challenging time for humanitarian intervention, as it faced strong international criticism before being contested by the end of the decade. In France, François Mitterrand completed his presidency and was replaced by President Jacques Chirac, whose first mandate lasted from 1995 to 2002. Both Mitterrand and Chirac had to work with governments from the opposite end of the political spectrum: the first *cohabitation* took place from 1993 to 1995 and forced left-wing President Mitterrand to work with a right-wing government led by Edouard Balladur, while right-wing President Chirac had to work with a left-wing government led by Lionel Jospin during the second *cohabitation*, which occurred between 1997 and 2002. This chapter investigates whether, how and why France continued to play a central role in human protection and whether its conception and practice of human protection impacted – and was impacted by – humanitarian intervention and the increasing international contestation it was facing.

In order to do this, the chapter is divided into four main sections. The first section clarifies the context of France's relationship to human protection by investigating the norm contestation faced by humanitarian intervention – and more specifically, the role played by France in deepening this contestation – along with the challenges faced by France during its participation in UN interventions undertaken for humanitarian purposes. The second argues that despite this challenging context, the various executives did not promote a normative rollback, and emphasises the role played by France's domestic norm of human protection. The third explains that in order to fulfil France's perceived duty to protect without endangering its rank, and to address some domestic and international constraints, France's practice of human protection, however, evolved considerably and contributed greatly to the reinforcement of the global trend of delegating humanitarian intervention to multilateral organisations and adopting more robust strategies in the field. The last section illustrates these changes by continuing the case study of France's involvement in former Yugoslavia and, more specifically, by focusing on its interventions in Bosnia and Herzegovina and Kosovo.

## A challenging context to which France contributed

First, it is important to investigate the context at the time and, more specifically, the challenges faced by humanitarian intervention and French troops in the field.

### The norm contestation of humanitarian intervention and the role played by France: the Rwandan genocide

As mentioned in Chapter 1, for a principle to become an international norm, it needs to be internalised by the members of the international community. This process was compromised for humanitarian intervention as it rapidly faced key challenges and contestation during the second half of the 1990s. In particular, as explained in more depth in this chapter, both the failure of the UN to prevent mass atrocities from being committed in Rwanda and Srebrenica, and the lack of authorisation by the UN Security Council of an intervention in Kosovo in spite of the atrocities committed, contributed to the contestation of the international principle by the international community (Evans 2008a, 3). Additionally, the lack of transparency in the intent of the intervening states, the human loss they had to face, the selectivity of the response and the low success rate of the interventions fuelled the growing international contestation (Bellamy and Wheeler 2011, 514–515). Strong criticism was also directed specifically towards the UN's incapacity to intervene to protect. Its lack of political will, funding, institutional capacity and practical competence were particularly emphasised (Bellamy, Williams and Griffin 2004, 81).

This section of the chapter focuses on how France added to this criticism through its actions. As mentioned in Chapter 2, the humanitarian approach adopted by Mitterrand's various executives in Bosnia and Herzegovina had been criticised for its ineffectiveness. But it was France's controversial response to the Rwandan genocide during Mitterrand's second *cohabitation* that was particularly damaging to the international principle.[1]

France's controversial response to the Rwandan genocide

The ties between France and Rwanda can be traced back to General Charles de Gaulle's presidency (1959–69), when France supported Rwanda's process of independence from Belgium and its membership of the UN (Quilès 1998, 18). However, Franco-Rwandan relations intensified mainly under Mitterrand's presidency, when France became "Rwanda's most important ally" (Kroslak 2007, 3). This strong cooperation was clearly visible in October 1990, when France helped the Hutu-led government repel the attacks of the Rwandan Patriotic Front (RPF) that were coming from Uganda, by undertaking *Opération Noroît* (Adelman and Suhrke 2004, 486; Jones 2007, 141; Kroslak 2007, 3; McNulty 2000, 109).[2]

On 6 April 1994 the genocide which led to the death of between 400,000 and 800,000 Tutsis and moderate Hutus in a hundred days began. It was triggered by the shooting of the Mystère Falcon aircraft carrying President Juvénal Habyarimana of Rwanda and President Cyprien Ntaryamira of Burundi, though the extermination project had been discovered as early as January 1994 by the Force Commander of UNAMIR (United Nations Assistance Mission for Rwanda),[3] General Roméo Dallaire, but had been ignored by the UN at the time (Wheeler 2000, 215).

In light of the level of violence, France undertook *Opération Amaryllis* from 8 to 14 April 1994. Despite the fact that the operation was short and was simply meant to evacuate French and foreign personnel from Rwanda (Quilès 1998, 265), it rapidly sparked strong criticism (Staunton 2016, 301). In fact, its limited scope constituted one of the main sources of criticism: France had extensive means available to put an end to the genocide in its early stage, but the mandate of the operation was very limited and focused on evacuating people rather than putting an end to the atrocities. It could be argued that France may not have realised that the world was about to witness a genocide with a killing rate faster than that of the Holocaust, yet the fact that *Opération Amaryllis* was deployed so rapidly suggests otherwise. As Kroslak explains, "other critical events in Rwanda over the previous three and a half years did not cause the French government to take similar measures. It thus does not seem far-fetched to argue that Paris, and others, expected a considerable worsening of the situation" (2007, 220). General Christian Quesnot, advisor on the military cooperation with Rwanda, confirmed Kroslak's suspicion by arguing that "the politicians, like the military, immediately understood that we were heading towards massacres beyond measure" (in Nouzille 2010, 392). Similarly, Hubert Védrine, one of the President's close advisors at the time, explained that on hearing about the attack, "President Mitterrand predict[ed] the most tragic consequences" (1996, 700).

*Opération Amaryllis* was also criticised for not being impartial. It indeed provided assistance to the Rwandan Armed Forces (Forces Armées Rwandaises). In particular, Kroslak argues that "the French used UNAMIR vehicles to move Rwandans of known extremist background to the airport, where they were flown out of the country" (2007, 224). Additionally, the Rwandans who benefited from the evacuation were mainly Hutus and were part of Habyarimana's regime or his family, while the Tutsis were left behind (McGreal 2007; Saint-Exupéry 1998).

The controversy over the French response to the genocide did not end there, but instead deepened with *Opération Turquoise* (Staunton 2016, 301–302). Because UNAMIR II would not be operational for several months, France volunteered to send troops (Mérimée 1994). In light of the ties between France and the Habyarimana regime, concerns rapidly emerged from Rwanda and the international community, and also from within France (Subtil 1994). However, in view of the delays faced by UNAMIR II, the fact that no other country was willing to intervene, and the fact that the French executive guaranteed that it would be an impartial, multinational humanitarian intervention (see UN Security Council 1994a, 5–6), the Security Council gave its approval on 22 June 1994, for two months, with the Chapter VII mandate requested by France (UN Security Council 1994b). The next day, *Opération Turquoise* began, and so did the criticism of it.

First, France's intentions were questioned (Staunton 2016, 301–302). This can be explained by the fact that the timing of the operation was surprising. In light of the news reports explaining that France had contributed to the training of the Rwandan army – and, therefore, of some of the *génocidaires* – "French public opinion wavered between horror and shame" (Gounin 2009, 46; see also McNulty 2000, 105). As a consequence, Mitterrand was pressured to intervene to put an end to the genocide, but also "in the hope of washing off any genocidal bloodspots in the baptismal waters of 'humanitarian' action" (Prunier 1997, 296). However, it is interesting to note that despite this public pressure, Mitterrand decided to intervene only when the genocide was practically over, since *Opération Turquoise* was deployed after the RPF had started to make extensive progress (Adelman 2000, 432). The timing of the intervention was even more surprising in that the deployment of *Turquoise* the day after its authorisation by the UN showed that France was capable of mobilising troops rapidly.

Second, the timing of the operation was not the only aspect of the intervention that led to questions regarding France's intent. The extent and nature of the force deployed by France were also surprising. As Findlay points out, "France deployed from neighbouring Zaïre a force of over 3,000 [and] had over 100 armoured vehicles, a battery of heavy 120-mm marine mortars, 2 light Gazelle and 8 heavy Super Puma helicopters, and air cover provided by 4 Jaguar fighter bombers, 4 Mirage ground-attack aircraft and 4 Mirages for reconnaissance" (2002, 282). This represented a particularly strong and heavily armed force for a humanitarian intervention. The scope of this force, and also the rapidity with which it was deployed, would have been particularly useful to UNAMIR II since it was desperately in need of troops in order to be operational. Instead, France undertook the operation almost unilaterally: "as of 25 July, the troop contingent consisted of 2,555 French soldiers and [only] 339 African soldiers" (Ladsous 1994).

Third, the outcomes of the operation also generated strong criticism because they were also controversial (Staunton 2016, 302). In particular, the French troops allowed some of the *génocidaires* to take refuge in the humanitarian protected zone they had created, thereby facilitating their escape to Zaire (Fleitz 2002, 156). They also refused to hand over to the UN some Hutus who were suspected of having taken part in the genocide and denied the RPF access to the humanitarian zone, even though it was now in control of the government (Wheeler 2000, 234; Fleitz 2002, 156). According to the Mucyo report produced for the Rwandan government in 2007, France's lack of impartiality even went beyond the protection of some of the *génocidaires*: "French troops collaborated with the *Interahamwe*. ... This cooperation was either active when the troops gave the instruction to the *Interahamwe* to continue killing, or passive when they let the *Interahamwe* kill under their eyes" (Mucyo et al. 2008, 181).[4]

Consequently, as Gounin explains, the controversy about France's involvement in Rwanda did not end with the fact that it had allowed an undemocratic regime to remain in power for years, or with its having ignored the early warning signs that suggested that a genocide was being planned and was likely to occur. It extended to the nature of France's response during the genocide and the actions of its troops during the two interventions it undertook (2009, 45). Given Mitterrand's commitment to human protection, and in light of the importance of this commitment in terms of France's identity and the associated diplomatic and strategic interests, the French executive's response to the genocide needs to be explained.

Making sense of the French response

The majority of the academic literature has argued that the French response to the genocide was not necessarily surprising, since the French supported several regimes – including dictatorial ones – in the region.[5] In light of the political, strategic, cultural and economic implications of France's relationship with francophone Africa (Cumming 1995, 396; Renou 2002, 6–8), France was indeed often believed to be turning a blind eye when it came to the nature of specific regimes as long as they were pro-French, since this helped it remain "more than a middle-size European state" (Gregory 2000b, 436). Renou has counted "eight defence agreements and 24 military technical assistance agreements" signed between France and francophone states between 1960 and 1993 (2002, 10), and it was common for *réseaux* ("networks of contacts between French and African officials, businessmen and intelligence operatives": Cumming 2013a, 26) to be developed and for personalised relationships between the African and the French leaders to emerge (Staunton 2016, 305–306).

This kind of explanation, however, fails to take into account the fact that Rwanda should actually have been of limited interest to France, since it was not a former colony and had only limited natural resources (Staunton 2016, 306). This argument is supported by the Quilès report produced for the French National Assembly, which explains that "this little African state, enclave, overpopulated and without resources, did not really justify the level of attention it received. As underlined by Minister of Foreign Affairs, Mr Hubert Védrine, ... this country 'did not represent any particular strategic interest'" (1998, 30).

This claim of 'business as usual' also fails to take into account the evolution of the context in francophone Africa at the time, for a process of democratisation had begun at the beginning of the 1990s (Staunton 2016, 307). As Schmidt explains, "with the end of the Cold War, France could afford to cut many of [the ties it had with unsavoury dictators], and the emergence of popular pro-democratic movements across *Francophone* Africa made severing them a necessity" (2013, 188). At the Franco-African Summit at La Baule in 1990, Mitterrand had made French aid dependent on democratisation efforts (Mitterrand 1990), thereby suggesting that he was aware of this shift and willing to support it. This declaration was rapidly put into practice: as Cumming explains, the executive "suspended development aid to Zaïre in October 1991 and Togo in February 1993 for their refusal to undertake reforms, and withheld 30m francs worth of subsidies from Bénin until it had shown clear signs of its commitment to democracy" (1995, 390).

Finally, and as mentioned previously, in addition to not explaining why France was involved with the regime of a relatively poor African state and was willing to be seen on the wrong side of the democratisation process in the continent, this account fails to take into account the efforts made by Mitterrand's various executives since the end of the 1980s to promote human protection. Not only had France been committed to human protection in light of the perceived idea that it was the 'homeland of human rights', but this strong commitment allowed the promotion of France's rank in what was perceived to be a challenging time for France internationally.

As Staunton explains, France's response to the genocide thus raises a key question: what was so important about Rwanda that it could justify undermining France's diplomatic efforts – and the strategic interests associated – to keep its allies in a small African state which did not have many natural resources or a colonial past with France (2016, 308)? Based on the comments of Gérard Prunier (1997), a key advisor of the executive during the genocide, and some members of Mitterrand's past and current executive at the time, the key to understanding France's support of the *génocidaire* regime lies in taking into account the influence of the Fashoda syndrome – and the perceived associated threat to France's rank – on the President (Staunton 2016, 308–311). As mentioned in Chapter 2, even though it was mainly Mitterrand who was affected by the syndrome rather than his entire executive (François Léotard in Kroslak 2007, 112), it played an important part in the design of France's foreign policy at the time, since Mitterrand handled Franco-African relationships – including the Franco-Rwandan relationship – almost exclusively by making them a *domaine réservé* (Amalric 2008; Kroslak 2007, 57,101).

According to Prunier, the syndrome "is the main reason – and practically the only one – why Paris intervened so quickly and so deeply in the growing Rwandese crisis" (1997, 105). Bernard Kouchner, who was in Rwanda at the time and is one of the few officials willing to talk about the ambiguous response of the executive, confirmed this theory by explaining that "big political mistakes were made, [for] arrogant France wanted to fight the British because it [was] Uganda and also the Americans who trained Kagame" (2014). Even the Quilès report discussed the influence of the syndrome on the French President by highlighting that it was visible as early as 1957, when Mitterrand was Minister of Justice and blamed the British for the challenges emerging from the decolonisation of France's former colonies: "all the troubles that we have had in West Africa have nothing to do with a desire for independence, but with a rivalry between the French and the British blocs. It was British agents who fomented all our troubles" (in Quilès 1998, 31).

It is essential to take the influence of the syndrome on Mitterrand into account because it helps to explain the French involvement in Rwanda despite its lack of substantial natural resources or colonial past with France (Staunton 2016, 309). As the Quilès report explicated, France's interest can be explained by Rwanda's geographic location, for it "[constituted] a privileged place of observation of the changes occurring in the region" (Quilès 1998, 31–32). Indeed, it was not only at the frontier of the francophone zone, but also shared a frontier with Zaire, which was of particular interest to France for its rich natural resources (Quilès 1998, 31) and was also, according to the French, coveted by the Americans (Léotard in Gregory 2000b, 441).

The influence of the syndrome also explains why Mitterrand was willing to support an undemocratic leader – Habyarimana – for years, while defining the RPF as a foreign threat rather than a legitimate ethnic group of

Rwanda (Staunton 2016, 309). Prunier argues that this decision was visible as early as 1990, when the executive defined the attack undertaken by the RPF as "an invasion ... by a group of rebels coming from Uganda [which] was a typical test-case – an obvious 'Anglo-Saxon' plot to destabilise one of 'ours', and one we needed to stop right away if we did not want to see a dangerous spread of the disease" (1997, 106). Defining the RPF as an external threat rather than an ethnic group of Rwanda allowed Mitterrand and his executive at the time to treat it as a common enemy of France and Rwanda without breaking the commitment it had made in 1990 (Mitterrand 1990) that France would no longer intervene in the domestic affairs of African states. Prunier thus argues that "this is how Paris found itself backing an ailing dictatorship in a tiny distant country producing only bananas and a declining coffee crop without even asking for political reform as a price for its support" (1997, 107), since fighting the RPF became "a way of fighting it out with the 'Anglo-Saxon' enemy by proxy, without the need for a major war" (1997, 111).

Finally, the Fashoda syndrome allows us to make sense of the timing, means and scope of *Opération Turquoise* (Staunton 2016, 309–310). In terms of the timing of the French response, the influence of the syndrome is visible in the fact that *Turquoise* was triggered by a declaration from the South African President Nelson Mandela. According to Prunier (1997, 281), despite the pressure of public opinion, it was indeed Mandela's declaration on 13 June 1994, explaining that South Africa was considering an intervention, that led Mitterrand to react rapidly. It can also be argued that the deployment of a large and heavily armed force, and the fact that France intervened only in south-east Rwanda, outside UNAMIR II, and offered refuge to suspected *génocidaires* can be explained by the executive's will to protect France's interests by helping – in the spirit of the Fashoda syndrome – the pro-French Hutus to remain powerful. This idea is supported by Wheeler, who argues that "the mission was to maintain what was left of French influence by securing the power base of those Hutus refugees who were fleeing from the victorious RPF" (2000, 233).

It is important to emphasise that despite the level of controversy around *Opération Turquoise*, France's response to the genocide did not represent a wish on the part of the executive to reconsider France's commitment to human protection worldwide. Mitterrand's executive remained committed to promoting human protection, and so did its successors. Additionally, it is interesting to note that even during the French interventions in Rwanda, France's domestic norm of human protection continued to exert a strong influence on the French executive. As Bellamy argues, "attempts to present non-compliant behaviour as compliant provide counter-factual validity to the norm itself" (2012, 221), and the executive indeed went to great lengths to deny any links with the *génocidaires* and to depict the French operation as a legitimate humanitarian intervention. Claims that a second genocide was being committed by the RPF against the Hutus even began to emerge in a desperate attempt to legitimise France's presence and actions (see for instance Mitterrand in *Courrier International* 2004).

Therefore, rather than being seen as an overall shift in France's commitment to human protection, the French response should be seen as a failed attempt by the executive at the time to negotiate two – in this specific case, contradicting – objectives of France's foreign policy in light of the influence of the Fashoda syndrome on the President: the promotion of human protection on the one hand, and the promotion of France's rank against the 'Anglo-Saxons' in Africa on the other. The French response to the genocide remains a dark episode of its history, but it also considerably weakened the international principle of humanitarian intervention by validating some of the key criticisms raised by its detractors: its inability to prevent atrocities and the idea that states intervened only to protect their own interests.

### The challenges faced by France during its participation in interventions undertaken for humanitarian purposes

In addition to this context of norm contestation, France's commitment to human protection was challenged by the failures it had to face when participating in UN interventions undertaken for humanitarian purposes. In particular, the three main operations in which France was involved during the first half of the 1990s – UNTAC, UNOSOM and UNPROFOR in former Yugoslavia – are particularly representative of the challenges experienced by France and how they strongly impacted the various French executives.

In Cambodia, France was heavily involved both diplomatically and militarily from the beginning of the conflict. In particular, Mitterrand's executive at the time had co-hosted the Paris Peace Conference in 1991. France had also participated in both UNAMIC and UNTAC (Gregory 2000a, 59–60; Morillon 1998, 88; Smouts 1998, 19), which at the time of its creation was the UN's most ambitious intervention ever undertaken (Bellamy, Williams and Griffin 2004, 123).

Nevertheless, challenges rapidly emerged, and the operation became difficult to undertake when the parties increasingly violated the 1991 Peace Agreement and began to target UN troops (Bellamy, Williams and Griffin 2004, 124–125). In light of these challenges, and given that UNTAC still managed to oversee the elections in June 1993, its mandate was not renewed (UN Security Council 1993k), and the UN and French troops had to leave Cambodia even though it was unstable and was still facing key issues. When appraising the operation, the French Brigadier-General Robert Rideau – who was UNTAC's second-in-command of the military component from 1 October 1992 to 3 June 1993 – explained that "the good and the mediocre [ran] side by side" (in Morillon 1998, 88). He emphasised in particular the fact that demobilisation and demilitarisation failed repeatedly, highlighted the difficulty UN forces had in remaining impartial in a changing context and stressed the fact that the rehabilitation of the country continued to be limited (in Morillon 1998, 88).

Beyond the borders of Cambodia, this relative failure of UNTAC had a strong impact on French soldiers and the French executive, who began to experience the difficulties linked to UN operations, in particular in conflicts where the peace to be kept was non-existent or very fragile (Smouts 1998, 20). As a consequence, Gregory argues, French troops "left Cambodia with few illusions about the ability of the UN to impose peace in an unstable political context or to engineer the reconciliation of those who had suffered or been adversaries during a conflict" (2000a, 60).

In Somalia, similar lessons were learnt. France supported the creation of UNOSOM I in April 1992 (UN Security Council 1992a), which was the first intervention where the UN Security Council explicitly linked the use of force and humanitarian emergency (Wheeler 2000, 172; UN Security Council 1992c). It also took an active part in Operation Restore Hope and UNOSOM II.[6] The former benefited from about 2,000 French troops from 9 December 1992 to 18 December 1993 (Smouts 1998, 20), while the latter received an average of 1,104 soldiers per month between May and November 1993 (UN 1993).

Nevertheless, the success of UNOSOM II was rapidly compromised when "left with the task of disarming the various warring factions, [it] was inevitably drawn into Somalia's fractious clan politics" (Bellamy, Williams and Griffin 2004, 158). After the deaths of eighteen American peacekeepers on 3 October 1993, the United States announced the withdrawal of its troops despite the fact that they constituted the largest contingent of the operation (UN 1993). Because allied forces were pulling out and tensions were high, Mitterrand's executive at the time also decided to withdraw the majority of French troops in December 1993 (UN 1993) from what was described as "the lost war of humanitarian assistance" (Guillot 1994, 37). Therefore what should have been "the triumph of the very French notion of 'right of humanitarian intervention'" (Smouts 1998, 20) became one of the UN's biggest failures since no solution was found to reach a sustainable peace (Gregory 2000a, 60). As a consequence, like that in Cambodia, this failure raised questions among French troops and the executive about the way human protection was being undertaken and the role the blue helmets could – and should – play (Smouts 1998, 20).

Likewise, in Bosnia and Herzegovina French troops had to face key difficulties. As explained in Chapter 2, France had been heavily involved in the conflict both diplomatically and militarily. Nevertheless, UNPROFOR's mission rapidly became difficult to undertake as the Serbs' attacks intensified (as illustrated for instance, by the bombing of the Markale market in Sarajevo in February 1994 and the overrun of the safe area of Srebrenica in July 1995, which are discussed in more depth in the last main section of this chapter). Additionally, the constant evolution of the UN mandates, along with operational limits, made the intervention challenging.

Last but not least, UNPROFOR was challenging for the French troops, for the Serbs' attacks were not limited to the civilians, but also included attacks against UN forces. This targeting of UN troops led to the deaths of fifty-three French soldiers and the wounding of 580 others between February 1992 and December 1995 (Smouts 1998, 21). Therefore, as the last main section of this chapter shows in more depth, from 1994 the constant humiliation of the UN and French troops by the Serbs, the failure of UNPROFOR to effectively protect civilians and the increasing amount of French casualties considerably impacted both Mitterrand's and Chirac's executives (Bozo 2012, 221; Soulet 2012).

All these difficulties in Cambodia, Somalia and Bosnia and Herzegovina were particularly problematic for the various French executives because, as explained in Chapter 2, participating in UN interventions was meant to help France fulfil its duty in light of its history, values and rank, while having the advantage of bolstering its rank by promoting its image and military power. Instead, the interventions were beginning to endanger its rank by making it appear weak and incapable of addressing key emergencies.

## A lack of normative rollback

In light of the growing international contestation around humanitarian intervention, the key challenges faced by France in the field and the subsequent threat to France's rank, a normative rollback from either Mitterrand's or Chirac's executives could have been expected. Nevertheless, despite these factors, they did not question the need for a right to intervene to protect to exist, which was mainly what humanitarian intervention stood for. At most, they simply criticised how humanitarian intervention had been implemented – in particular, as the next sections show in more depth, Chirac condemned the limited scope of the UN mandates – and acted as if an international right to intervene to address humanitarian emergencies already existed and was here to stay (Staunton 2018, 375).

Therefore the various French executives focused their efforts on justifying France's involvement in specific interventions and influencing how they were undertaken, rather than debating whether or not they should take place. They also continued to promote and draft key resolutions for the UN Security Council so that the international community could monitor and address humanitarian emergencies as it did in the early 1990s. As illustrated by Table 1, France co-drafted eighty-eight draft resolutions to the UN Security Council between 1994 and 1999.

Given the challenges faced by humanitarian intervention, and also by France in the field, this lack of rollback raises a key question: why did the various executives abstain from taking part in the international contestation? A logical explanation could be that humanitarian intervention had already been internalised by France, and consequently, was action-binding. Nevertheless, even though the international principle did allow France to undertake interventions for humanitarian purposes, the executives never used it to justify or explain France's involvement. Rather, as in the early 1990s, they referred to France's domestic norm of human protection. Like Mitterrand's, Chirac's executives indeed continued to emphasise the idea that France had a duty to protect and a consequent right to intervene not only because of its history and values, but also in light of its status as "more than a middle sized power" (Chirac 1995a).

For instance, in 1995, Chirac explained that troops were present in "Bosnia, Croatia, Africa, Lebanon and everywhere in the world, where, in the name of a certain conception of France, universal values need to be defended" (1995b). A few months later, he argued that the French population was the "heir of a long history. ... It is not anything to be French. It is rights that need to be preserved. It is responsibilities that need to be fulfilled. ... Our country is the bearer of a message. A message of fraternity, of tolerance and of justice. It is how I see France. ... A France faithful to its history, to its values, and determined to defend them" (1995c). Similarly, in 2001 he declared, "Human rights, the concern for the human being and their dignity, have been a passion of France for a long time now. The French nation was among the first to declare human rights as universal and sacred. The French nation has always wanted to be in the avant-garde of the fight for freedom" (Chirac 2007, 433). He also explained that "the duty of great powers, and of France in particular, is to work, wherever they can, towards the maintenance of peace and the prevention of conflicts" (Chirac 2011, 126).

The fact that it was the domestic norm that kept driving France's conception of, and contribution to, human protection is not surprising since,

**Table 1** Draft resolutions to the UN Security Council co-drafted by France, 1994–99

| Date | Focus | Draft resolution |
|------|-------|------------------|
| 1994 | Former Yugoslavia | S/1994/224 (4 March); S/1994/465 (21 April); S/1994/487 (27 April); S/1994/857 (21 July); S/1994/1084 (22 September); S/1994/1085 (22 September); S/1994/1120 (30 September); S/1994/1316 (19 November); S/1994/1317 (19 November) |
| | Israel and Palestine | S/1994/280 (11 March) |
| | Haiti | S/1994/541 (6 May); S/1994/776 (30 June); S/1994/904 (31 July); S/1994/1109 (29 September); S/1994/1163 (15 October); S/1994/1354 (28 November) |
| | Rwanda | S/1994/571 (16 May); S/1994/737 (21 June); S/1994/775 (1 July); S/1994/1168 (8 November) |
| | Iraq | S/1994/1164 (15 October) |
| | Somalia | S/1994/1119 (30 September) |
| 1995 | Former Yugoslavia | S/1995/21 (11 January); S/1995/244 (30 March); S/1995/242 (31 March); S/1995/243 (31 March); S/1995/311 (18 April); S/1995/319 (21 April); S/1995/395 (17 May); S/1995/478 (15 June); S/1995/537 (5 July); S/1995/560 (12 July); S/1995/789 (14 September); S/1995/940 (9 November); S/1995/978 (22 November); S/1995/979 (12 November); S/1995/994 (30 November); S/1995/996 (30 November); S/1995/995 (30 November); S/1995/1033 (15 December); S/1995/1047 (19 December) |
| | Haiti | S/1995/85 (30 January); S/1995/629 (31 July) |
| | Burundi | S/1995/724 (28 August) |
| | Western Sahara | S/1995/523 (30 June) |
| 1996 | Former Yugoslavia | S/1996/23 (15 January); S/1996/392 (29 May); S/1996/866 (21 October); S/1996/979 (26 November); S/1996/1032 (12 December) |
| | Lebanon | S/1996/304 (18 April) |
| | Afghanistan | S/1996/865 (22 October) |
| | Great Lakes region | S/1996/943 (15 November) |
| | Haiti | S/1996/1002 (4 December) |

**Table 1** Draft resolutions to the UN Security Council co-drafted by France, 1994–99 (Continued)

| Date | Focus | Draft resolution |
|------|-------|------------------|
| 1997 | Former Yugoslavia | S/1997/371 (15 May); S/1997/405 (28 May); S/1997/472 (19 June); S/1997/538 (14 July); S/1997/948 (4 December); S/1997/989 (19 December); S/1997/990 (19 December) |
| | Haiti | S/1997/589 (29 July); S/1997/931 (28 November) |
| | Israel and Palestine | S/1997/199 (7 March) |
| 1998 | Former Yugoslavia (including Kosovo) | S/1998/284 (31 March); S/1998/386 (13 May); S/1998/502 (15 June); S/1998/642 (15 July); S/1998/648 (16 July); S/1998/668 (21 July); S/1998/699 (30 July); S/1998/882 (23 September); S/1998/992 (24 October); S/1998/1082 (17 November) |
| | Iraq | S/1998/1038 (5 November); S/1998/1112 (24 November) |
| | Haiti | S/1998/1117 (25 November) |
| | Afghanistan | S/1998/810 (28 August) |
| | Rwanda | S/1998/353 (30 April) |
| 1999 | Former Yugoslavia (including Kosovo) | S/1999/39 (15 January); S/1999/79 (28 January); S/1999/201 (25 February); S/1999/661 (10 June); S/1999/688 (18 June) |
| | Angola | S/1999/27 (12 January) |
| | Central African Republic | S/1999/122 (26 February) |
| | East Timor | S/1999/1083 (25 October) |
| | Haiti | S/1999/1202 (30 November) |
| | Western Sahara | S/1999/1239 (14 December) |

Source: Data compiled using the United Nations Bibliographic Information System.

as Chapter 1 explained, the influence of a principle or emerging norm is only proportional to its strength, and by the mid-1990s humanitarian intervention was already weakened by the international criticism it faced. In contrast, the domestic norm was strong and thus very influential. Consequently, even though humanitarian intervention allowed the various executives to intervene to protect endangered populations, as in the early 1990s, it was mainly the influence of the domestic norm that led the various French executives to play a central role in human protection.

This also led France to promote a broad understanding of human protection that was not limited to specific populations, situations or means to intervene.

It is interesting to note that by simply assuming that the right to intervene already existed and that it was the way the international community had practised humanitarian intervention that was problematic, France did not stop the norm contestation faced by the international principle, nor did it take part in the discussions on the way forward. As a result, in contrast to its role in the early 1990s, it played a limited normative role during the second half of the decade.

### A shift in France's practice of human protection

Even though there was a lack of normative rollback, France considerably shifted the way it promoted human protection in the field, in particular during the first years of Chirac's first term. It continued to intervene for humanitarian purposes by deploying an average of 6,803 troops between 1994 and 1999 despite the high level of casualties faced in the early 1990s (IISS 1993; 1994; 1995; 1996; 1997; 1998; 1999), yet it focused its efforts on Europe instead of intervening worldwide, favoured intervening via multilateral organisations such as NATO rather than the UN and used a more coercive approach.

#### A period of introspection at the end of Mitterrand's presidency

This shift of practice was gradual and began with a period of introspection during the second *cohabitation*, which was materialised in the 1994 *livre blanc* (white paper) on defence (Grégoire 2002, 2–3; Gregory 2000a, 62). The document is important not only because it assessed the foreign and defence policies undertaken so far and suggested ways forward, but also because no publication of this sort had been undertaken since 1972. After re-emphasising that France had "international responsibilities [resulting] from its obligations as a permanent member of the Security Council, its history, its particular vocation" (Long 1994, 25), it introduced some important shifts in terms of France's practice of human protection.

First, the report emphasised the need for France to take part only in UN operations that fulfilled "precise political and organisational conditions" (Long 1994, 41). Five conditions were outlined, among which were the need to have a clear idea of the political goals of the operation; the necessity for the operation to be in line with France's strategic priorities and the interests it aims to promote in the world; the requirement to define a clear division of responsibilities between the different intervening actors; the need to determine the duration and exit strategy before the intervention begins; and the necessity to make sure that the way the operation is executed is approved at the political, national and multinational levels (Long 1994, 42–43). In other words, for the first time, some restrictions on when and how to intervene to protect were explicitly defined.

The *livre blanc* also suggested that France could no longer intervene worldwide for humanitarian purposes and had to find new ways to support human protection by promoting, in particular, the importance of prevention. It argued that prevention could be used in order to avoid "the appearance of situations that are potentially dangerous and direct and indirect threats; prevent the use of force; contain the crises and conflicts at the lowest level possible" (Long 1994, 59–60). The report thus encouraged the use of political, diplomatic, economic, politico-military and military means in order to develop and implement France's capacities in terms of prevention (Long 1994, 59, 84–85).

Last but not least, the report showed that Mitterrand's executive during the second *cohabitation* was beginning to change the way it perceived the UN. In contrast to its view in the early 1990s, it now emphasised not only the strengths of the UN but also its limits: "the expectations of the UN are multiplying and sometimes the gathering, commands and coordination of the considerable resources that are necessary exceed the capacities of the Organisation of United Nations" (Long 1994, 41). This shift was not surprising in view of the challenges faced by the UN interventions in which France took part, and given that the Minister of Defence had declared in January 1994, "the term 'thing' used by de Gaulle is probably underestimating reality. There is a real crisis at the UN ... It is struck by a certain form of incapacity, a military incapacity" (Léotard in Tardy 1999, 242).

Consequently, the report encouraged the delegation of some of the interventions undertaken for humanitarian purposes to regional and multilateral organisations. In particular, it emphasised the importance of strengthening the European Union and cooperating more with NATO (Long 1994, 26, 31–37) since the organisation could lend "powerful means which probably only it today is able to gather and coordinate" (Long 1994, 35). These reflections continued as the failures of the UN operations progressed – especially in former Yugoslavia, where France was heavily involved and committed – and were facilitated by Chirac's election in 1995.

*A shift of institutional framework*

The first noticeable shift that took place during Chirac's presidency related to the institutional framework chosen to intervene to protect endangered populations. As suggested in the 1994 *livre blanc* and by the numerous declarations of the Minister of Defence, Léotard, during the

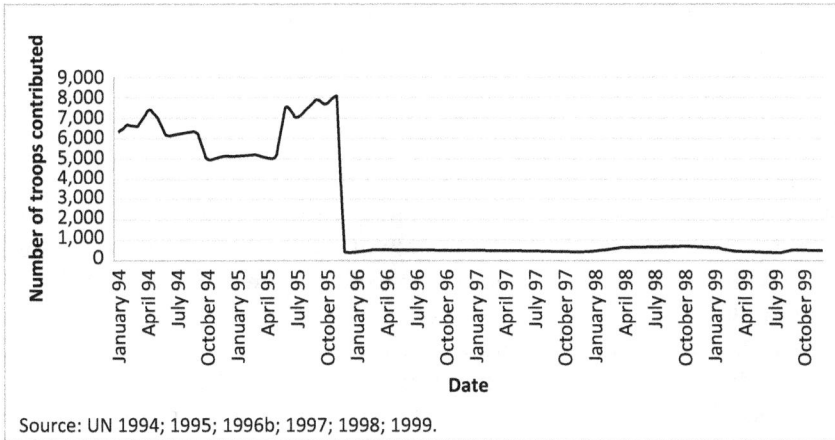

Source: UN 1994; 1995; 1996b; 1997; 1998; 1999.

Note: Data not available for December 1998.

**Graph 4** France's troop contributions to the UN, January 1994 – December 1999

*cohabitation*,[7] Chirac's various executives reconsidered France's heavy military commitment to UN interventions undertaken for humanitarian purposes. As Graph 4 shows, a clear shift is particularly visible in December 1995, when the monthly French troop contribution dropped from 8,115 to 475, making France the twenty-fourth UN troop contributor instead of the leading one (UN 1995).

This shift of practice can partly be explained by the new international context. As mentioned previously, in light of the failures faced by UN interventions, its capacity to intervene to protect was questioned, and states that were originally supportive of its interventions became reluctant to contribute troops. For instance, as mentioned earlier, the United States refused to intervene heavily in the field after the death of some of its peacekeepers in Somalia in 1993. Moreover, when states did decide to intervene, they favoured doing so unilaterally or through multilateral institutions like NATO rather than the UN (Bellamy, Williams and Griffin 2004, 85). As a consequence, the UN progressively reduced the amount of humanitarian interventions it authorised and delegated their undertaking. Nevertheless, even though this shift was not unique to France, France helped to reinforce the trend by withdrawing the UN's leading troop contributor.

This reduction did not mean that the French executive stopped promoting the importance of the UN (see for instance Chirac 2003, in Chirac 2007, 69). The UN was seen as central to peace and security, and also to France's rank, given its permanent seat at the Security Council. Consequently, the various executives continued to promote its importance and, as illustrated by Table 1, proposed over eighty-eight draft resolutions on humanitarian emergencies to the Security Council. The UN thus increasingly became "a place of expression and political legitimacy rather than a privileged place for action" (Tardy 2002, 931).

The decline in troop contributions also did not mean that France stopped intervening for humanitarian purposes. For instance, in February 1996 Chirac announced a modernisation of the French army and a fivefold increase in the number of troops capable of being deployed rapidly abroad (Vie Publique 2011). Even during the third *cohabitation*, which began in June 1997, left-wing Prime Minister Jospin argued that "France has neither the freedom nor the will to withdraw from the world. It does not intend to renounce either its universal vocation, its world influence or its economic interests. Faithful to its tradition, it wishes instead to participate in the definition of global balance and contribute to the respect of international law and human rights, as well as to actions which aim to promote peace" (1997a). As illustrated by Graph 5, France's goal was indeed not to stop intervening, but rather to intervene differently, through multilateral organisations such as NATO and later the European Union instead of the UN.

The will of the executives to intervene via the European Union is not surprising, for "France ha[d] been in the forefront of the Western European states' pursuit of European integration for 50 years" (Grégoire 2002, 10) and the European Union was seen as a way to counterbalance the influence of the United States and promote France's rank. In particular, Mitterrand, along with German Chancellor Helmut Kohl, played a central role in the construction of the European Union in order to build a powerful and independent Europe (Bossuat 2012, 195; Bozo 2012, 182, 190, 199–200). From a security and foreign policy point of view, three important milestones were achieved during his presidency. The first was the signature of the Treaty of Maastricht in February 1992, which created the European Union and thus the Common Foreign and Security Policy (European Union 1992; Vie Publique 2011).[8] Second, during the fifty-ninth French–German Summit at La Rochelle in May 1992, Mitterrand and Kohl established the Eurocorps, which became operational in November 1995 (Eurocorps 2013). Lastly, at the Council of Ministers of the Western European Union held in June 1992 near Bonn, the Petersberg tasks were created (Vie Publique 2011). Article II.4 of the ministerial declaration "outlined the following three purposes for which military units could be deployed: humanitarian and rescue tasks; peacekeeping tasks; tasks of combat forces in crisis management, including peacemaking" (Western European Union 1992). The tasks were then included in the 1997 Amsterdam Treaty (Grégoire 2002, 11).

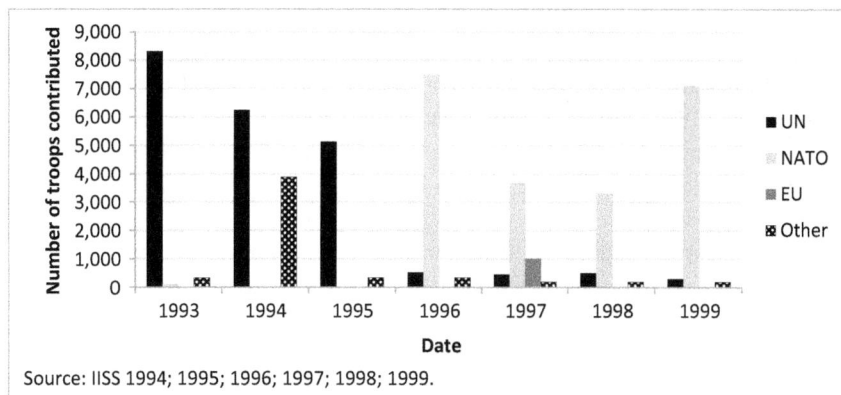

Source: IISS 1994; 1995; 1996; 1997; 1998; 1999.

Note: This graph does not take into account troops deployed outside France owing to security agreements or headquarters situated overseas. Even though it is useful in showing a trend in France's troop contribution, it is not fully representative since the data available reflects France's contribution in specific months of the year only (June for 1993, 1994 and 1995; August for 1996, 1997, 1998 and 1999).

**Graph 5** France's troop contributions to international organisations for humanitarian purposes, 1993–99

Chirac followed the legacy of his predecessor in order to promote the emergence of a European foreign policy and a military force that would allow the fulfilment of the Petersberg tasks. In a key speech in June 1996 he declared, "Europe can and must affirm itself again as one of the great centres of decision and action in the world" and emphasised the central role France should play in the development of this powerful Europe (in Chirac 2007, 174). In December 1998, during the Franco-British Summit organised in Saint-Malo, some strong French lobbying led to a ground-breaking Franco-British common declaration (Bozo 2012, 245) which emphasised that "the Union must have the capacity for autonomous action, backed up by credible military forces, the means to decide to use them and a readiness to do so, in order to respond to international crises" (Foreign and Commonwealth Office of the United Kindgom 1998). In the mean-time, Chirac also pursued the development of the Eurocorps, and at the Franco-German Defence and Security Summit held in Toulouse in May 1999, he and the Chancellor of Germany, Gerhard Schröder, proposed to transform it into a Rapid Reaction Corps, which was rapidly approved by other member states (Eurocorps 2013; Vie Publique 2011).

A few months later, at the European Summit held in June 1999 in Cologne, France also supported the creation of the European Security and Defence Policy, and an EU military committee was created in order to help build a European military force to prevent crises and manage conflicts (Vie Publique 2011). The first concrete step towards the creation of that military force was undertaken at the Helsinki Council of Ministers in December 1999, when the European Union committed itself to creating an autonomous defence force of up to 60,000 soldiers which would be capable of addressing humanitarian emergencies (Bossuat 2012, 192; Vie Publique 2011).

However, even though Chirac put a strong emphasis on the European Union, he was aware that the construction of a European defence and military force capable of addressing humanitarian emergencies would take time, and the conflict in Bosnia and Herzegovina had proved that the European Union was not ready to address a conflict that had the potential to destabilise the continent (Bryant 2000, 26). Consequently, he also undertook a stronger cooperation with NATO and promoted the role of Europe within the organisation. The relationship between France and NATO had been complex ever since the 1966 decision of President de Gaulle to remain a member of the organisation but to withdraw from its integrated military command structure (de Gaulle 1966). Some progress had been achieved in 1994 during the *cohabitation* when France agreed to the creation of the Combined Joint Task Forces, which could be put under the command of either Americans or Europeans (Bryant 2000, 27; de Russé 2010, 20).

Chirac intensified this change of position towards NATO (Bryant 2000, 27–28) in order to allow France to continue intervening multilaterally for humanitarian purposes with stronger mandates and more extensive means. He declared that France could be fully reintegrated into the organisation, and as a first step towards that goal, he announced in December 1995 that France was re-joining the Council of Ministers of NATO and its military council (Bozo 2012, 223; Nouzille 2010, 461; Vie Publique 2011). In February 1996, in front of the United States Congress, he explained that France's full reintegration of the military structure could happen "if the European identity [could] be fully affirmed" (Chirac 1996). The reintegration nevertheless rapidly failed, despite the progress achieved at the Berlin Summit.[9] This can be explained by the fact that the Americans refused to give the command of the Naples headquarters to a European commandant (Bryant 2000, 31–32; Nouzille 2010, 474; Vie Publique 2011), and also because left-wing Jospin, who became Prime Minister in 1997 as a result of the third *cohabitation*, was opposed to the project (Bozo 2012, 239; Jospin in Jauvert 2011).

Nevertheless, even though France was still not part of the integrated military command structure, the diplomatic progress achieved and the limits faced by the UN and the European Union led France's support of

NATO's interventions to increase from 1996. As Graph 5 illustrates, NATO mobilised the majority of the French troops deployed abroad for humanitarian purposes: France's contribution averaged 5,393 troops per year between 1996 and 1999, in contrast to the 437 troops deployed under the UN flag (IISS 1996; 1997; 1998; 1999). As explained in more depth in the next section on former Yugoslavia, Védrine argued that "we had come to the conclusion that [NATO] was the only organisation available in Europe which was capable of gathering men, coordinating them, ensuring the logistics and communications, and exercising a sufficient deterrent function" (in Weber 1999, 27).

Additionally, intervening through NATO rather than the UN meant that France could fulfil its perceived duty to protect in light of its history, values and rank, while promoting – rather than endangering – its status, since NATO's interventions relied on stronger mandates and more extensive means. Chirac indeed believed that France's rank was an intrinsic part of its identity and was determined to protect it. For instance, in 1995 he explained that France "has important assets: it is the fourth economic and commercial power in the world, it is one of the five permanent members of the Security Council, it is a nuclear power, and the first troop contributor to the UN. We are not a middle-size country. France also has a humanist and universalist tradition which is strongly linked to human rights and democracy" (1995a).

A good illustration of Chirac's determination to promote France's rank can be seen as early as 1995, when he decided to resume French nuclear testing (Lombart 2007b, 380). In spite of the high level of international criticism, these tests were deemed necessary in order to "maintain a reliable and secure deterrent power for our country" (Chirac 1996, in Chirac 2007, 175) and were thus undertaken before France signed the Comprehensive Test Ban Treaty a year later (Dalloz 2002, 215; Lombart 2007b, 380). Chirac's determination to promote France's rank was facilitated by the fact that it was shared by his various executives. For instance, in May 1995 the Minister of Foreign Affairs, Alain Juppé, declared in front of the National Assembly, "France can and must affirm its vocation to world power" (in Dalloz 2002, 224). The executives therefore adjusted the way France practised human protection so that fulfilling France's duty in light of its history, values and rank would also promote France's status.

This shift of strategy also allowed Chirac's various executives to address some of the criticisms made by public opinion. As Utley explains, during Mitterrand's presidency, "the national authorities were often perceived to be reacting to events, especially in the former Yugoslavia, doing too little too late, and acting as much from concern over domestic political calculations as from concerns to further the rule of international law" (2000, 180). Intervening through NATO with a more robust approach helped to address some of these concerns.

## A military focus on Europe

In addition to the shift of institutional framework, a second important shift in the way France intervened to protect endangered populations during Chirac's first mandate lay in the geographic locations. As Graph 6 shows, and as illustrated by the next section on France's involvement in former Yugoslavia, France mainly intervened militarily in Europe for humanitarian purposes.

As mentioned previously, this change did not represent an evolution in France's conception of human protection, but can be explained by a shift of strategy and a change of circumstances. France's military capacities were stretched by its involvement in various interventions worldwide, and there was thus a need to address the increasing tensions regarding "France's military capabilities, force structures, and military doctrines – and the perennial problem of finance" (Utley 2000, 180). There was also a sense that France should intervene in fewer operations so that it could do so

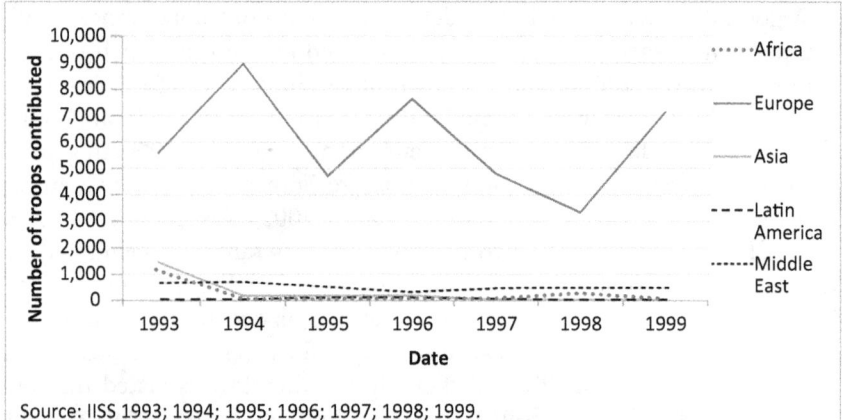

Source: IISS 1993; 1994; 1995; 1996; 1997; 1998; 1999.

Note: This graph does not take into account troops deployed outside France owing to security agreements or headquarters situated overseas. Even though it is useful in showing a trend in France's troop contribution, it is not fully representative since the data available reflects France's contribution at a specific period of the year only (June for 1993, 1994 and 1995; August for 1996, 1997, 1998 and 1999). For instance, the intervention in Rwanda is not represented here because the intervention only started in July.

**Graph 6** Evolution of France's troop contributions to interventions for humanitarian purposes by geographic area, 1993–99

more robustly and avoid endangering its rank. The fact that a major humanitarian crisis was taking place on the European continent and that France had been involved since its beginning made it an obvious choice of focus.

Additionally, in contrast to the shift from the UN to NATO, which was mainly a deliberate choice of Chirac's various executives, the focus on the European Union needs to be contextualised as it too can be explained by various factors that were not necessarily in Chirac's executives' control. In particular, France needed to rethink its presence in Africa following the cooperation of Mitterrand's executive with the *génocidaire* regime in Rwanda. As Renou explains, "France was perceived as the accomplice of criminals, as a power ready to do anything to keep control of the *Franco-phone* part of the continent" (2002, 13–14). Even though Chirac was particularly committed to Africa, to the point that he is often referred to as "Chirac the African" or the "friend of Africa" (Claude 2007, 906), he also rapidly became constrained in his African policy by his socialist Prime Minister Jospin. Using the slogan *ni ingérence, ni indifférence* (neither interference (or intrusion) nor intervention) (Leymarie 2002), Jospin was indeed determined to stop the French interventions in the continent (Banégas and Marchal 2013, 187–188). This was apparent when "the new administration of Lionel Jospin announced substantial cuts in France's standing forces in Africa" (Gregory 2000b, 441), and in 1998, when the Ministry of Cooperation, which was mainly in charge of dealing with Franco-African cooperation, was absorbed by the Ministry of Foreign Affairs (Claude 2007, 915). It was further illustrated in 1999, when a putsch took place in Côte d'Ivoire and France did not intervene (Fall 2004, 78; Leymarie 2002).

The strength of France's commitment to intervene for humanitarian purposes in Europe did not mean that it stopped promoting other human protection initiatives elsewhere. For instance, its diplomatic efforts to solve the Israeli–Palestinian conflict deserve to be mentioned (see Allaire and Goulliard 2002, 215–222; Bozo 2012, 231–232; Lombart 2007b, 382–383). But most importantly, in Africa, France emphasised the importance of training regional forces so that they could intervene – instead of French troops – when a crisis occurred. On 23 May 1997 France joined forces with the United Kingdom and the United States in order to promote "an 'Afri-canisation of regional security'", by creating a "trilateral peacekeeping initiative" (Gregory 2000b, 442). As Gregory explains, "the United Kingdom ... established a regional Peacekeeping Training Centre at Harare in Zimbabwe and the United States [began] to implement its African Crisis Response Initiative (ACRI)" (2000b, 442). As part of this initiative, France started the Renforcement des Capacités Africaines de Maintien de la Paix

(RECAMP, Reinforcement of African Peacekeeping Capacities) programme and opened up the École de Maintien de la Paix (School of Peacekeeping) in Zambakro in Côte d'Ivoire (Gregory 2000b, 442–443; Hansen 2008; Renou 2002, 20; Tardy 2002, 936).

The idea of the RECAMP programme was presented to various African states (both francophone and non-francophone) during the summer of 1997 and was officially pitched to the UN in December 1997 (Borgis 2004, 118). The goal was "to train a sizeable African force (up to 4–5,000 troops by the end of 2000) in the techniques of peacekeeping and to equip and support the force appropriately for rapid intervention in regional crisis" (Gregory 2000b, 442). The programme was based on four key characteristics: "multilateralism, ... availability to all the African states, ... transparency of contributions, ... and the non-permanence of the forces" (Diop 2004, 127–128).

After the establishment of the first RECAMP centre in Dakar and the undertaking of the first exercise, 'Guidimakha', in February 1998 in Mali, Mauritania and Senegal (Borgis 2004, 118; Gregory 2000b, 443), the programme continued to expand. For instance, the Senegalese troops who took part in the United Nations Organization Mission in the Democratic Republic of the Congo (MONUC) from November 1999 were "equipped, trained and transported by France" (Tardy 2002, 936). Consequently, as Doudou Salla Diop, the Senegalese Ambassador in France, explained, the French executive's strategy in the continent at the time was not to do less, but to do differently (2004, 127). This collaboration between France, the United Kingdom and the United States was significant because, as discussed in the first section of this chapter, tensions were high between France and its Anglo-Saxon partners when it came to African issues during Mitterrand's presidency. As Védrine explains, the goal of the executive at the time was to promote human protection while "overcom[ing] the antagonism and rivalries inherited from the past, the infamous Fashoda syndrome" (2002, 866).

Thus during the second half of the 1990s, France remained committed to intervening for humanitarian purposes but considerably changed its strategy. It focused its military efforts on Europe (favouring diplomacy and training elsewhere), and mainly undertook its operations with NATO, rather than the UN, while working towards the development of the European Union's capacity to intervene to protect. It is important to emphasise that this shift did not reflect a modification of France's conception of human protection, or of its domestic norm. Chirac's various executives continued to promote a broad understanding of human protection that was not limited to specific populations or situations, and kept emphasising the role France had to play in human protection in light of its history, values and rank. However, they changed France's practice of human protection to reconcile it with the promotion of France's rank and take into account technical and budgetary constraints. In other words, the importance of France's rank contributed to its playing a central role in human protection, and also impacted how it practised it. While this shift of strategy was partly influenced by the way the international community practised humanitarian intervention, France also influenced the way the international community practised humanitarian intervention: by withdrawing the UN's principal troop contributor, it reinforced the tendency of the UN to delegate the undertaking of humanitarian interventions to multilateral organisations and the organisations' use of stronger mandates.

## Former Yugoslavia

The shifts described above can be seen in France's main interventions at the time: the operations in Bosnia and Herzegovina and Kosovo.

### Bosnia and Herzegovina

As explained in Chapter 2, France was heavily involved in Bosnia and Herzegovina, and the resolution of this conflict constituted a priority for Mitterrand. He had chosen to intervene through the UN and had adopted a humanitarian strategy. Despite the French support for the creation of safe areas, this strategy was not drastically changed during the first year of the second *cohabitation*, though some shifts began to take place. A call to use force to deliver humanitarian assistance was promoted in December 1993 by the Minister of Foreign Affairs, Juppé, and the Defence Minister, Léotard, under the slogan *ou on tire ou on se tire* (either we shoot or we get out) (Guillot 1994, 39). Additionally, the right-wing government began raising strong criticisms towards the Secretary General and Yasushi Akashi – the Secretary General's personal representative for the war in the former Yugoslavia – and condemned the fact that "they had consumed generals at an inmoderate rate" (Guillot 1994, 39). They also began promoting a stronger involvement by the United States and NATO, in particular during the NATO Summit held in Brussels in January (Juppé in Assemblée Nationale 1994, 682; Guillot 1994, 39; Macleod 1997, 257).

These shifts towards a more robust approach and away from the UN deepened after the bombing of the Markale market in Sarajevo in February 1994 (Rollet 2006, 46; Smouts 1997, 41). The executive "called on NATO to declare a deadline for lifting the siege of that city and to threaten to bomb Serb positions if the deadline were [sic] not met" (Macleod 1997, 256–257). The success of the ultimatum was seen as a "diplomatic victory" for France, and for Juppé in particular (Rollet 2006, 46). As Macleod explains, "the French obtained much more [than the pull-back from the Serb military]. They succeeded in involving the United States directly in the peace process for the first time" (1997, 257). France also supported the creation in April 1994 of the Contact Group – which would be composed of France, the United States, the United Kingdom and Germany – in order to try to solve the conflict because the UN seemed to have reached a stalemate (Tardy 1999, 253). However, despite these changes, France's strategy was not entirely revisited during the *cohabitation*. As Védrine argued, France's "operational capacity" was made stronger during the *cohabitation*, but its overall strategy remained focused on the delivery of humanitarian aid and the negotiation of a diplomatic solution (Guillot 1994, 38; Védrine in Rollet 2006, 46).

When Chirac became President in May 1995, he further intensified France's strategy to the extent that his arrival in power can be seen as the turning point in France's strategy in former Yugoslavia (see Chirac 2011, 111; Juppé 2001). He promoted a more robust strategy in order to put a stop to the mass atrocities and end the humiliation of the French troops on the ground. France was indeed no longer promoting the use of force to simply support humanitarian intervention; it was willing to use force to impose peace. As a consequence, and as explained by Zic, "France moved from trying to minimise NATO's role, to actively calling for NATO and US political and military involvement" (2000, 18).

This wish for a stronger strategy was partly sparked by the intensification of the conflict (Soulet 2012; Tardy 1999, 271). In particular, as soon as Chirac was elected in May 1995, the Serbs took 174 French troops hostage after dressing up as French peacekeepers and used them as a human shield (McQueen 2005, 94; Rollet 2006, 47; Soulet 2012). President Chirac, who considered that this public humiliation was the last straw, ordered for the first time the use of force to free the hostages (Chirac in Nouzille 2010, 430–431).

Additionally, the new executive began lobbying for a stronger response from the international community (Macleod 1997, 259; Soulet 2012). For instance, four weeks after his election, Chirac undertook his first international visit to the United States to discuss with President Bill Clinton the need for "more forceful action" (Sutton 2007, 298). Throughout the summer of 1995 Chirac's executive also "put forward a series of proposals aimed at strengthening the military aspects of United Nations and NATO actions in Bosnia" (Macleod 1997, 259). Last but not least, Chirac agreed with the British Prime Minister, John Major, to create and deploy a Rapid Reaction Force (RRF) (Soulet 2012). With the United Kingdom's support followed by Denmark's, the RRF was born and 12,500 troops were deployed from June after the agreement of the UN Security Council (Macleod 1997, 260; UN Security Council 1995; Zic 2000, 20–21).

Nevertheless, the RRF and the UN were not able to prevent the Serbs from taking two of the six safe areas – Srebrenica and Žepa. In light of this failure and taking into account the near collapse of Goražde and Bihać and the provocation of the Serbs by the new attacks on Sarajevo, the international community progressively changed its strategy in favour of the more robust response advocated by France and the United States (Macleod 1997, 260). On 30 August 1995 NATO launched Operation Deliberate Force. Although NATO and the RRF interventions were not the only factors that led to the end of the violence (McQueen 2005, 89; Wheeler 2000, 256–257), the conflict was over in four months.

It is interesting to note that the involvement of the United States, promoted by France during the year leading up to the intervention, ended up limiting France's role during the final stage of the conflict, since the majority of Operation Deliberate Force was undertaken by the United States, and France and the other European powers were not included in the Dayton negotiations (Macleod 1997, 259, 262; Tardy 1999, 298–300). However, France's participation in the operation via the RRF remained important, and the Americans agreed to have the signing of the Dayton Agreement in Paris on 14 December 1995 so as to acknowledge the diplomatic contribution made by France throughout the conflict (Nouzille 2010, 453; Soulet 2012).

The French presence in Bosnia and Herzegovina continued even after the signature of the Dayton Agreement (Soulet 2012). France participated heavily in IFOR (Implementation Force), also known as Operation Joint Endeavour, a NATO operation undertaken under UN mandate from December 1995 to December 1996 to implement the agreement, and in SFOR (Stabilisation Force), a NATO operation led from December 1996 to December 2004 to stabilise the country. Finally, as discussed in Chapter 4, France was involved from December 2004 in the European Union's operation EUFOR (European Force) Althea.

*Kosovo*

The intervention in Kosovo was another central moment of Chirac's presidency and a key illustration of the shift in the practice of human protection during the second half of the 1990s. The tensions between the Serbs and the Albanians in the region of Kosovo, in which Albanians constituted a majority (90 per cent), were not new. However, the relations between the two ethnic groups had deteriorated in 1989 when President Slobodan Milosevic "stripped Kosovo of its autonomy and pulled her back more closely under Serbia and a newly oppressive political control" (Wilton 2008, 364). In February 1998 the violence intensified into a conflict which, as the Independent International Commission on Kosovo (IICK) explained, can be divided into two phases: "in the first phase of the conflict from February 1998 to March 1999, casualties were relatively low … [and] [m]ore than 400,000 people were driven from their homes", while "in the period March 24, 1999 to June 19, 1999, the Commission estimates the number of killings in the neighbourhood of 10,000, with the vast majority of the victims being Kosovar Albanians killed by FRY [Federal Republic of Yugoslavia] forces. Approximately 863,000 civilians sought or were forced into refuge outside Kosovo and an additional 590,000 were internally displaced" (IICK 2000, 2).

The French executive at the time rapidly began to play a role in the conflict resolution, to the point that Bryant has argued that it was "a key player at all stages and in all dimensions of the Kosovo crisis" (2000, 35). France's role should, however, not be exaggerated, for the United States' contribution was unparalleled: it was the key player in the resolution of this crisis.[10] However, Chirac was committed to resolving the conflict from the start, and even though this was still a period of *cohabitation*, the President and the government agreed on the strategy to follow (Tourard 2000, 202).

Various factors influenced the decision of the French executive to become involved. First, as the Quilès and Lamy report explained, France's involvement was needed because the stability of south-east Europe was being endangered (1999, 29–30; see also Chirac and Jospin in Davidson 2011, 87–88). The influence of France's domestic norm of human protection also needs to be taken into account. The executive was concerned about the humanitarian emergency and believed it had a duty to put an end to it in light of France's history, values and rank. For instance, on 8 June 1998 Chirac explained, "when I was elected, we had a dramatic situation in Bosnia. The UN soldiers were humiliated and I decided to react very firmly and to create the special force, the Rapid Reaction Force, and the situation rapidly improved. I have the same will for Kosovo, the same determination. We cannot accept the ethnic cleansing policies. We cannot and we have to be very firm" (1998).

France's involvement in Kosovo also had the advantage of allowing it to fulfil its perceived duty while promoting its rank (Macleod and Voyer-Léger 2004, 80). As Chirac explained in 1999, it helped promote its status as European leader: "[be] assured that France, as it has done since the beginning of the conflict in the former Yugoslavia, will fulfil all of its responsibilities. It owes it to its European ambition" (in Davidson 2011, 89–90). Similarly, as Davidson explains, it partly intended "to further [France's] aims on European security and defence integration, and to maximise its influence over the United States" (2011, 92).

From a diplomatic point of view, France's involvement began as early as November 1997, when the French Minister of Foreign Affairs, Védrine and the German Minister of Foreign Affairs, Klaus Kinkel, wrote a letter to President Milosevic asking him to address the situation (Védrine in Weber 1999, 23). They suggested a "special status" for Kosovo, which would consist of a middle ground between the status quo and independence (Quilès and Lamy 1999, 13). While the letter had little impact, since it was ignored by Milosevic, the 1999 report to the French Parliament argued that it "is of particular importance. It marks, first of all, the beginning of the renewed interest of the international community in the Kosovar question. Then it identifies the elements that will constantly be put forward to promote the resolution of the crisis. Finally, it warns the Yugoslav President of the consequences of an obstinate tension over the status of Kosovo" (Quilès and Lamy 1999, 13).

When the Contact Group was reactivated at the beginning of 1998,[11] France tried to play "a catalytic role at [its] heart" (Jospin in Davidson 2011, 89). But France's diplomatic involvement became particularly visible in 1999 when, in light of the intensification of the violence and the failure of diplomatic solutions, Védrine suggested to the Contact Group that a peace conference be organised in order to promote "diplomatic pressure" and give diplomacy one more chance (Védrine in Weber 1999, 26). This conference was held in February 1999 in Rambouillet (near Paris) under the co-presidency of France and the United Kingdom. Védrine argued that "in Rambouillet, we have negotiated relentlessly" (in Weber 1999, 28), but the conference ended inconclusively. On 13 March 1999 talks resumed at the Centre Kléber in Paris, where the co-chairs – Védrine and the British Foreign Secretary, Robin Cook – "opened the proceedings by insisting that the negotiations must produce a quick result and would be wound up in a week if there were no agreement" (Bellamy 2002, 146). The talks ended five days later when Milosevic refused to sign the agreement.

After the failure of the peace negotiations, because the humanitarian situation was deteriorating – "FRY forces were engaged in a well planned campaign of … 'ethnic cleansing', intended to drive many, if not all, Kosovar Albanians from Kosovo, destroy the foundations of their society, and prevent them from returning" (IICK 2000, 88) – the Contact Group decided that a military intervention was necessary (Védrine in Weber 1999, 30). Védrine argued that "we had tried everything, that the situation is no longer tolerable, that we thus need to put an end to this, and that the use of force is inevitable" (in Weber 1999, 30).

On 24 March 1999 NATO's Operation Allied Force began, with the aim of forcing Milosevic to accept a peace agreement (Wilton 2008, 366). In his speech to the French people on 29 March 1999, Chirac explained that "Europe cannot accept on its territory a man and a regime which, for almost ten years, has engaged in Slovenia, Croatia, Bosnia and now Kosovo in operations of ethnic cleansing, in assassinations and massacres, in the destabilisation of the whole region" (1999a). He then declared that "in view of the stubborn refusal of the Serbian government and of its President, ... the government and myself, with our unanimous allies, [have taken] the decision to engage in military action" (1999a).

Even though the United States made the largest contribution, France played a key part: it was the largest non-US contributor to Operation Allied Force and offered the full range of its military means to NATO. It thus undertook "12 to 13 per cent of the attack missions, 20 per cent of the intelligence missions and ... 8 per cent of the air defence" (Quilès and Lamy 1999, 100). It is also important to note that French troops were also deployed in Macedonia from December 1998 as part of the Kosovo Veri-fication Mission of the Organization for Security and Co-operation in Europe (OSCE), which had been authorised by Resolution 1199. As the 1999 report to the French Parliament explained, "the number of French troops regularly increased, from 500 in December 1998 to 1,160 in Febru-ary, then 2,340 in mid-March 1999" (Quilès and Lamy 1999, 102).

Similarly, following Milosevic's agreement to withdraw troops from Kosovo and the resultant end of the NATO air strikes, the Kosovo Force (KFOR) was deployed on 12 June 1999 following UN Security Council Resolution 1244. By August 1999 France had contributed 5,500 troops (Quilès and Lamy 1999, 104). Its involvement in Kosovo carried on beyond 1999, for the various French executives decided to contribute troops, and sometimes lead, the four missions that were created by the European Union and NATO in order to stabilise and rebuild Kosovo: KFOR, the United Nations Interim Administration Mission in Kosovo (UNMIK), the European Union Rule of Law Mission (EULEX) in Kosovo and the OSCE Mission in Kosovo (OMIK).

Even though France's contribution – both diplomatically and militarily – to the conflict resolution was important, it was not always deemed beneficial. Beyond the criticisms that have been directed at the inter-national community's response,[12] France's approach to the conflict resolu-tion was also criticised at times, especially by the Americans, who had a very different strategy. Wesley Clark, NATO's Supreme Commander in Europe, explained that the United States was willing to go "after the heart of Milosevic's power" while the French wanted to find a solution to the situation in Kosovo while "avoiding actions that might antagonise or damage Serbia further" (2001, 239). Some might argue that there was a will on France's part to protect Milosevic and the Serbs, but as Chirac's strong response to the conflict in Bosnia and Herzegovina showed, this was not the case. Rather, the French executive – and other European states (see for instance Clark 2001, 273) – feared the consequences of alienating Milosevic and aimed to promote a political outcome until it was clear that only force could impose a compromise.

These contrasting strategies became visible in the early stages of the conflict. For instance, in April 1998, while the French showed their will to use diplomatic pressure on Milosevic,[13] they "indicated that they would not be prepared to consider imposing comprehensive sanctions against Yugoslavia as the US proposed" (Bellamy 2002, 79) despite Kofi Annan's warning to the Security Council that the situation on the ground was deteriorating. This position rapidly evolved, and a few months later France was willing to support punitive air strikes (Bellamy 2002, 81), but it reflected the fear the French had of alienating Milosevic.

This approach led the French executive at the time to make major concessions to the Serbs during the negotiations they led in Rambouillet. For instance, driven by the will to find a diplomatic solution to the conflict – especially if that solution was brokered in France – and in light of the reluctance of the Serbs to reach a compromise and to accept the presence of an interposition force, Védrine and Cook "importantly, erroneously, and disastrously for the Kosovar Albanians", argued in front of the Serb media that the Kosovar Albanians should give up their demand for independence (Bellamy 2002, 139). While explaining that "the status quo is unacceptable", Védrine argued, "we have a responsibility to resist complete independence!" (in Weber 1999, 27). As Bellamy explains, "this diplomatic initiative only compounded Kosovar Albanian disquiet with the way the negotiations were progressing and reduced the likelihood of reaching agreement still further" (2002, 139).

This approach to the resolution of the conflict also led the French to adopt a conservative attitude during the beginning of the NATO campaign by refusing to authorise strikes on sensitive targets. Clark recalled that the French justified their position by arguing that "the best way to pressure Milosevic was to ensure that he had more to lose in the future than he had already lost. In other words, they seemed to be saying, if he feels like he's already lost everything, he'll have no incentive to stop" (2001, 239). He was, however, critical of this approach, believing that "we were a long way from that point. And if we didn't increase the pressure on him, our own people would grow discouraged" (2001, 239).

In light of these key differences in strategies, but also in order to make sure that France played a central role in the conflict resolution, the French executive insisted on being part of the decision-making process when it came to determining where the strikes would occur, especially in terms of civilian targets (Priest 1999). As Bellamy explains, "Chirac demanded direct personal involvement in target selection and the three leaders [Chirac, British Prime Minister Tony Blair and Clinton] agreed a set of guidelines that gave each direct input on the selection of civilian targets" (2002, 161). Consequently, Louis Gautier, one of Jospin's advisors, argued that France "was able in Kosovo to impose itself in the decision making process and affect strategy" (in Davidson 2011, 86–87). This request, however, frustrated Clark, who argued that it was slowing down the process (Priest 1999).

Before concluding, it is important to specify that even though Operation Allied Force took place without the explicit authorisation of the Security Council, this did not mean that the French executive at the time considered that the Council's approval was no longer necessary for intervention in the future and that the UN was no longer relevant. Even during Operation Allied Force, Chirac continued to emphasise his will to cooperate with the UN and the importance of the institution (see for example, Chirac 1999b; 1999c; 1999d), and so did the French Permanent Representative to the UN (see, for instance, Alain Dejammet in UN Security Council 1999, 12). Védrine also underlines the fact that Kosovo "had to remain an isolated case" (2000). Thus what was advocated was a reconsideration not of the authority of the Council, but rather of the way it functioned so that it could address situations like Kosovo.

The French involvement in Bosnia and Herzegovina and Kosovo illustrates both the French executive's support to human protection and its shift of practice. First, it shows the increasing focus put on Europe. Second, it highlights the progressive shift away from the UN in favour of NATO and the European Union. Finally, it demonstrates that this progressive shift of institutional framework was accompanied by a shift from a humanitarian strategy to a more coercive one when deemed necessary.

## Conclusion

During the second half of the 1990s, France remained supportive of human protection. Despite the changes of executives, the difficulties experienced in the field by France's troops during their participation in UN interventions for humanitarian purposes and the international criticism of humanitarian intervention – to which France contributed – the various French executives never questioned the need for a right to intervene to be internationally recognised and continued to intervene for humanitarian purposes. This lack of normative rollback could have been the result of the internalisation of humanitarian intervention by France, but there is no evidence that validates this claim, and this is not surprising, since a norm's influence is only proportional to its strength, and humanitarian intervention was an internationally contested principle during the second half of the 1990s. In contrast, Mitterrand's and Chirac's executives continued to emphasise the idea that in light of its history, values and rank, France had a special role to play in human protection.

France's role was, however, much more limited and controversial than in the early 1990s. First, it contributed to the contestation of humanitarian intervention by undertaking a controversial intervention in Rwanda using humanitarian claims. Additionally, in light of the backlash of *Opération Turquoise*, technical and budgetary constraints, a change of both the domestic and international contexts and the need to reconcile France's promotion of human protection with its rank, it concentrated its military interventions in Europe rather than intervening worldwide, favouring diplomacy and training elsewhere. It also increasingly intervened through multilateral interventions, mostly led by NATO rather than the UN, thus shifting away from the humanitarian approach used at the beginning of the 1990s in favour of more coercive – but also contentious – operations.

It is interesting to note that in contrast to the situation in 1988–93, France impacted human protection mainly through its practice rather than through its normative contribution. Its normative impact was indeed limited since it did not stop the international contestation of the principle, nor did it help address its limits. In contrast, its practice helped shape the way the international community practised humanitarian intervention: even though the change in its practice of human protection was partly influenced by the way the international community implemented humanitarian intervention, France did indeed reinforce the international trend of delegating humanitarian interventions to multilateral organisations and to using more coercive mandates. It also contributed to fuelling some of the main criticisms directed towards humanitarian intervention, such as the idea that it was undertaken to promote the interests of intervening states (Rwanda), did not respect the sovereignty of states (Bosnia and Herzegovina) and was illegal (Kosovo).

### Notes

1 For a more in-depth discussion of France's involvement in the Rwandan genocide and the rationale behind it, see Staunton (2016).
2 The RPF is a group constituted mainly of English-speaking Tutsis, as many Tutsis had to take refuge in neighbouring English-speaking countries such as Uganda after their defeat during the Hutu Revolution in the early 1960s. They

were asking for the right to return and for a multi-party democracy (Ramsbotham and Woodhouse 1999, 210).

3 UNAMIR was established by Security Council Resolution 872 of 5 October 1993 (UN Security Council 1993l).

4 The *Interahamwe* were Hutu militia who participated in the genocide.

5 For a more detailed overview of the various accounts trying to make sense of France's response, see Staunton (2016, 302–308).

6 Operation Restore Hope was undertaken under the command of the United States to provide a secure environment for the delivery of humanitarian aid. UNOSOM II was established by the Security Council's Resolution 814 in March 1993. Its mandate "was to take appropriate action, including enforcement measures, to establish throughout Somalia a secure environment for humanitarian assistance" (UN 1996a).

7 See in particular Léotard in Tardy (1999, 242); Léotard (1995, 207).

8 See in particular Article 5.J.1 and 5.J.2.

9 The Berlin Summit was held in June 1996 and led to recognition of the existence of the European Security and Defence Policy within NATO.

10 For instance, the United States carried out 60 to 80 per cent of the air strikes of Operation Allied Force (Quilès and Lamy 1999, 98).

11 As mentioned previously, the Contact Group consisted of France, the United Kingdom, Germany, Italy, the United States and Russia and had originally been created to solve the conflict in Bosnia and Herzegovina.

12 In particular, NATO's air strikes led Milosevic to accelerate his campaign of ethnic cleansing. They thus accelerated the displacement and expulsion of the Kosovar Albanian population (IICK 2000, 92–93). Additionally, as Wheeler explains, "if NATO's intervention in Kosovo was successful in restoring to the Albanians the civil and political rights that Milosevic's policy of repression had stripped away, it failed to stop a new round of ethnic cleansing, as thousands of Serbs fled in fear of Albanians seeking revenge" (2000, 274).

13 Following their letter on November 1997, Védrine and Kinkel visited Milosevic in Belgrade in March 1998 to again promote a diplomatic resolution to the conflict (Quilès and Lamy 1999, 14).

# 4

# From norm entrepreneur to 'part of the problem': France and the emergence of the responsibility to protect (2000–2004)

At the end of the 1990s, the international community questioned how to promote human rights without endangering state sovereignty. In response, the early 2000s saw the emergence of a new concept, R2P, in order to allow states to continue protecting beyond their borders, while addressing the issues raised by humanitarian intervention.[1] During this period President Jacques Chirac was in power thanks to his re-election in 2002.[2] Between 1997 and 2002 he had to work with a left-wing government led by Prime Minister Lionel Jospin, before the right wing won the legislative elections in 2002, allowing him to work alongside a government from his own party.

In order to better understand France's conception of, and contribution to, human protection during the early 2000s, this chapter investigates whether France played a role in the emergence of R2P between 2000 and 2004 and whether the international concept impacted France in any way. To achieve this, it is divided into two main sections. The first argues that even though Chirac's various executives continued to promote the importance of human protection, and in particular the idea that because of its history, values and rank France had a special role to play, France did not take part in the emergence of R2P. In view of France's commitment to human protection since the 1980s, and in particular its role as norm entrepreneur in the emergence of humanitarian intervention, this lack of direct contribution is surprising and is therefore investigated. The book argues that France was excluded from the discussions on R2P after the international community deemed its conception and practice of human protection controversial and outdated.

The second section analyses France's ongoing commitment to human protection despite its exclusion from the negotiating table. During the lead-up to the Iraq War, France showed that it was willing to stand up for its conception of human protection and that its voice still mattered. Additionally, Chirac's executives remained committed to intervening militarily for humanitarian purposes and thus continued to contribute to shaping the way the international community practised human protection. The lack of involvement of France in the emergence of R2P, combined with the fact that the concept was not recognised until the 2005 World Summit, meant that it had no influence on France's conception of human protection during the early 2000s. In contrast, France's domestic norm of human protection helped drive its ongoing commitment to protection while its associated obsession with its rank helped determine how it fulfilled its perceived duty.

## The exclusion of France from the emergence of R2P

As demonstrated in Chapter 3, the international contestation of humanitarian intervention grew increasingly strong during the second half of the 1990s. By 1995 humanitarian intervention was already being heavily criticised in view of the "catastrophic mission failures in Angola, Somalia, Bosnia and Rwanda, characterised by the failure of UN [troops] to protect themselves and those under their care" (Bellamy 2011, 171). The delegation of humanitarian intervention by the UN to regional organisations did not stop the criticism, for, as Gierycz explains, these interventions "were not necessarily more successful" (2010, 111). The fact that an "illegal but legitimate" intervention took place in Kosovo (IICK 2000, 4) was deemed problematic by the supporters of humanitarian intervention. It was also the last straw for those sceptical about humanitarian intervention because "the NATO action created basic reservations that a concept of humanitarian intervention could be misused in order to interfere in the internal matters of states, to undermine their sovereignty, and to depose 'inconvenient' leaders" (Gierycz 2010, 112).

As a consequence, by the end of the decade, the international community was divided between those who considered that the right to intervene in the domestic affairs of a state in mass atrocity situations was a necessity, and those who argued that it would continue to lead to intolerable violations of state sovereignty, which is a core principle of the UN Charter.[3] Gareth Evans explains this best:

> Every general discussion in the UN General Assembly and other international forums, and nearly every difficult individual case that arose, became a political battlefield with two warring armies. On the one side were those, mostly from the global North, who, in situations of catastrophic human rights violations, could not see beyond humanitarian intervention, the 'right to intervene' with military force. On the other side were those, mostly from the global South, who were often prepared to concede that grave rights violations were occurring but were resolutely determined to maintain the

continued resonance, and indeed primacy, of the traditional non-intervention concept of national sovereignty. ... The debate was intense and very bitter, and the twentieth century ended with it utterly unresolved in the UN or anywhere else. (2008a, 30)

## The emergence of R2P without France

With the debate unresolved by the end of the 1990s, UN Secretary General Kofi Annan asked in 2000 in his Millennium report, "if humanitarian intervention is indeed an unacceptable assault on sovereignty, how should we respond to a Rwanda, to a Srebrenica – to gross and systemic violations of human rights that offend every precept of our common humanity?" (Annan 2000, 48). In 2001 the Canadian government established the ICISS in order to answer Annan's call or, more specifically, "when, if ever, it is appropriate for states to take coercive – and in particular military – action, against another state for the purpose of protecting people at risk in that other state" (ICISS 2001, vii). In its report *The Responsibility to Protect*, the Commission argued that both states and the international community have a responsibility to protect populations from four crimes: genocide, crimes against humanity, war crimes and ethnic cleansing. Three responsibilities were identified: to prevent, to react and to rebuild. It thus concluded that "the principle of non-intervention yields to the international responsibility to protect" (ICISS 2001, xi).

By doing so, the report did not disregard the importance of sovereignty, since this would have sealed the fate of R2P by leading to the same divisions humanitarian intervention had generated. Rather, the Commission aimed to reconcile the international community by arguing that "sovereignty and human rights are two sides of the same coin" (Bellamy 2009a, 33), and that promoting the former did not lead to violating the latter. The ICISS accomplished this goal by promoting the concept of 'sovereignty as responsibility', which had emerged during the 1990s thanks to the work of Francis Deng, Roberta Cohen and Annan (Bellamy 2009a, chapter 1; Glanville 2010, 233–234; 2012, 9–10). In contrast to a traditional, post-Second World War understanding of sovereignty, this concept argues that sovereignty and non-intervention are "conditional upon the performance of sovereign responsibilities for the protection of populations" (Glanville 2012, 9).

In 2004 the High-Level Panel on Threats, Challenges and Change published a report called *A More Secure World: Our Shared Responsibility* which called for the support of the concept of R2P (UN General Assembly 2004). Three months later, Annan also encouraged states to support the concept (Annan 2005; Glanville 2012, 11; Weiss 2012b, 437). This took place in September 2005, when member states unanimously endorsed R2P at the UN World Summit. In particular, Article 139 of the World Summit Outcome Document argued that:

> The international community, through the United Nations, also has the responsibility to use appropriate diplomatic, humanitarian and other peaceful means, in accordance with Chapters VI and VIII of the Charter, to help protect populations from genocide, war crimes, ethnic cleansing and crimes against humanity. In this context, we are prepared to take collective action, in a timely and decisive manner, through the Security Council, in accordance with the Charter, including Chapter VII, on a case-by-case basis and in cooperation with relevant regional organisations as appropriate, should peaceful means be inadequate and national authorities manifestly fail to protect their populations from genocide, war crimes, ethnic cleansing and crimes against humanity. (UN General Assembly 2005)

Given its commitment to human protection since the 1980s, and in particular, in light of its role as norm entrepreneur in the emergence of humanitarian intervention, it would not seem far-fetched to expect France to have played a central role in the emergence of R2P. Nevertheless, no French representative – not even Bernard Kouchner – was present at the negotiating table (Staunton 2018, 375–376). This is surprising because, as mentioned in Chapter 2, Evans, one of the co-chairs of the ICISS, has argued that "in making the response to mass atrocities the single most debated foreign policy issue of the decade, rather than one that could comfortably be ignored by policymakers, his contribution was outstanding" (2008a, 32).

*Making sense of France's absence from the ICISS: France, a 'part of the problem'*

A logical explanation for France's absence from the ICISS could have been that it was mainly composed of representatives from the global South, in order to signal that their concerns had been heard and taken seriously. However, this was not the case, for it regrouped key advocates of human protection from all around the world, including Security Council veto powers. In particular, in addition to the five members from the global South,[4] the ICISS was composed of Evans (co-chair, Australia), Gisèle Côté-Harper (Canada), Lee Hamilton (United States), Michael Ignatieff (Canada), Vladimir Lukin (Russia), Klaus Naumann (Germany) and Cornelio Sommaruga (Switzerland). This lack of a French presence makes us question why France was not represented.

This lack of representation was not caused by an oversight or a lack of interest on France's part, but by a deliberate decision of the Commission (Staunton 2018, 376; see also Jeangène Vilmer 2012, 89–90). Kouchner and

Mario Bettati argued that it was a political move to attempt to exclude France from the human protection arena (Kouchner 2014; Bettati 2014), while Bettati also contended that old personal rivalries were at play as former colleagues of the Red Cross were lobbying against France's inclusion in the Commission (Bettati 2014). Evans confirmed that France was deliberately excluded from the Commission, but not for the reasons put forward by Kouchner and Bettati. He explained in an interview with the author that "the French were part of the problem" (Evans 2013b; see also Ramesh Thakur 2008, in Jeangène Vilmer 2012, 90) because by the end of the 1990s, many members of the international community deemed France's position on human protection to be controversial and outdated.

This perception of France's position – and the subsequent shift from norm entrepreneur to 'part of the problem' – can first be explained by the fact that throughout the 1990s, the various French executives appeared to be promoting only a right – rather than a duty and a right – to intervene (Staunton 2018, 376). For instance, Evans argued that "there was so much, so much antagonism towards the notion of a right. ... No matter what [the new members of the Security Council and newly independent states] were willing to sign up to, they were not prepared to sign up to a generalised right, a *droit*" (2013b).[5] Similarly, Cohen and Deng explain that the French contribution can be summarised as "the idea of a right to humanitarian intervention (*'le droit d'ingérence'*) ... . The international community, it was argued, should have a right to intervene when governments obstructed access to populations in need or deliberately subjected them to starvation or other abuses" (2016, 75). While these commentators associate France with a "right to humanitarian intervention", they do not mention the idea of a *devoir* to protect that had influenced the various French executives since the 1980s.

This understanding of France's conception of human protection is not surprising, for key French personalities such as François Mitterrand, Chirac and Kouchner had clearly defined the distinctions – but also the links – between *droit* and *devoir d'ingérence* domestically during the 1987 International Conference on Humanitarian Law and Ethics in Paris; however, they failed to clearly do so internationally. In particular, during Chirac's presidency, the need for the international community to intervene was often emphasised but the idea of a 'responsibility' to do so was mainly linked to France specifically (see for instance Chirac 1995b).

The fact that France had been actively intervening militarily for humanitarian purposes since 1992 and had often done so using a coercive approach also contributed to France's exclusion from the ICISS. Not only had France deployed an average of around 7,000 troops between 1992 and 1999, but it increasingly chose to intervene to protect through multilateral institutions such as NATO, which favoured more robust interventions. Chirac's push for a robust strategy in Bosnia and Herzegovina was a good illustration of France's willingness to use coercive intervention, and so was its support for, and participation in, NATO's intervention in Kosovo. Consequently, France's conception of human protection was seen as promoting coercive intervention, which was precisely what those sceptical of humanitarian intervention were concerned about. Additionally, the impact of France's controversial intervention in Rwanda cannot be underestimated as it fuelled the claim that France used humanitarian narratives as a pretext for undertaking interest-based interventions.

Given that these factors led the international community to see France's position as controversial and outdated, and taking into account the fact that finding a compromise between the states in favour of intervening to protect and those concerned with the implication such interventions had on their sovereignty would already be challenging, the ICISS felt it had to exclude the French from the global conversation about a new framework for human protection. This allowed it to send a strong signal to those who were sceptical of humanitarian intervention and to rally support behind the work of the Commission (Staunton 2018, 376).

## An ongoing commitment to human protection

France's exclusion from the ICISS led it to play no role in the emergence of R2P, and it also meant that R2P had no impact on Chirac's various executives during the early 2000s. In fact, like most of the international community, they showed no sign of explicit endorsement of R2P before the 2005 World Summit.[6] Nevertheless, as this section shows, they continued to promote human protection both diplomatically and militarily. This support can partly be explained by the influence of France's domestic norm of human protection.

Chirac's executives indeed continued to promote the idea that France had a special role to play in the promotion of human protection in light of its history, values and rank. For instance, Chirac declared in 2001, "Human rights, the concern for the human being and their dignity, have been a passion of France for a long time now" (in Chirac 2007, 433). He also explained in front of the French ambassadors that "history, the responsibilities that our country assumes and the vision that we have of the world dictate the orientations [of our foreign policy]" (Chirac 2002). Similarly, left-wing Prime Minister Jospin argued during the *cohabitation* that "in a world which, on a daily basis, offers too many examples of human rights violations, attacks on the freedom of conscience and expression, and acts that are contrary to human dignity, France, owing to its history, its place on the international scene and its fight for democracy, deserves to be the spokesperson of those who are deprived of their basic rights" (1997b). The Minister of Foreign Affairs, Dominique de Villepin (2002–04), also explained in 2002 that:

> France has the vocation and the ambition to play a great role. It also has the means to do so. … Its position in Europe, its membership of the G8, of NATO, of the UN Security Council, impart it a real power of mobilisation. All through our history, our nation has felt invested with a particular mission on the world stage, as a carrier of values that it wants to share with other populations. Today our singular and generous vocation to universality constitutes our asset and our opportunity. (in Macleod and Voyer-Léger 2004, 85)

### A voice that still matters: France and the Iraq War

In light of the influence of the domestic norm, and even though it was excluded from the initial discussions on R2P, France showed that it was willing to stand up and protect its understanding of human protection and that its voice still mattered. A good illustration of its influence is its firm and somewhat surprising position on the Iraq War. In 2003 what would become the coalition led by the United States argued that an intervention was necessary in light of the presence of weapons of mass destruction and the ties of the regime with the terrorist group al-Qaeda. When this argument was questioned and contested by some members of the international community – including France – the coalition also argued that the intervention was needed on humanitarian grounds in light of the atrocities that had been committed by Saddam Hussein over the years (see for instance Bush and Blair 2003).

Despite the support of Denmark, the United Kingdom, Hungary, Italy, Poland, Slovakia and the 'Vilnius Ten' in January–February 2003 (Melandri 2013, 142), the French executive at the time continued to emphasise that an intervention should not be considered, or at least that it could not be considered yet. In a notorious speech to the UN Security Council, de Villepin declared on 14 February 2003, "the use of force cannot be justified today" (2003b; see also de Villepin 2003a). On 10 March 2003 President Chirac revealed at a press conference that if a resolution allowing the use of force against Iraq was put forward to the Security Council, "no matter what the circumstances are, France will vote 'no' because it considers, tonight, that there is no need to make war to achieve the objective that we have decided" (in Chirac 2007, 252–253). In light of the criticisms coming from France, and also from several other members of the Security Council, on 17 March, the United States, the United Kingdom and Spain decided to give an ultimatum to Saddam Hussein instead of putting their resolution forward (Ploton 2003, 100).

France's stance in Iraq can first be explained by the fact that the executive at the time believed that if Iraq was hiding weapons of mass destruction, they could be handled using diplomacy and UN inspections (Nouzille 2010, 601; Tardy 2003, 111). It also questioned the alleged links of Saddam Hussein's regime with al-Qaeda. As de Villepin argued in front of the Security Council, "there is an alternative to war: to disarm Iraq through inspections. [...] Ten days ago, the US Secretary of State, Mr Powell, reported the alleged links between al-Qaeda and the regime in Baghdad. Given the present state of our research and intelligence, in liaison with our allies, nothing allows us to establish such links" (2003b).

Nevertheless, some would argue that France could still have intervened, or at least supported an intervention, on a humanitarian basis – as it did in 1991 – to put an end to the atrocities committed by Saddam Hussein since 1979.[7] Yet France remained determined to refuse to authorise military action and showed that it was prepared to damage France's relationship with the world's hegemonic power in order to do so (see for instance Bozo 2012, 251; Melandri 2013, 145–147; Nouzille 2010, 615). This decision can partly be explained by the fact that an intervention in Iraq would have been in contradiction to its approach to human protection.

Since the 1990s France had mainly intervened to protect populations after specific emergencies had emerged, which was not the case here. Additionally, even though France was not opposed to the use of force under specific circumstances, the executive at the time did not believe that the regime change promoted by the coalition would be beneficial (Vaïsse 2003; Tardy 2003, 112). As de Villepin explained in January 2003, "it is one thing to intervene militarily in Iraq, to attack the regime of Saddam Hussein, to drive out Saddam Hussein and bring down the regime. It is another to have a united Iraq" (2003a). A month later, he also argued to the Security Council that "premature resort to the military option would have serious consequences ... it would reinforce the feeling of injustice, aggravate tensions and threaten to open the way to other conflicts" (2003b). Similarly, Chirac argued on 16 February that "the consequences of war would be considerable in human terms. In political terms, it would destabilize the entire region" (in Graff and Crumley 2003). Even after the intervention had begun, Chirac argued that he was hoping that it would not lead to a "humanitarian catastrophe" (2003) and that he was sceptical that a peace imposed by the coalition could have a positive outcome (see Chirac in Nouzille 2010, 663).

Consequently, the executive continued to work towards preventing the intervention from being authorised by the UN Security Council. As de Villepin explained in front of the Council,

> In this temple that is the United Nations, we are the caretakers of an ideal, we are the caretakers of a conscience. The heavy responsibility and the immense honour that are ours have to make us give priority to disarmament in peace. This message comes to you today from an old country, France, from a continent like mine, Europe, that has known wars, occupation and barbarity. A country that does not forget and knows everything it owes to the freedom-fighters who came from America and elsewhere. And yet has never ceased to stand upright in the face of history and before mankind. Faithful to its values, it wishes resolutely to act with all the members of the international community. It believes in our ability to build a better world together. (2003b)

Thus even though France did not play a role in the emergence of R2P, it showed that it was determined to stand up for its conception of human protection, even if it meant going against the world's hegemonic powers. While France did not stop the war from taking place, it played a central role in preventing its legitimisation by the Security Council.

During the first half of the 2000s, Chirac's various executives also put forward some important proposals in order to improve how the international community was handling humanitarian crises. For instance, in 2000 the Minister of Foreign Affairs Hubert Védrine argued that a lot of the issues associated with humanitarian intervention were linked to the fact that many interventions lacked legitimacy and that the international community could not always react. As a consequence, he called for an enlarged Security Council of twenty-four members where the permanent members would "solemnly renounce use of the veto power once it prevents the Security Council from looking at the fate of a population under imminent threat and taking every action possible to assist it" (Védrine 2009, 259).

Looking back on his presidencies, Chirac gave a very positive summary of France's contribution to human protection under his leadership:

> Since 1995, our country has affirmed itself as one of the most determined to work for the maintenance of peace and the prevention of conflicts ... . France has assumed its responsibilities in this regard, when the situation required, as much in Bosnia as in Kosovo, by taking the initiative in concerted military operations in which the only objective was to end humanitarian dramas that had become intolerable. ... But it is also opposed, with an equal firmness, to any decision likely to aggravate relations between populations under the cover of normalising these relations and to exacerbate the factors of incomprehension and resentment. (2011, 414)

*An ongoing commitment to militarily intervene to protect*

As hinted in Chirac's statement, France remained committed to intervening militarily for humanitarian purposes in various theatres during the early 2000s. Influenced by the domestic norm of human protection, France deployed an average of 9,062 troops a year between 2000 and 2004 for humanitarian purposes (IISS 2000; 2001; 2002; 2003; 2004). Some continuity can be seen with the first years of Chirac's mandate: a commitment to focus France's efforts in Europe, to intervene through NATO rather than the UN and to build the European Union's capacity to intervene. But the various executives also renewed some of the practice from the early 1990s by intervening in Africa, even if, in the case of *Opération Licorne*, it meant intervening unilaterally and, initially, without the UN Security Council's approval.

The choice of institutional framework

During the second half of the 1990s, the various French executives had questioned the capacity of the UN to undertake successful interventions for humanitarian purposes, but they never stopped promoting the idea that it was the only legitimate institution capable of authorising such interventions, even during the intervention in Kosovo. As mentioned previously in the discussion of the Iraq War, the early 2000s were no different. Chirac explained in 2001 that "France [saw] in the UN the principal element of an emerging world governance" (in Lombart 2007b, 386). Nevertheless, as at the beginning of Chirac's presidency, French support for the institution was mainly limited to the diplomatic sphere: as illustrated by Graph 7, its military contributions to the UN's operations undertaken for humanitarian purposes remained marginal in comparison to those it made to NATO's.

France indeed participated in eighteen of the twenty-five interventions undertaken by the UN between 2000 and 2004, but its troop contribution was mainly concentrated in Lebanon (UNIFIL), Bosnia and Herzegovina (UNMIBH – United Nations Mission in Bosnia Herzegovina) and Côte d'Ivoire (UNOCI – United Nations Operation in Côte d'Ivoire),[8] and the level of troops contributed was relatively small: an average of 223 troops per month for UNIFIL, 175 for UNMIBH and 105 for UNOCI. This meant that France remained between the fifteenth and the thirty-first troop contributor of the UN (UN 2000; 2001; 2002; 2003; 2004).

In contrast, France remained committed to intervening to protect through NATO, and it kept actively working towards the development of the European Union's capacity to intervene. Additionally, when neither institution was willing to intervene rapidly to protect in Côte d'Ivoire,

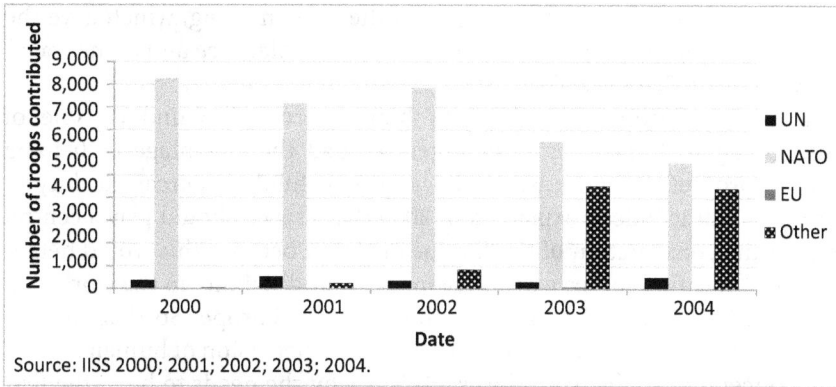

Source: IISS 2000; 2001; 2002; 2003; 2004.

Note: This graph does not take into account troops deployed outside France owing to security agreements, France's contribution to Operation Enduring Freedom in Afghanistan or headquarters situated overseas (with the exception of the troops in Côte d'Ivoire from 2002 since they were used for *Opération Licorne*). Even though it is useful in showing a trend in France's troop contribution, it is not fully representative since the data available reflects France's contribution in August of each year only.

**Graph 7**  France's troop contributions to interventions for humanitarian purposes by international institution, 2000–04

France undertook a unilateral intervention without – at least initially – the consent of the UN Security Council. Because this will to intervene unilaterally was limited to a specific intervention in Africa and did not reflect a new trend in France's practice of human protection – for its aim was always to favour multilateral interventions – it is discussed in the next section, "An ongoing commitment to Europe, but a renewed military presence in Africa", where France's approach to human protection in Africa is investigated.

During the first half of the 2000s, the French executives pursued their efforts to develop the European Union's capacity to address humanitarian emergencies. This commitment was not surprising in view of France's efforts to develop the European Union's response capacity since the 1980s, and also in light of the fact that, to borrow Chirac's words, "Kosovo confirmed the necessity [of European defence], I would even say its urgency" (1999e, 805). According to the President, the European Union not only had to be able to intervene to address crises in its own backyard for security reasons, but also had to play a role in the promotion of human rights beyond Europe in light of its identity. For instance, on 27 June 2000 Chirac explained that the European Union was "a promoter and implanter of progress in the world. What unites Germany and France and their partners, is of course their populations' profound aspirations to peace. But it is also, and maybe first of all, a specific idea of the human being, which gave the European project its vision of freedom, dignity, tolerance and democracy" (in Chirac 2007, 285–286).

A strong Europe committed to human protection and capable of responding to humanitarian emergencies had the advantage of helping France promote its rank while allowing it to fulfil its perceived duty to protect. Chirac indeed explained in 2005 that France should play a central role in the construction of the European Union because this would help it fulfil its "vocation to serve peace, democracy and stability in the world" (in Chirac 2007, 342) and allow it to "be strong in Europe. So that she can remain herself. So that she can make her voice, her vision of human beings, her conception of the world heard. This is why she needs to be in the first rank of the European nations" (Chirac 1998, in Bossuat 2012, 196).

During the early 2000s Chirac's executives consequently pushed for the development of the European Union's capacity to protect by promoting key initiatives that would complement the progress it had achieved.[9] At the Nice Summit of December 2000, which was hosted by France and prioritised by Chirac (Madelin 2002, 745), three new organisations were created as a result of Franco-German cooperation in order to improve the European Union's capacity to respond rapidly to crises (European Institute 2009; Stark 2002, 978). The first was the Political and Security Committee, which "monitors the international situation in the areas covered by the Common Foreign and Security Policy (CFSP) and the Common Security and Defence Policy (CSDP) [and] plays a central role in the definition of and follow-up to the European Union's response to a crisis" (European Union 2011). It was complemented by the Military Committee of the European Union, which is "the supreme military body within the Council of the EU [and] is the forum for military consultation and cooperation between the EU Member States in the field of conflict prevention and crisis management" (European Union 2006a). Last but not least, the Military Staff of the European Union was created to constitute "the source of the EU's military expertise [in addition to] perform[ing] early warning, situation assessment and strategic planning for Petersberg tasks (humanitarian missions, peacekeeping and crisis management) and all EU-led operations" (European Union 2006b).

Additionally, France – along with Germany and the United Kingdom – suggested in February 2004 the creation of thirteen rapid reaction units that would be "inter-army, ... 1,500 troops each, and that could be deployed in less than fifteen days" (Buffotot 2005, 43–44). The units, now known as the European Union Battlegroup, are under the authority of the Council of the European Union and reached operating capacity at the beginning of 2007 (EEAS 2017).

On top of these diplomatic contributions, France also participated heavily in the operations undertaken by the European Union, even though they remained limited in scale and scope, beginning with *Opération Concordia* in Macedonia from March to December 2003. It mobilised around 300 troops, of which half were provided by France (Petiteville 2006, 93). It aimed, "at the explicit request of the FYROM [Former Yugoslav Republic of Macedonia] government, to contribute further to a stable secure environment and to allow the implementation of the August 2001 Ohrid Framework Agreement" (European Union 2015c).

In June 2003 the European Union also intervened outside Europe with *Opération Artémis* in the DRC. The intervention was authorised by UN Security Council Resolution 1484 of 30 May 2003 and aimed "inter alia, at contributing to the stabilisation of the security conditions and the improvement of the humanitarian situation in Bunia" (European Union 2015b). Germany and France shared the command (Boniface 2008, 60), and most of the troops were provided by France, "which acted as the 'Framework Nation' and established operational headquarters in Paris" (Francia and Medina Abellan 2006, 155). The intervention lasted only until September 2003, but in 2005 Chirac emphasised its importance: "*Opération Artémis* demonstrated the ability of the European Union to lead, in a situation of emergency, autonomous peacekeeping operations, in a difficult environment and several thousand kilometres from its frontiers" (in Chirac 2007, 338).

Finally, France also participated in the European Union's *Opération Althea* in Bosnia and Herzegovina, launched in December 2004, by contributing around 450 troops until the beginning of 2009 (France Diplomatie 2010). *Althea's* goal has been to "[ensure] a Safe and Secure Environment (SASE) in the country" and "[support] combined and collective training activities and exercise with the Armed Forces of BiH [Bosnia and Herzegovina]" (EEAS 2019; European Union 2015a).

Despite these achievements, the development of the European Union's capacity to respond to humanitarian crises was nevertheless slow, as illustrated by the small scope and scale of its interventions. Consequently, as in the previous years, Chirac's executives continued to intervene heavily to protect through NATO, while promoting the role of the European Union within the organisation. As Graph 7 has shown, between 2000 and 2004 an average of 6,851 French troops per month took part in the interventions NATO undertook for humanitarian purposes (IISS 2000; 2001; 2002; 2003; 2004). France's military contribution was particularly important to NATO's interventions in Bosnia and Herzegovina, Kosovo and Afghanistan.[10]

In Bosnia and Herzegovina, France participated in SFOR, which was authorised on 12 December 1996 by Resolution 1088 and whose "primary task was to contribute to a safe and secure environment conducive to civil and political reconstruction" (NATO 2014). The goal of the intervention was the "support of wider international efforts to build peace and stability in the area" (NATO 2018). Alain Dejammet, French Permanent Represent-ative to the UN, emphasised to the Security Council France's "commitment to continue to be vigilant and to mobilise our resources and our energies so as to contribute to ensuring that peace, law and justice prevail" (in UN Security Council 1999, 12). As a consequence, France's contribution was considerable since an average of 2,120 troops a year was deployed between 2000 and 2004 (IISS 2000; 2001; 2003; 2004). In Kosovo, France's military commitment was also substantial since between the creation of KFOR in June 1999 and 2004, an average of 4,363 troops a year were contributed (IISS 1999; 2000; 2001; 2002; 2003; 2004).

Finally, France committed troops to the International Security Assis-tance Force (ISAF) in Afghanistan, with an average of about 488 troops a year between 2002 and 2004 (IISS 2002; 2003; 2004). ISAF was established by Resolution 1386, which was passed by the Security Council on 20 December 2001 "to assist the Afghan Interim Authority in the mainte-nance of security in Kabul and its surrounding areas, so that the Afghan Interim Authority as well as the personnel of the United Nations can operate in a secure environment" (UN Security Council 2001).

To a certain extent, this ongoing commitment to intervene to protect through NATO can be seen as surprising because, as explained above, Chirac's executives refused to take part in the war against Iraq and, con-sequently, tensions were high between France and the United States from 2003 onwards. Additionally, Biscop and Coelmont emphasise the idea that "during the first administration of President George W. Bush (2001–2004), European confidence in NATO was gravely undermined by the US attitude towards the alliance", in particular because of the United States' tendency to do "warfare by committee" rather than use the coalition (2012, 101).

Nevertheless, even though the Iraq War constituted one of the most heated moments in the Franco-American relationship, and despite the reluctance of the United States to accept large contributions for its war in Afghanistan (Biscop and Coelmont 2012, 101), the various French execu-tives emphasised the importance of the friendship. For instance, in 2004, Chirac declared, "the solidarity between France and the United States is inscribed in the past and in the future. On the Iraq question, let's avoid dramatising. We should not consider divorce every time there is a fight between a couple. There are other solutions. Anything that can call into question the transatlantic link, the friendship between Europe and the United States, France and the United States, is dangerous and pointless" (in Nouzille 2010, 661).

Additionally, as mentioned previously, this will to continue intervening for humanitarian purposes through NATO can be explained by the fact that the European Union was not ready to address key humanitarian emergencies and that it needed NATO. As Chirac explained in 2004, "building a credible European defence obviously does not consist of building Europe against the United States, as we sometimes hear. It consists of giving Europe the capacity to exercise its responsibilities autonomously, either in liaison with the Atlantic Alliance or within it" (in Chirac 2007, 90). Furthermore, the UN continued to limit the amount of interventions it undertook, and its interventions had proved to be largely unsuccessful at the beginning of the 1990s. In contrast, the interventions undertaken by France through NATO had some positive outcomes and relied on strong mandates that allowed French troops more leeway than UN interventions. Consequently, intervening through NATO allowed France to fulfil its perceived duty to protect while promoting its rank.

## An ongoing commitment in Europe, but a renewed military presence in Africa

In terms of the geographic area it favoured for interventions undertaken for humanitarian purposes, France remained strongly present in Europe. As Graph 8 shows, between 52 and 94 per cent of the troops deployed for humanitarian purposes between 2000 and 2004 were in the European continent. In particular, as explained above, France played a key role in operations taking place in Bosnia and Herzegovina (SFOR and *Opération Althea*) and Kosovo (KFOR).

Nevertheless, during the first half of the 2000s, France's presence outside Europe grew progressively. This can partly be explained by the fact that the activism of Minister of Foreign Affairs de Villepin echoed that of his predecessor, Védrine, despite their different political affiliations.[11] Charillon explains that with de Villepin there was a "systematic reaffirmation of the French presence on all the big dossiers, from the Middle East to Kashmir, including Afghanistan and Madagascar" (2002, 922). The French diplomatic efforts were particularly visible in the Middle East. Chirac emphasised throughout his presidency his wish to see the Israeli–Palestinian conflict resolved through the creation of a Palestinian state that would satisfy both Israel and Palestine. As illustrated by the Peace Conference organised in Paris in October 2000, he tried to use diplomatic tools and the Franco-Israeli relationship to achieve this objective (see for instance a speech of 2004, in Chirac 2007, 263–268).

Additionally, in Lebanon, Chirac's executives remained involved in peacekeeping and the reconstruction of the country.[12] For instance,

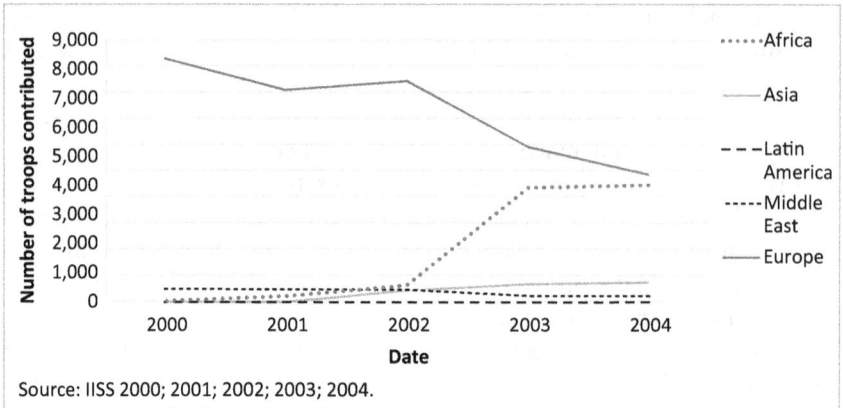

Source: IISS 2000; 2001; 2002; 2003; 2004.

Note: This graph does not take into account troops deployed outside France owing to security agreements, France's contribution to Operation Enduring Freedom in Afghanistan or headquarters situated overseas (with the exception of the troops in Côte d'Ivoire from 2002 since they were used for *Opération Licorne*). Even though it is useful in showing a trend in France's troop contribution, it is not fully representative since the data available reflects France's contribution in August of each year only.

**Graph 8** Evolution of France's troop contributions to interventions for humanitarian purposes by geographic area, 2000–04

following the withdrawal of Israeli troops in 2000, France hosted two international conferences for Lebanon in February 2001 and November 2002 (Filiu 2013, 207). In 2002 Chirac declared before the Lebanese Parliament, "here is the message that France wished to bring you today. Here is the message from the heart: France loves Lebanon and will always be with it, to work towards peace, cooperation and prosperity" (in Chirac 2007, 275). Furthermore, from 2003 Chirac also tried to pressure Bashar al-Assad to withdraw his troops,[13] and France's diplomatic efforts partly led to the adoption by the Security Council of Resolution 1559 (Filiu 2013, 208). Without referring directly to Syria, the resolution condemned the occupation by "[reaffirming] its call for the strict respect of the sovereignty, territorial integrity, unity, and political independence of Lebanon under the sole and exclusive authority of the Government of Lebanon throughout Lebanon; [and calling] upon all remaining foreign forces to withdraw from Lebanon" (UN Security Council 2004b). Lastly, France's contribution to UNIFIL remained stable between 2000 and 2004, averaging 223 troops a year (UN 2000; 2001; 2002; 2003; 2004).

Although France's presence in Europe and its diplomatic commitment in the Middle East are not surprising considering that they were already noticeable during the second half of the 1990s, a rupture was visible in

Africa. As explained in Chapter 3, France had to withdraw militarily from the continent from 1995 following the controversial role it had played during the Rwandan genocide. This shift away from military interventions was also sparked by the context of *cohabitation* after Prime Minister Jospin pushed for a policy of *ni ingérence, ni indifférence*. His influence became particularly visible when a putsch by General Robert Gueï took place in Côte d'Ivoire in 1999: France did not intervene, despite Chirac's sympathy for the Henri Bédié regime and even though the two states had secret agreements that could have justified a French intervention (Banégas and Marchal 2013, 188). As former minister Philippe Madelin recalls, the *cohabitation* played a central role in this lack of intervention, since "in spite of the pressure applied by the President, the Prime Minister indeed refuse[d] to make the French troops present intervene" (2002, 730). There-fore between 1995 and 2002 France did not militarily intervene in the continent for humanitarian purposes and instead took part in the training of African peacekeepers.

From 2000, through RECAMP, France indeed continued to promote the intervention of African troops – rather than French ones – to address humanitarian crises. For instance, two multilateral interventions took place in Gabon in 2000 and in Austral and East Africa in 2000–02 (*Opéra-tion Tanzanite*) (Benoit 2004, 105). Additionally, the various executives emphasised France's wish to increase the cooperation of the European Union in Africa. For instance, in December 2005 France pushed for the development of a European strategy for Africa (Balleix 2011, 97), which eventually led to the undertaking of *Opération Artémis* as previously discussed.

Besides these continuities, the activism of Chirac's various executives, combined with the influence of France's domestic norm of human protec-tion and the end of the *cohabitation* in May 2002, led France to renew its direct military involvement for humanitarian purposes in Africa. This was not surprising, since "Chirac has always cultivated an attraction to Africa, in keeping with his Gaullist heritage but also due to his personal fondness for non-Western civilisations" (Banégas and Marchal 2013, 180). In August 2002 Chirac signalled to the French ambassadors that he wanted to end Jospin's *ni ingérence, ni indifférence* policy by explaining:

> more than ever, France seeks to be present alongside Africans to help them integrate into the modern world, to prevent crises that could tear apart the continent, to overcome the immense difficulties faced by countries which are exiting conflicts. France will mobilise itself in all the concerned inter-national platforms. She will remind others that, if Africa needs us, states from the global North will need a stable and prosperous Africa all the more. (Chirac 2002)

As a result, France's financial contribution, which had been in decline since 1994, increased to 0.7 per cent of its gross domestic product in 2003 (Banégas and Marchal 2013, 193).

Additionally, in 2002 France heavily intervened in Côte d'Ivoire unilaterally, and without the UN Security Council's approval, before intervening in 2003 in the DRC through the European Union. The European Union's *Opération Artémis* in the DRC has already been discussed in the section "The choice of institutional framework" above. The rest of this section focuses on the intervention in Côte d'Ivoire. When on 19 September 2002 the rebels of the Patriotic Movement of Côte d'Ivoire attempted a *coup d'état* and took over the north of the state, the French executive rapidly reacted by deploying a unilateral intervention: *Opération Licorne*, on 22 September (Hofnung 2011, 79). *Licorne*, which was originally dispatched to ensure the repatriation of French citizens, was asked by President Laurent Gbagbo to monitor the ceasefire signed on 17 October between the north, controlled by the rebels, and the south under the authority of the government (Hofnung 2011, 82; Ministère de la Défense 2012). *Licorne* froze the conflict in order to prevent further crimes from taking place (Bovcon 2009, 16) and "to set up 'the necessary conditions in search of a political solution'" (French Senate (2006) in Charbonneau 2008, 289).

Given that France was often accused of neo-colonialism when intervening in Africa, especially after the Rwandan genocide, the fact that the executive at the time decided to intervene unilaterally, without the authorisation of the Security Council, can appear surprising. However, it is important to emphasise that France had a strong relationship with its former colony and that French troops were already present in the country because of a military agreement (Domergue-Cloarec 2005, 94). Additionally, in 2004 the Defence Minister, Michèle Alliot-Marie, justified the intervention by arguing that "a show of force serve[d] to avoid the resort to force" (in Charbonneau 2008, 290). Champagne de Labriolle, number two of the African cell of the Elysée, also argued that "in contrast to the policy of Jospin, our position [was] to not exclude an intervention in principle, because it [was] deterrent. ... No one should be able to think that they can govern haphazardly without action from France" (in Banégas and Marchal 2013, 193). The idea was not to argue that France would start constantly intervening unilaterally in Africa, since as explained previously, multilateral interventions were still favoured by Chirac's various executives. Rather, the intervention aimed to show that the *ni ingérence, ni indifférence* period was over and that, in light of its perceived duty, France was willing – and able – to intervene to protect, even if it meant having to face some criticism from sceptics.

Despite the five military accords that were signed between France and Côte d'Ivoire between 1961 and 1980 (Domergue-Cloarec 2005, 94), France adopted a neutral position because, as Bovcon explains, it did not want to support the rebels who attempted a *coup*, but also did not want to back "Laurent Gbagbo, because of his contentious ascension to power in 2000 amidst what he himself described as 'calamitous conditions', the exacerbation of his xenophobic politics of *Ivoirité* after the elections, and the violation of the human rights by his militia groups" (2009, 8).

The mission became more complex than the executive had originally hoped as both parties became wary of France's intentions. The rebels argued that France was biased towards the Gbagbo regime, while the latter was convinced of French support of the rebels and of France's wish to "recolonise Côte d'Ivoire" following its refusal to apply the defence accords that linked the two states (Boniface 2008, 64; Hofnung 2011, 82–83). Additionally, two new rebel movements were created: the Ivorian Popular Movement of the Great West (Mouvement Populaire Ivoirien du Grand Ouest) and the Movement for Justice and Peace (Mouvement pour la Justice et la Paix) (Hofnung 2011, 88). They took over Man and Danané in the west, thereby complicating the French monitoring of the ceasefire (Ministère de la Défense 2012) and forcing France to deploy troops to the south and the west (Hofnung 2011, 89).

In order to reach a rapid solution to the conflict and in light of the failure of the negotiations organised since October 2002 by the Economic Community of West African States (ECOWAS) in Togo (Hofnung 2011, 93), the French executive decided to organise a peace meeting in Linas-Marcoussis, just outside Paris, from 15 to 23 January 2003 (Bovcon 2009, 10). In order to promote multilateralism, Secretary General Annan, President of the African Union Thabo Mbeki, President of ECOWAS Abdoulaye Wade, President of Gabon Omar Bongo Ondimba and President of the European Commission Romano Prodi were all invited (Lombart 2007b, 385). However, President Gbagbo was not present at the negotiations, since only the various heads of political parties were invited (Hofnung 2011, 94). This move considerably degraded the relationship between the Ivorian President and the French Minister of Foreign Affairs, de Villepin (Hofnung 2011, 99).

The task faced at Linas-Marcoussis was complex: as explained by Bakong, the crisis in Côte d'Ivoire had emerged out of "the result of a combination of three regional, economic and political factors linked to the domestic social situation created by the manipulation of the idea of *ivoirité*" (2012, 225). Nevertheless, after intense and heated discussions, an agreement was reached. Hofnung explains that "a very precise roadmap was established: from the nationality code to the conditions of access to property, via the independence of the media and justice" (2011, 95). It was also agreed that a reconciliation government – including the rebel groups – would govern until the next elections in 2005 (Hofnung 2011, 95). President Gbagbo was presented with the *fait accompli*, but still agreed to sign the final agreement at the Kléber negotiations held in Paris in January 2003 (Hofnung 2011, 96).

Because tensions remained high and a large French community still lived in Côte d'Ivoire (Hofnung 2011, 97, 99), *Opération Licorne* was maintained after the signature of the agreement. On 4 February 2003, almost five months after the beginning of the French intervention, the UN Security Council passed Resolution 1464, giving it the legitimacy and legality it was missing (UN Security Council 2003). The resolution also authorised ECOWAS and French forces "to take the necessary steps to guarantee the security and freedom of movement of their personnel and to ensure, without prejudice to the responsibilities of the Government of National Reconciliation, the protection of civilians immediately threatened with physical violence within their zones of operation, using the means available to them" (UN Security Council 2003).

Additionally, on 27 February 2004 Resolution 1528 created UNOCI to monitor the ceasefire and support humanitarian assistance and "authorize[d] for a period of 12 months from 4 April 2004 the French forces to use all necessary means in order to support UNOCI" (UN Security Council 2004a). As Graph 9 shows, France contributed troops to UNOCI, but this contribution was marginal in comparison to the troops deployed under *Licorne*.

A peace summit was organised in Ghana in July 2004 and eventually led to the Accra Agreements, which reiterated the main measures agreed upon in Linas-Marcoussis and requested that the disarmament begin before 15 October (Hofnung 2011, 106). Nevertheless, the accord rapidly became void when, in spite of the presence of *Licorne* and UNOCI, President Gbagbo began attacking various regions of Côte d'Ivoire along with the French base in Bouaké on 6 November 2004, killing nine French soldiers and wounding thirty-three others (Bakong 2012, 228–229). The French retaliated immediately by destroying the air force capacity of the army, provoking violent anti-French protests throughout the country (Hofnung 2011, 114). Tensions intensified when, for unclear reasons, the French army opened fire on protestors on 7 November 2004 (Charbonneau 2008, 291).

Nevertheless, France did not leave, and on 15 November 2004 the Security Council passed Resolution 1572. It established an immediate arms embargo and threatened economic sanctions to be implemented "on 15 December 2004, unless the Security Council shall determine before then

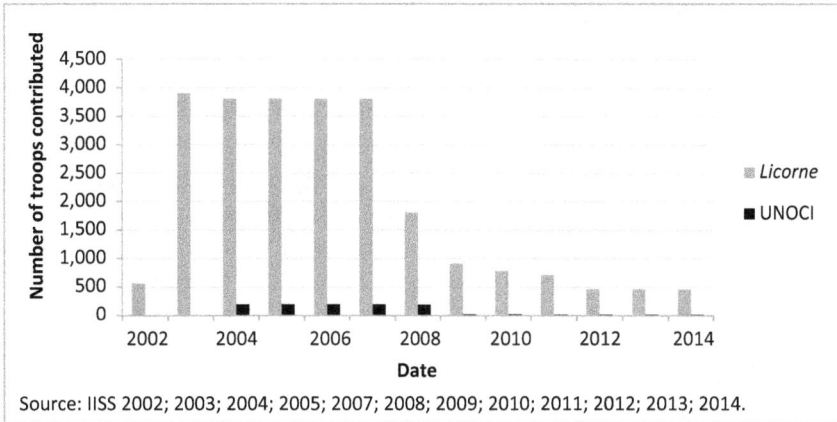

Source: IISS 2002; 2003; 2004; 2005; 2007; 2008; 2009; 2010; 2011; 2012; 2013; 2014.

Note: This graph does not take into account troops deployed outside France owing to security agreements, France's contribution to Operation Enduring Freedom in Afghanistan or headquarters situated overseas (with the exception of the troops in Côte d'Ivoire from 2002 since they were used for *Opération Licorne*). Even though it is useful in showing a trend in France's troop contribution, it is not fully representative since the data available reflect France's contribution in August of each year only.

**Graph 9**  France's interventions in Côte d'Ivoire, 2002–14

that the signatories of the Linas-Marcoussis and Accra III Agreements have implemented all their commitments under the Accra III Agreement and are embarked towards full implementation of the Linas-Marcoussis Agreement" (UN Security Council 2004c).

Following the November crisis with the French troops, Mbeki was put in charge of restoring peace negotiations (Hofnung 2011, 127). An agreement was signed in Pretoria on 6 April 2005, re-emphasising the measures agreed at Linas-Marcoussis (Hofnung 2011, 187). Nevertheless, these efforts again failed, with various massacres being committed and tensions remaining high. A solution was not found until March 2007, when an inter-Ivorian agreement was signed in Ouagadougou: Gbagbo remained President, and Guillaume Soro became Prime Minister (Hofnung 2011, 188). However, as Chapter 5 explains, tensions were re-ignited with the 2010 presidential election, when Gbagbo refused to acknowledge the victory of Alassane Ouattara, his political opponent, even though it had officially been recognised by the African Union and the Security Council in its Resolution 1962 (Hofnung 2011, 188; Ministère de la Défense 2012). Throughout these years, *Licorne* remained in Côte d'Ivoire and assisted with the stabilisation of the situation (Ministère de la Défense 2014), and the operation did not end until January 2015 (Ministère de la Défense 2015).

The French intervention in Côte d'Ivoire is particularly important because it shows that as soon as the *cohabitation* was over, Chirac's executive was willing to intervene in Africa, especially since the situation allowed France to fulfil its perceived duty to protect while promoting its rank in the region. It thus confirms the idea that France's focus on Europe in the second half of the 1990s was not an attempt to shift its conception of human protection, but rather a necessity in order to adjust to the changing domestic and international contexts. In contrast, the conflicts in former Yugoslavia being contained and the *cohabitation* no longer restraining Chirac's actions, his new executive was determined to signal that it was willing – and able – to intervene for humanitarian purposes, even in Africa, and despite the fact that this could be perceived by its critics as an attempt at neo-colonialism.

Even though France intervened unilaterally and without – at least initially – the authorisation of the UN Security Council, it would be misleading to argue that the French executive at the time believed that it no longer needed the approval of the Security Council. As mentioned previously, it attached a great importance to the institution, especially in light of the power that its permanent seat at the Security Council gave France. Côte d'Ivoire was not about the UN: it was about signalling the end of the *ni ingérence, ni indifférence* era and the central role France still aimed to play in human protection in Africa.

## Conclusion

In contrast to the late 1980s and early 1990s, when France played the role of norm entrepreneur of humanitarian intervention, it did not take part in the emergence of R2P. This lack of participation was sparked by the fact that the international community had deemed its conception of human protection to be controversial and outdated. By failing to promote internationally the idea that France intervened only to fulfil a perceived duty to protect, by supporting coercive interventions and by responding in such a controversial way to the Rwandan genocide, France indeed became associated with humanitarian intervention and, subsequently, with its limitations. As a consequence, the ICISS aimed to move away from the French conception of human protection – or at least, from what it understood to be France's conception – by excluding it from the discussions that led to the emergence of R2P.

This lack of involvement did not mean that France stopped promoting and implementing human protection. By preventing the intervention in Iraq from receiving the authorisation of the UN Security Council, the French executive at the time showed that France's voice still mattered and that it was willing to stand up and promote its conception of human protection, even if it meant going against the United States. Additionally, despite the lack of a normative contribution to R2P, France contributed to the promotion of human protection through its practice, for an average of 9,062 French troops a year were deployed between 2000 and 2004 to protect endangered populations.

Some continuity can be seen with the first mandate of Chirac: France continued to intervene in Europe, through NATO rather than the UN, and continued to increase the European Union's capacity to intervene for humanitarian purposes. But Chirac's executives also renewed some of France's practice from the early 1990s by intervening in Africa after the *cohabitation* ended, even if, in the case of *Opération Licorne*, it meant intervening unilaterally and without the initial approval of the UN Security Council. By heavily intervening for humanitarian purposes, France, in its ongoing practice of human protection, once again helped shape the way the international community practised human protection, and in particular, it facilitated the delegation by the UN of interventions undertaken for humanitarian purposes to multilateral institutions.

While France's domestic norm of human protection continued to influence the various French executives, the same cannot be said about R2P. Because France had played no role in the emergence of the concept, R2P indeed had no impact on France. Therefore its conception of human protection was again mainly influenced by the idea that in light of its history, values and rank, France had a perceived duty to protect, while its contribution was determined by the will to fulfil this duty while promoting its rank.

## Notes

1 Because R2P was not endorsed by the international community until 2005, this chapter mainly refers to R2P as a concept rather than a principle or norm.

2 It is useful to note that Chirac's opponent in the second round of the presidential election was extreme-right candidate Jean-Marie Le Pen, even though the polls predicted that left-wing candidate and former Prime Minister Lionel Jospin would go through. The climate was thus very tense in France.

3 See Article 2(4).

4 The members from the global South were Mohamed Sahnoun (co-chair, Algeria), Fidel Ramos (Philippines), Cyril Rmaphosa (South Africa), Eduardo Stein (Guatemala) and Ramesh Thakur (India).

5 Repetition by Evans.

6 France was supportive of the ideas R2P stood for before then (see for instance Rochereau de la Sablière in UN Security Council 2004d), but the first explicit and official endorsement of R2P was at the 2005 World Summit.

7 See the arguments put forward by authors such as Tesón (2005).

8 The UN interventions in which France took part were: the United Nations Peacebuilding Support Office (BONUCA), the United Nations Verification Mission in Guatemala (MINUGUA), UNTSO, UNIFIL, MINURSO, UNMIK, the United Nations Mission in Sierra Leone (UNAMSIL), the United Nations Transitional Administration in East Timor (UNTAET), MONUC, the United Nations Mission in Ethiopia and Eritrea (UNMEE), the United Nations Mission in Liberia (UNMIL), UNOCI, the United Nations Stabilization Mission in Haiti (MINUSTAH), the United Nations Civilian Police Mission in Haiti (MIPONUH), UNIKOM, UNMIBH, the United Nations Observer Mission in Georgia (UNOMIG) and the United Nations Mission in the Central African Republic (MINURCA).

9 For instance, in November 2000 the European Union obtained a military commitment from all member states (with the exception of Denmark) to fulfil the 1999 Helsinki Headline Goal. This was the first step of the European RRF (European Institute 2009). Additionally, at the Gothenburg Summit of June 2001, the European Union adopted the Programme for the Prevention of Violent Conflicts and agreed to "set clear political priorities for preventive actions, improve its early warning, action and policy coherence, enhance its instruments for long- and short-term prevention, and build effective partnerships for prevention" (European Union 2001, 3). Another key milestone was the publication in 2003 of the report "A secure Europe in a better world: European security strategy", which was adopted by the European Council of 12–13 December 2003. The report identified regional conflicts as a global challenge that should concern the European Union by explaining that they can not only threaten the interests of member states, but are also a key concern since "they destroy human lives and social and physical infrastructures; they threaten minorities, fundamental freedoms and human rights" (European Union 2003, 4).

10 This statement refers to the International Security Assistance Force and not to Operation Enduring Freedom, which the French executive did not consider to be an intervention for humanitarian purposes.

11 Because of the *cohabitation*, Védrine was left-wing Minister of Foreign Affairs from June 1997 to May 2002, whereas de Villepin was right-wing Minister from May 2002 to March 2004.

12 France's involvement in Lebanon went back to 1860, when it had intervened in order to save Maronite populations, and it had remained involved ever since. In 1982, when the Lebanese war broke out following the Israeli occupation, France sent humanitarian aid to Beirut and the south of the country and mobilised the interventional community (in particular, Resolution 512 on the protection of civilians in the conflict was passed following a French initiative) (El Moustaoui 2011, 291–292). It has also contributed troops to UNIFIL since 1978 (Ambassade de France au Liban 2019).

13 Syrian troops had been present in Lebanon since 1976.

**5**

# France and the development of the responsibility to protect: consolidator or threat (2005–2011)?

R2P was unanimously endorsed by member states at the UN World Summit in September 2005. Some key distinctions can, however, be noticed between the definition put forward by the ICISS and the one adopted in the World Summit Outcome Document. For instance, the three responsibilities emphasised in the ICISS report – to prevent, to react and to rebuild – did not appear in the World Summit Outcome Document, and the use of force was made conditional on the approval of the UN Security Council (see UN General Assembly 2005, paragraphs 138 and 139).

Between 2005 and 2011, R2P continued to develop and gained increasing international traction, as illustrated by the fact that the UN Security Council passed twelve resolutions referring to the principle.[1] This development was not always easy, for even after endorsing R2P in 2005, some states remained concerned that it would be used as an instrument for undue Western influence (Bellamy 2009a, 94–95). An important milestone took place in 2009 when the UN Secretary General Ban Ki-Moon released the first of his annual reports on R2P in order to facilitate its development. The report was called "Implementing the responsibility to protect" and defined a three-pillar strategy where the first pillar promotes the states' responsibility to protect their own population, the second pillar calls for "the international community to assist States in meeting those obligations", and the third pillar argues that the international community has to "respond collectively in a timely and decisive manner" when a state fails to fulfil its responsibilities (Ban 2009, 8–9).[2] However, it is important to note that the consultations that preceded this report were partly undertaken to get R2P back on track (Bellamy 2011, 33). Two years later, the first coercive R2P military intervention was undertaken, without host consent, in Libya. As explained in the Introduction, this intervention was a turning point because it created an 'oughtness' for states – and the international community more generally – to protect the Libyan population from the repression of the Muammar Gaddafi regime (see Glanville 2016, 185). It can thus be argued that while 2005 was the year R2P became an international principle rather than a concept, 2011 was the year it transitioned from being an international principle to being an international norm.

The period 2005–12 also corresponded to the last sixteen months of Jacques Chirac's presidency (1995–2007) and to Nicolas Sarkozy's entire presidency (2007–12).[3] Because the right wing won the legislative elections, Sarkozy was able to work with a government and Parliament from the same political party as his own. Nevertheless, as this chapter explains, he tried to undertake a strategy of *ouverture* (opening) by including left-wing ministers. This led Bernard Kouchner, the father of the *devoir d'ingérence*, to be Minister of Foreign Affairs from May 2007 to November 2010, before being replaced by Michèle Alliot-Marie (November 2010 – February 2011) and Alain Juppé (February 2011 – May 2012), both from the right wing.

As explained in Chapter 4, R2P and France's conception of human protection had no impact on each other during the early 2000s. The goal of this chapter is to investigate whether and how this relationship evolved after R2P was endorsed by the international community in 2005. It is useful to emphasise that in light of the focus of the book on military intervention, this chapter discusses France's relationship to R2P with a strong emphasis on the use of force under pillar three. To achieve this, it is divided into three main sections. Two sections analyse the impact France had on the development of the international principle. The first section discusses France's growing role as norm consolidator, while the second section analyses how and why France endangered the international principle at times. The third section discusses the influence of R2P on France's conception and practice of human protection. It argues that even though there is evidence that it began to restrain when and how France could intervene to protect, the influence of the international principle remained limited. In contrast, the domestic norm remained influential and contributed to France intervening to protect beyond cases defined as R2P situations by the Security Council, in a way that aimed to fulfil France's perceived duty while promoting its rank.

## Strong support for R2P

In order to understand the relationship between R2P and France's conception of human protection, it is important to first define the impact that the various French executives had on the international principle during this period. This section focuses on France's positive impact.

*Strong diplomatic support*

At the 2005 World Summit, the Minister of Foreign Affairs Dominique de Villepin declared, "let us ... learn what experience has to teach us, be it in Iraq, in the Middle East, in Côte d'Ivoire, Afghanistan or Haiti, and in all the regional crises that destabilise the world. Where division has brought about failure, we must together find new ways forward. Where unity has enabled us to achieve initial success, we must persevere. New principles are needed, such as the responsibility to protect" (2005). Although unsurprising in view of the context and the audience de Villepin was addressing, this statement constituted the first official endorsement of R2P by France. Following the World Summit, Chirac's executive at the time also voted in favour of the first two UN Security Council resolutions referring to R2P: Resolution 1653 on the DRC and Burundi, and Resolution 1674 on the protection of civilians.

However, France's support of the international principle began to increase in August 2006 (Staunton 2018, 377). Despite the different executives appointed with the election of Sarkozy in 2007 and the multiple changes of ministers of foreign affairs, France began to co-draft the UN Security Council resolutions referring to R2P and emphasised its importance in its statements.[4] For instance, in regard to Resolution 1894 on the protection of civilians, the French Permanent Representative, Gérard Araud, declared, "I should like to take the opportunity provided by this meeting of the Security Council to commend the General Assembly's recent reaffirmation of the concept of R2P. The Security Council has a special responsibility under that concept. ... In its action in the Council, France is always mindful of that responsibility. We will spare no effort to operationalize that concept" (in UN Security Council 2009).

France's support was also visible beyond the Security Council. For instance, when in 2009 the Secretary General presented his report "Implementing the responsibility to protect" (Ban 2009), the French Representative, Jean-Pierre Lacroix, emphasised the progress made by R2P and argued that it was here to stay:

> The responsibility to protect therefore already largely exists. ... We are therefore meeting not to discuss the definition of the concept, but rather to debate the means to strengthen its implementation and its respect. ... France calls on nations, the international community and the United Nations as a whole to meet this challenge so that the world will never again witness such heinous crimes as genocide, war crimes, ethnic cleansing and crimes against humanity. France will be fully involved in that daily effort. (in UN General Assembly 2009, 9–10)

*France's military support for R2P: the intervention in Libya*

In addition to supporting R2P diplomatically, France became instrumental in the first military intervention undertaken under the R2P banner: the intervention in Libya in 2011. The beginning of Sarkozy's presidency had been the object of criticisms due to the rapprochement undertaken with the Gaddafi regime. In July 2007 Sarkozy announced the liberation of the Bulgarian nurses who had been imprisoned in Libya after being wrongly accused of infecting children with HIV (Tiersky 2008, 104). This was described as a key victory for Sarkozy, who had made the issue a priority of his electoral campaign. The freeing of the hostages was not meant to be in exchange for anything, but the next day a Franco-Libyan nuclear commercial agreement for the desalination of seawater was signed. Even though Sarkozy argued that the two were not linked and that this agreement had been in negotiation "for the last eighteen months" (Sarkozy in *L'Express* 2007), it generated much controversy (Tiersky 2008, 104).

The controversy intensified when Gaddafi was invited for an official visit, which coincided with the international human rights day in December 2007. France was not the only state to operate a rapprochement with the Libyan leader: as Ian Black explained in 2009 "many things [were] going his way; Western oil companies and investors [were] flocking to Tripoli, domestic repression ha[d] eased somewhat and even tourism [was] developing" (in Hehir 2013, 2). Nevertheless, the visit was heavily criticised, including within the executive. Rama Yade, Secretary of State for Human Rights, declared that France "does not only take its prestige from its economic power, but also from the principles and values that make France a country like no other. ... Colonel Gaddafi must understand that our country is not a doormat on which a leader, terrorist or not, can come and wipe their feet with the blood of their crimes. France must not receive this kiss of death" (in Segaunes and Vernet 2007). The controversy increased further when Gaddafi denied Sarkozy's claim that the two had discussed the question of human rights in Libya (*Le Figaro* 2007).

This rapprochement with the Gaddafi regime ended, however, in 2011, when peaceful protests held against the regime in mid-February were met with violence. In contrast to its actions during the Tunisian Revolution of a few months earlier,[5] France was one of the first states to heavily criticise the violence orchestrated by the Libyan dictator (see Sarkozy in *Libération* 2011). When the opposition created the Transnational National Council, the French executive quickly signalled its shift of position towards Gaddafi by being the first state to recognise the Council on 10 March as "the legitimate representation of the Libyan population", and by announcing that a French ambassador would be sent (*Le Point* 2011a). Nevertheless, this diplomatic endorsement was not enough, for by mid-March Gaddafi's forces had made real progress and were threatening to take back Benghazi – the opposition's epicentre in the east (Freeman 2011).

Along with the United Kingdom, France made sure that the violence perpetrated in Libya remained predominant in what was a busy news cycle, and began lobbying for a military intervention. In light of Franco-British pressure, the UN Security Council rapidly responded to the violence and Gaddafi's declarations that "officers have been deployed in all tribes and regions so that they can purify all decisions from these cockroaches. ... Any Libyan who takes arms against Libya will be executed" (in Miller 2011). After issuing a press statement on 22 February to express concerns about the situation in Libya, the Council passed Resolutions 1970 and 1973, both co-drafted by France.

The French executive at the time played a central role in lobbying key actors such as Russia and China not to veto the resolutions. Juppé personally explained France's position to the Council by arguing:

> we must not give free rein to warmongers; we must not abandon civilian populations, the victims of brutal repression, to their fate; we must not allow the rule of law and international morality to be trampled underfoot. For this reason, France sought to contribute its utmost to the international momentum by working alongside the United Kingdom, the United States and others to prepare the draft resolution before the Council. ... If [this resolution] is adopted, we are prepared to act with Member States – in particular Arab States – that wish to do so. We do not have much time left. It is a matter of days, perhaps even hours. Every hour and day that goes by means a further clampdown and repression for the freedom-loving civilian population, in particular the people of Benghazi. Every hour and day that goes by increases the burden of responsibility on our shoulders. (UN Security Council 2011a)

After recalling the Libyan authorities' responsibility to protect its population, Resolution 1970 called for an immediate end to the violence, announced an arms embargo and referred the situation to the International Criminal Court (UN Security Council 2011c). Resolution 1973 went even further by authorising member states "to take all necessary measures, notwithstanding paragraph 9 of resolution 1970 (2011), to protect civilians and civilian populated areas under threat of attack in the Libyan Arab Jamahiriya, including Benghazi" (UN Security Council 2011d).

Following the adoption of Resolution 1973, Sarkozy announced to the French population that "in agreement with our partners, [France's] air forces will oppose any aggression committed by Colonel Gaddafi's planes. ... Some Arab nations have chosen to free themselves from the servitude in which they have felt imprisoned for too long. ... In the midst of the difficulties and trials of all kinds they have to confront, these Arab nations need our help and our support. It is our duty. ... Our determination is total" (Sarkozy 2011c). It is interesting to note that Sarkozy's executive was initially favourable to an intervention through a "coalition of the willing" rather than NATO, but this decision was rapidly reconsidered in light of the extent of NATO's means (Chivvis 2012, 71–72).

France's heavy participation in NATO's Operation Unified Protector was undertaken through *Opération Harmattan*, which officially began on 19 March 2011 with the objective of implementing Resolution 1973 by (1) ensuring respect for the no-fly zone, (2) reducing the Gaddafi regime's capacity for defence and (3) undertaking attacks on military objectives that could threaten the Libyan population (Ministère de la Défense 2011a). France's military participation was one of the strongest: mobilising up to 4,200 soldiers, France undertook 5,600 operations (4,000 of them using the French air force), which corresponded to "25% of the operations, 35% of the offensive missions and 20% of the strikes of the coalition" (Ministère de la Défense 2011b). In addition to this strong participation in NATO's intervention, the French executive decided to send trainers and military supplies – "rocket launchers, assault rifles, machine guns and especially Milan anti-tank missiles" – to the rebel forces from May 2011 (Gelie 2011).

Therefore, even though France was not a norm entrepreneur of R2P since it played no role in its emergence, it can be argued that from 2006 it became a norm consolidator on the global stage by making sure that the international principle was being debated and implemented by the international community.

## The endangering of R2P

However, in light of how France understood the international principle, its support was not always beneficial to the development of R2P. As explained in Chapter 1, it is common for differences in understanding to emerge during the early stages of a norm's emergence, especially during the localisation process. This can be explained by the fact that norms are often broadly defined in order to facilitate their endorsement by the international community. States need to be able to build congruence between the transnational emerging norm and local beliefs and practices, and the lack of clarity of norms facilitates this process (Acharya 2004, 241). For instance, as Gallagher explains, some of the terms chosen in the World Summit Outcome Document – such as "timely and decisive manner" and "manifest failing" – were particularly ambiguous (2014). This lack of clarity explains why even several years after the international endorsement of R2P, some states comprehended it as "persuading states to fulfil their protection responsibilities and providing mutual assistance on a consensual basis", while others saw it in a broader way, "as a response to the dilemmas of humanitarian intervention" (Bellamy 2011, 8). It is thus important to comprehend how the various French executives defined R2P and to derive from this an account of what they were actually supporting. The rest of this section concentrates mainly on Sarkozy's various executives' interpretation of R2P, since France's engagement with the international principle only became prevalent during his presidency.

*A specific understanding of R2P*

It is interesting to note that even though the World Summit Outcome Document did not refer to R2P as containing three responsibilities as the original ICISS report had done, Sarkozy's executives embraced the ICISS's formula. For instance, the 2008 *livre blanc* on the Foreign and European Policy of France explained that R2P "entails a triple dimension: responsibility to prevent, responsibility to intervene,[6] if need be with armed forces, and the responsibility to reconstruct" (Juppé and Schweitzer 2008, 48).

This understanding meant that, like the majority of the international community, Sarkozy's executives particularly emphasised the importance of prevention and saw the use of force as a last resort (Staunton 2018, 377). For instance, at the UN General Assembly debate in 2009, France's representative Lacroix defined prevention as the "key element" of R2P (in UN General Assembly 2009, 10). Similarly, following the passing of Resolution 1894 on the protection of civilians, Araud explained that "it is not just a matter of intervening in serious crises to put an end to the most heinous crimes; it is also a matter of acting beforehand to prevent such crimes and of strengthening warning systems for situations where there is the potential for such crimes" (in UN Security Council 2009, 15). Last but not least, during the discussion of the presidential statement 2011/18 on the maintenance of international peace and security, the Minister of Foreign Affairs Juppé explained, "resolving crises is the duty of our Council, as is preventing them. France believes that preventive diplomacy in all its aspects is a key element of the just and effective governance to which my country aspires with all its heart" (in UN Security Council 2011b, 14).

Despite what the international community thought of France's conception of human protection in the late 1990s, this emphasis on prevention was nothing new and had actually been promoted by the various executives since the mid-1990s. For instance, the 1994 *livre blanc* on defence argued that prevention could be used in order to "prevent the appearance of situations that are potentially dangerous and direct and indirect threats; prevent the use of force; contain the crises and conflicts at the lowest level possible" (Long 1994, 59–60). The report thus encouraged the use of political, diplomatic, economic, politico-military and military means in order to undertake and develop France's capacities in terms of prevention (Long 1994, 60, 84–85).

That being said, Sarkozy's various executives also emphasised the idea that although prevention should be a priority, pillar three should not be neglected when prevention failed. For instance, in 2009 Lacroix explained to the General Assembly that "the responsibility to protect would not be complete without the third pillar, which gives it its full meaning – that is, the international community's reaction when one of the four crimes is being or is about to be committed" (in UN General Assembly 2009, 10). He emphasised that it was not limited "to actions taken under Chapter VII [since it] also includes the whole host of measures for peaceful settlement of disputes provided for in Chapters VI and VIII of the Charter of the United Nations" (Lacroix in UN General Assembly 2009, 10), yet military actions were not excluded when deemed necessary (see also Mallet and Ministère de la Défense 2008, 130).

This conception of R2P put France among the minority of states that saw R2P as more than a "consensual" tool to protect, yet the real essence of France's conception of the international principle lies in the way it under-stood its historic roots (Staunton 2018, 377). Sarkozy's various executives rejected the idea that the principle was new and argued that it had French roots by associating it with the domestic norm of human protection and, more specifically, with the way it was defined in the 1980s. For instance, Kouchner – who was again Minister of Foreign Affairs at the time – argued that "France invented the *droit d'ingérence*. .... The Security Council talks about 'the responsibility to protect'. It is the same thing" (in Védrine 2009, 245–246). Similarly, in 2010 Kouchner argued in front of the UN General Assembly that General Assembly Resolution 43/131 (1988) on "Humanitarian assistance to victims of natural disasters and similar emergency situations" and Security Council Resolution 688 (1991) on Iraq were "two historical moments that lay down the first foundations of the *droit d'ingérence*, which has become the responsibility to protect" (2010). Comparably, in 2009, in front of the General Assembly, Lacroix declared that R2P's "emergence was made possible, let me remind you, by the conceptual leap made in the 1990s with the emergence of the right of humanitarian interference as formulated by France and by Bernard Kouchner, and which was ratified by several General Assembly resolutions" (in UN General Assembly 2009, 9).

Claims of this kind could be seen as unsurprising coming from Kouchner and his representatives, but they were shared by other members of Sarkozy's various executives, including Kouchner's successor as Minister of Foreign Affairs. In 2011 Juppé argued that "France has played a decisive role in inscribing [R2P] in international law – I am thinking of the visionary action of Mario Bettati and of Bernard Kouchner" (2011). Similarly, in 2011 Sarkozy explained in relation to the conflicts in Côte d'Ivoire and Libya that "with these two crises, the Security Council allowed us to form, for the first time, a principle of action, which France managed to make the UN adopt in 2005: the responsibility to protect" (Sarkozy 2011a). Therefore, apart from de Villepin's speech in 2005 which insinuated that R2P was new by declaring "new principles are needed, such as the responsibility to protect" (de Villepin 2005), the declarations made thereafter consistently linked the two concepts, or at the very least argued that R2P had French roots because the idea that the international community has a 'duty' to intervene in cases of humanitarian crisis had been promoted by France's domestic norm since the end of the 1980s.

This association of R2P with France's conception of human protection is quite surprising given that the ICISS had purposefully excluded France from the negotiating table. As noted previously, Gareth Evans explained the basis of this exclusion in clear and unambiguous terms: "the French were part of the problem" (2013b). Therefore the fact that no French representative was invited to take part in the ICISS was no coincidence, since there was a will to dissociate R2P from France.

Additionally, the claim that R2P has French roots is questionable since there are some key distinctions between the international principle and the *devoir d'ingérence* (see also Jeangène Vilmer 2012, 88–89). The most important one lies in the definition of sovereignty. The *devoir d'ingérence* relies on a Westphalian conception of sovereignty, which necessarily counterpoises sovereignty and intervention,[7] yet R2P is based on 'sovereignty as responsibility', in which "sovereignty and human rights are two sides of the same coin, and not opposing principles locked in interminable struggle" (Bellamy 2009a, 33). Additionally, the tools available under R2P are broader than those under the *devoir d'ingérence* since the former is not only about reacting militarily to a humanitarian crisis: "the R2P agenda ... comprises more complex and subtle responses to mass atrocities than the use of force, ranging from prevention to post-conflict rebuilding to protecting civilians at risk" (Weiss 2012b, 434). Finally, R2P is meant to cover four categories of crime exclusively: genocide, ethnic cleansing, war crimes and crimes against humanity.

It is difficult to explain why the various executives did not seem to see – or refused to articulate – these key distinctions, but three factors can be emphasised (Staunton 2018, 378). First, the role played by the domestic norm of human protection cannot be underestimated. It had been influential since the 1980s, and Sarkozy's presidency was no exception. Like their predecessors, he and his executives argued that in light of its history, values and rank, France had a special role to play in the promotion of human protection. For instance, he recalled in his description of his foreign policy objectives in 2007 that "France is herself when she promotes freedom against oppression and reason against chaos" (2007e, 150). Given that one of the key premises of R2P was to promote a responsibility – and not simply a right – of the international community to protect, it appears that France's own understanding of human protection, and more particularly the idea that right and duty had always been linked, misled the executives in their understanding of R2P, especially at a time when the principle was still being defined and negotiated by the international community.

Second, that being said, the obsession of Sarkozy's executives with France's rank also needs to be taken into account. Like François Mitter-rand and Chirac, Sarkozy was determined to promote France's rank (Bozo 2012, 272). Because France's image as a promoter of human rights and human protection helped to promote the idea that France is 'more than a middle sized power', taking the risk of losing this role by being seen as isolated from the international principle was very problematic. As Sarkozy argued in 2007, "guided by our values, our foreign policy needs to rely on a clear vision of the world and of the interests we defend. It is our identity as a nation that we express through this foreign policy" (2007d). Conse-quently, it does not seem far-fetched to argue that his executives began to link R2P with France's efforts since the 1980s, with the aim of ending the dissociation between France and R2P that had been promoted by the ICISS, so that France could maintain its key role in human protection and, consequently, its rank.

Third and finally, it appears that the role played by some influential members of the executive such as Kouchner and Mario Bettati contrib-uted to the linking of R2P with the *devoir d'ingérence*: both have argued that R2P was a political move to exclude the French from the human rights arena and, more particularly, an attempt to diminish their legacy in human protection (Bettati 2014; Kouchner 2014). It is therefore possible to argue that they promoted the idea that R2P and the *devoir d'ingérence* were similar so that they could reinstate France's place in the R2P story and maintain their legacy.

### Endangering the international principle

The implications of the association of R2P with France's domestic norm of human protection were important since, by refusing – or, at the very least, by failing – to understand the distinctions between the two, the executives promoted a broad understanding of the international principle in which the source of the humanitarian emergency should be broadly

defined, and where coercive military action should be undertaken if prevention and diplomacy fail. This specific conception of R2P meant that at
times, when trying to promote R2P, Sarkozy's various executives ended up
endangering the international principle. This can be seen particularly in
2008, when Cyclone Nargis hit Myanmar/Burma, and in 2011 during the
intervention in Libya (Staunton 2018, 378–379). Even though in both cases
France's intent was not to damage the international principle but rather to
support it, it ended up weakening – at least temporarily – the international
consensus around the principle by promoting a broad understanding
of R2P.

Myanmar/Burma

In 2008 Cyclone Nargis hit Myanmar/Burma and left a large part of the
region under water. Despite the fact that 2.5 million people were affected
by the cyclone, the Burmese government imposed restrictions on the delivery of international humanitarian aid, for instance by limiting the issuing
of visas for foreign aid workers and UN personnel (APR2P 2008, 2; Barber
2009, 3–4).

On 7 May 2008 French Minister of Foreign Affairs Kouchner suggested
that the UN Security Council use R2P in order to pressure the Burmese
junta into allowing access to international assistance: "we are seeing at
the United Nations if we can't implement the responsibility to protect,
given that food, boats and relief teams are there, and obtain a United
Nations' resolution which authorises the delivery (of aid) and imposes this
on the Burmese government" (in ICRtoP 2008). The idea that R2P could
be invoked during "overwhelming natural or environmental catastrophes,
where the state concerned is either unwilling or unable to cope, or call for
assistance, and significant loss of life is occurring or threatened" had originally been suggested in the ICISS report (2001, 33). However, this suggestion was not kept, for the World Summit Outcome Document explained
that R2P could be used in only four cases: genocide, ethnic cleansing, war
crimes and crimes against humanity (Nougayrède, Bolopion and Ferenczi
2008; UN General Assembly 2005).

Some might argue that Kouchner's proposal was an attempt to show
that his voice still mattered in human protection even though he was
not invited to be part of the ICISS. However, even if personal interests
were at play, this proposal was in line with France's conception of human
protection, which had promoted a broad understanding of human protection since the 1980s by not restricting it to specific populations or
sources of emergency (see for instance Bettati 1987, 26). The proposal
was even less surprising for coming from Kouchner, who had considerably

shaped this broad understanding of human protection in the late 1980s and early 1990s.

Evans has argued that, given that in 2008 R2P was still relatively new and therefore negotiations on what it entailed and excluded were still taking place, the proposition was not completely without merit (Evans 2013b). In particular, he explains that there was a need to clarify what constituted a crime against humanity: "if what the generals are now doing – effectively denying relief to hundreds of thousands of people at real and immediate risk of death – can itself be characterised as a crime against humanity, then the responsibility to protect principle does indeed cut in" (Evans 2008b).

As a consequence of this lack of clarity, Kouchner's call received some support. For instance, as Barber explains, "Australia's former Minister of Foreign Affairs, Alexander Downer, argued that 'the concept of responsibility to protect needs to be extended to humanitarian assistance', while Canada's Minister of Foreign Affairs, Lloyd Axworthy, said that the fundamental message of R2P is that there is no moral difference between an innocent person being killed by machete or AK-47 and starving to death or dying in a cholera epidemic that could have been avoided by proper international response" (Barber 2009, 33). Additionally, even though the European Union failed to agree on Kouchner's proposal, the "European Union's High Representative for the Common Foreign and Security Policy, Javier Solana, declared ... that the international community should 'use all possible means to get aid through to victims of Myanmar's cyclone'" (in Caballero-Anthony and Chng 2009, 140).

The idea that natural disasters could be used to call on R2P was, however, flatly rejected by two veto powers, Russia and China. They were supported by key international figures in the area of R2P who were concerned that this broad understanding of the principle would damage it. For instance, Ramesh Thakur (who was part of the ICISS) argued that "there would be no better way to damage the responsibility to protect beyond repair ... than to have humanitarian assistance delivered into Myanmar backed by Western soldiers fighting in the jungles of Southeast Asia again" (in Barber 2009, 4). Edward Luck, Special Advisor to the Secretary General on R2P, also argued that:

> it would be a misapplication of responsibility to protect principles to apply them at this point to the unfolding tragedy in Myanmar. The Outcome Document of the 2005 [World] Summit limited their application to four crimes and violations: genocide, crimes against humanity, war crimes and ethnic cleansing. We must focus our efforts on implementing these principles in these four cases, as there is no agreement among the Member States on applying them to other situations, no matter how disturbing and regrettable the circumstances. (in APR2P 2008, 8)

He then claimed that by referring to R2P in this situation, Kouchner had done "considerable damage" and "ha[d] made things more complex for those trying to promote trust in the concept" (in Nougayrède, Bolopion and Ferenczi 2008).

Interestingly, as suggested in the section "Subsidiarity" in Chapter 1, after temporarily endangering the international principle, France's attempt to broadly define R2P actually led to its strengthening (Staunton 2018, 379). While France's proposal sparked debate and led to controversy, it eventually contributed to reinforcing the international consensus around the international principle, since the majority of the international community agreed that Myanmar did not fall under R2P. In other words, by overstating its scope, France provided a catalyst for a re-articulation of R2P as a bounded concept.

## Libya

Another episode when, in light of the executive's broad understanding of the principle, France ended up endangering R2P occurred when it intervened with NATO in Libya in 2011. France's role in the intervention has already been examined, and so this discussion focuses on how the regime change promoted by France, the United Kingdom and the United States weakened the international principle.

At first, France's support for peace negotiations between the Gaddafi regime and the rebel forces suggested that regime change was not necessarily a goal of the French executive. However, once the intervention began, Barack Obama, David Cameron and Sarkozy simultaneously published a press statement in the *New York Times*, *The Times* and *Le Monde* to justify regime change:

> it is impossible to imagine a future for Libya with Gaddafi in power. ... It is unthinkable that someone who has tried to massacre his own people can play a part in their future government. The brave citizens of those towns that have held out against forces that have been mercilessly targeting them would face a fearful vengeance if the world accepted such an arrangement. It would be an unconscionable betrayal. Furthermore, it would condemn Libya to being not only a pariah state, but a failed state too. Gaddafi has promised to carry out terrorist attacks against civilian ships and airliners. And because he has lost the consent of his people any deal that leaves him in power would lead to further chaos and lawlessness. ... Gaddafi must go and go for good. (Obama, Cameron and Sarkozy 2011)

Throughout the military intervention, the French President always defended it and never came close to arguing that it went too far. For instance, before the UN General Assembly on 20 September 2011, he declared, "we intervened to assist the Libyans *révolutionnaires* and we are proud of it. ... Freedom is not without risk, but dictatorship is a guarantee of failure. ... France is proud and happy to have been a part of the coalition and if we had to do it again, we would" (Sarkozy 2011b).

Although NATO's intervention was initially well received in many Western countries because it prevented the Gaddafi regime from committing large-scale mass atrocities, NATO was also strongly criticised for undertaking regime change. This criticism became visible as early as 26 April 2011, when the African Union declared in an official report on Libya that "it should be left to Libyans to choose their leaders and that international actors should refrain from taking positions or making pronouncements that can only complicate the search for a solution. The role of the international community should be to help Libyans achieve their legitimate aspirations, in a nationally-owned and nationally-led process" (African Union 2011, 12). As Evans explained, the criticism intensified as the intervention went on, and "the Western coalition came under fierce attack by the BRICS countries – Brazil, Russia, India, China and South Africa – for exceeding its narrow civilian protection mandate, and being content with nothing less than regime change, which was finally accomplished with the overthrow of Gaddafi in October 2011" (2013a). As a consequence, the coalition was deemed responsible for damaging the weak international consensus around R2P, even though this was not its intention.

In contrast to that of Myanmar/Burma, the case of Libya provides a good example of an instance when the subsidiarity process ended up endangering R2P more extensively. By promoting a broad understanding and undertaking regime change, France and the coalition badly damaged the international consensus from which R2P benefited (see for instance Rieff 2011). This damage was not irrevocable, for R2P continued to develop beyond Libya in light of its regulative and constitutive effects (see Glanville 2016). However, its effects cannot be underestimated, as is illustrated by the international community's reluctance to intervene in Syria during a small available window at the beginning of the conflict. This episode shows how far the subsidiarity process can impact an international norm, even at a stage of its development where it benefits from a relatively strong international consensus (Staunton 2018, 379). Consequently, even though France can be seen as a norm consolidator of R2P from 2006 in view of its active support both diplomatically and militarily, it sometimes ended up endangering the emerging principle instead of promoting it.

## The influence of R2P on France: a growing yet limited impact

The influence of Sarkozy's various executives on R2P having been addressed, this section focuses on the impact of R2P on France's conception and implementation of human protection.

### Some signs of influence

The year 2008 was important for R2P in France. The French executive showed that it was willing to be a norm implementer by including R2P in its own foreign policy. In the 2008 *livre blanc* on France's foreign and European policy, which is meant to be a guideline for the period 2008–20, R2P was defined as a key objective of French foreign policy. Setting out a ten-step approach to promote human rights, the report called for "the prevention and repression of massive violations of human rights, in particular in light of our responsibility to protect, and the cooperation with the penal international justice" (Juppé and Schweitzer 2008, 48).

Additionally, the 2008 *livre blanc* on defence and national security emphasised the idea that France might intervene militarily in situations falling under R2P (Mallet and Ministère de la Défense 2008, 74, 76, 130). It explained that "it is expected that France will remain a highly sought-after contributor. Its participation ... will usually include contingents that are relatively limited (around 1,000 to 5,000 men excluding the naval and aerial contingents) ... in several theatres, in remote geographic zones, often hard to access, with difficult physical, human and economic characteristics. These operations are long-term and face strong challenges that require permanent adaptation" (Mallet and Ministère de la Défense 2008, 130).

R2P's influence on France was also particularly visible when the French executive had to pull back from intervening in Myanmar/Burma after contestation by the international community (Staunton 2018, 379). This episode showed that the international principle was beginning to have a restraining impact on France's practice of human protection. It was not well received by the executive at the time since it led French diplomacy to be criticised and prevented France from intervening to protect.

### A limited impact

The impact of R2P on France nevertheless remained limited. This can be seen in the fact that Sarkozy's executives continued to promote a broad understanding of human protection. For instance, even though Kouchner's proposal to intervene in Myanmar/Burma was rejected in 2008, Lacroix reminded the General Assembly in 2009 that, while the UN Secretary General's report restricted the focus of R2P to four crimes, "France will also remain vigilant to ensure that natural disasters, when combined with deliberate inaction on the part of a Government that refuses to provide assistance to its population in distress or to ask the international community for aid, do not lead to human tragedies in which the international community can only look on helplessly" (in UN General Assembly 2009, 9).

Additionally, Sarkozy's various executives continued to intervene heavily for humanitarian purposes, even when the Security Council did not invoke R2P (Staunton 2018, 379–380). Even though the track record of Sarkozy's presidency in the area of human rights was more controversial than he would have hoped,[8] France deployed an average of 9,396 troops a year for humanitarian purposes between 2005 and 2011 (IISS 2005; 2007; 2008; 2009; 2010; 2011; 2012).[9] Moreover, as is illustrated by *Opération Harmattan* in Libya, these interventions were not always consensual and often went beyond a narrow civilian protection mandate in order to meet France's own conception of human protection rather than that of R2P.

The remainder of this section therefore aims to investigate France's military commitment to human protection beyond the R2P intervention in Libya and how and where France intervened militarily for humanitarian purposes. But before doing this, it is important to emphasise that this ongoing commitment to intervene to protect despite R2P's limited influence can partly be explained by the fact that the various French executives remained strongly influenced by France's domestic norm of human protection. This can be seen in the fact that they continued to promote the idea that in light of its history, values and rank, France has a special role to play in the promotion of human protection.

For instance, during the presidential electoral campaign, Sarkozy explained, "our pride lies in France's special vocation in the world. I will not compromise the values of our country, its independence and its alliances. I want France to carry weight on the world stage and fulfil its responsibility in managing global conflicts. ... I will never silence violations of human rights in the name of our economic interests. I will defend human rights wherever they are ignored or threatened" (Sarkozy 2007f, 15). Similarly, between the two rounds of the election, he referred to France as "the homeland of human rights" and declared, "I want to be President of a France defending freedom at home but also in the world. Because it is France's vocation. I want to be the President of the France of Human Rights. ... I do not want to simply speak about it, I want to act. Every time a woman or a child is martyred in the world, France will be at their side" (2007g). He added in his victory speech that this was "France's message, France's identity, France's history" (Sarkozy 2007b).

These declarations were rapidly reflected in Sarkozy's choice of Minister of Foreign Affairs, for as part of his policy of *ouverture* (opening), he appointed Kouchner. Although this decision was heavily criticised by the right wing, Sarkozy justified it by arguing, "I am among those who think that France still carries a message and values that resonate throughout the world, those of the Declaration of the Rights of Man and of the Citizen, of humanism, but also, more recently, of humanitarianism and the duty to protect as incarnated by men like Bernard Kouchner, whom I was happy to welcome to the government and put in charge of our diplomacy" (Sarkozy 2007d). A position of State Secretary for Human Rights was also created to support the Minister of Foreign Affairs.[10]

Similarly, as mentioned previously, the promotion of human rights became a central part of France's 2008 *livre blanc* on defence and national security, which explained that "the sovereignty of a state is first and foremost to protect its population. Neither the principle of non-interference in the internal affairs of a state nor the principle of the sovereignty of that state can thus be invoked to defend atrocities such as massacres and other forms of mass violation of international humanitarian law" (Mallet and Ministère de la Défense 2008, 123). It also contended that France had particular responsibilities to play in the UN owing to its permanent seat at the Security Council: "They [the permanent members of the UN Security Council, or P5] have the primary responsibility to prevent crises rather than reacting after they have occurred. It is to them, in particular, that the responsibility falls to reduce the divisions between opponents when conflicts erupt" (Mallet and Ministère de la Défense 2008, 115–116). Similarly, the *livre blanc* on France's foreign and European policy recalled that "France must seek to act in the world for peace, security and human rights" (Juppé and Schweitzer 2008, 44). Consequently, like their predecessors, Sarkozy's various executives remained committed to intervene, and like their predecessors, they tried to do so in a way that would also promote France's rank.

The choice of institutional framework

As Graph 10 shows, France continued to favour intervening for humanitarian purposes through NATO and the European Union, and via unilateral operations undertaken to support multilateral interventions (*Opération Licorne* in Côte d'Ivoire and *Opération Boali* in the CAR), while also increasing its troop contribution to UN interventions.

France's diplomatic support of the UN had been strong since the end of the Cold War, and the second half of the 2000s was no exception. For instance, in 2010 Kouchner, in his capacity as Minister of Foreign Affairs,

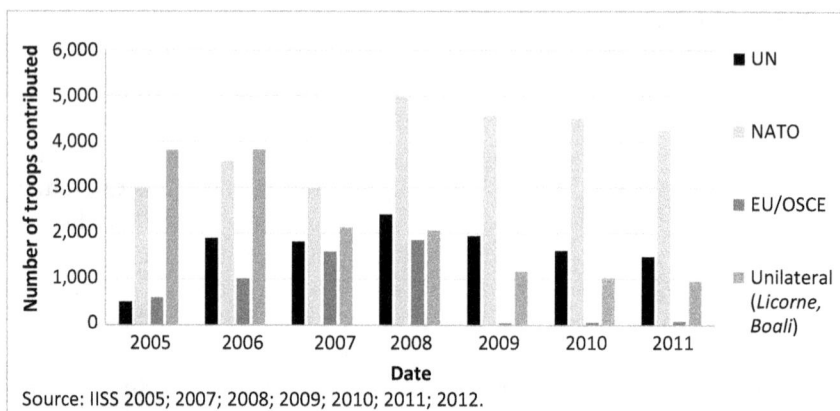

Source: IISS 2005; 2007; 2008; 2009; 2010; 2011; 2012.

Note: This graph does not take into account troops deployed outside France owing to security agreements or headquarters situated overseas (with the exception of the troops in Côte d'Ivoire from 2002 since they were used for *Opération Licorne*). With the exception of 2005 (August), it reflects the troop contribution in November of that year and therefore is not representative of the whole year. Additionally, it takes into account only troops on the ground and therefore is not representative of France's commitment to NATO's intervention in Libya in 2011, which was an air-strike-based intervention.

**Graph 10** France's troop contributions to interventions for humanitarian purposes by institutional framework, 2005–11

explained that France had a "sincere and fierce faith in the United Nations Organisation. … The United Nations is at the centre of the international life and needs to remain there. There is a simple reason for this: the UN is universal, it has a legitimacy that no other organisation can compete with. It is the only platform where multilateralism can fully develop" (2010; see also Mallet and Ministère de la Défense 2008, 114).

In order to consolidate the UN and help overcome its challenges, Sarkozy's executives continued to promote the need to undertake key reforms. In particular, like Hubert Védrine, Kouchner recommended an enlargement of the Security Council, since "it is not acceptable that the African continent does not have a single permanent representative. Nor it is acceptable that powers such as Japan, Germany, India and Brazil do not already hold a permanent seat" (Kouchner 2010). The idea was that a reformed Council would help reconcile legitimacy and efficacy within the institution and would thus benefit human protection (Mallet and Ministère de la Défense 2008, 116).

France's troop contribution to UN interventions undertaken for humanitarian purposes also increased from 806 to 1,900 in September 2006, a considerably higher number than the contributions made by the other P3 members, the United States and the United Kingdom (UN 2005; 2006;

2007; 2008; 2009; 2010; 2011; 2012).[11] Nevertheless, this shift should not be overestimated; even though an increase in the troop contribution made by France is undeniable, it was mainly caused by a growth of the number of troops deployed under UNIFIL, to which France had been committed since the 1970s. Additionally, even though France was willing to support UN interventions, *Opération Licorne* (which is discussed in more depth in the next section) shows that Sarkozy's various executives favoured intervening outside the UN, via unilateral operations – which aimed to support UN troops without being limited by their constraints – in order to not endanger France's rank.

Moreover, despite the fact that France participated in fifteen UN operations, its contribution was substantial for only three of them: UNIFIL in Lebanon, UNOCI and the United Nations Mission in the Central African Republic and Chad (MINURCAT) (UN 2005; 2006; 2007; 2008; 2009; 2010; 2011; 2012). Even then, as the next section shows, the troop contributions to UNOCI and MINURCAT were marginal in comparison to those deployed under *Opération Licorne* and EUFOR CAR/Chad. Consequently, with the exception of *Licorne*, as in the early 2000s, the European Union and NATO were favoured by France to intervene to protect.

France's relationship with the European Union took a hit on 29 May 2005, when 55 per cent of the French population rejected the Constitutional Treaty in a referendum organised by President Chirac (Charillon 2007, 140). This decision can be seen as the consequence of the discontent with Chirac's presidency rather than with the European Union (see Bozo 2012, 257), yet it was still perceived as a strong signal against the European Union. This was problematic given that the various executives wanted to increase the European Union's capacity for military intervention for humanitarian purposes, and it was also seen as a tool with which to promote France's rank. As the *livre blanc* on foreign and European policy explained, France's "place in the world will depend on the leading role that it will continue to play in the European enterprise" (Juppé and Schweitzer 2008, 37). Consequently, it argued, "Europe, for our diplomacy, is not one geographical area of action like the others, it is the first" (Juppé and Schweitzer 2008, 37).

In order to repair the damage caused by the referendum, Sarkozy made the strengthening of France's relationship with the European Union "the absolute priority of our foreign policy" (2007d). In his victory speech, he declared, "I want to appeal to our European partners, to whom our destiny is deeply linked, to tell them that all my life I have been a European; that I deeply believe, that I sincerely believe, in the European construction. And that tonight France is back in Europe" (2007b). On the day of his investiture, he went to Berlin to meet the German Chancellor, Angela Merkel, thereby signalling the importance of the European Union and of the renewal of the Franco-German partnership (de Charette 2008, 8).

In order to reinforce France's role in Europe and its capacity to intervene for humanitarian purposes, the executive spent the first year of Sarkozy's presidency working on the adoption of a 'mini treaty', which became the Lisbon Treaty in December 2007 (Bozo 2012, 261; Tiersky 2008, 102). Even though the treaty was criticised for offering too many concessions to the Euro-sceptics, it allowed France to prove its commitment to the European Union and got it out of an institutional stalemate (de Charette 2008, 8–9). Moreover, when France took over the European Union presidency on 1 July 2008, it adopted an ambitious agenda which included "moving forward with the EU's common foreign and security policy" (Tiersky 2008, 102).

Sarkozy's executives were specifically determined to work towards the development of the military capacity of the European Union so that it could rapidly intervene in crises, particularly humanitarian ones.[12] Even though a European defence and foreign policy had been in construction since the 1980s, and key milestones such as the creation of the CSDP at the Cologne Summit of 1999 and the Eurocorps in 2002 had been achieved over the years, the European Union remained weak in the mid-2000s. Sarkozy was thus determined to overcome these limits because, to use his words, "how can one speak of a European voice if it has to be silent when weapons speak? Europeans must be able to act on their own if necessary, and with their allies if they choose to" (2009b).

In particular, the Lisbon Treaty pushed by France was a key step in consolidating the CSDP since it created a "High Representative of the Union for Foreign Affairs and Security Policy", a solidarity clause and a clause of mutual assistance (Mallet and Ministère de la Défense 2008, 84). In addition to this diplomatic support, and as shown by Graph 10, France actively participated in the interventions undertaken by the European Union for humanitarian purposes. As mentioned in Chapter 4, when the European Union undertook an intervention in Bosnia and Herzegovina from December 2004 onwards in order to replace NATO, France was present. Although its troop contribution was smaller than those of other key European players such as Germany and the United Kingdom, it averaged 475 troops between 2005 and 2006 (IISS 2005; 2007). Similarly, the European Union undertook a second intervention in the DRC in June 2005 which aimed to promote stability during the elections. It was composed of 2,000 troops and France, along with Germany, made the biggest contribution (Petiteville 2006, 94).

France's commitment was even more visible during the European Union intervention in the CAR and Chad from January 2008 to March 2009. It aimed to address the tensions that had emerged following the strong influx of refugees going to Chad from Darfur and the CAR. The European Union decided to send troops to avoid a deterioration in the situation, showing that it could be "one of the major players involved in conflict management in Africa and a key partner of the AU [African Union] and UN" (Sicurelli 2010, 71). The mission thus had a wide mandate that ranged from "protecting civilians in danger, particularly refugees and displaced persons, ... to ensuring the security and freedom of movement of its own staff, UN staff and associated personnel" (European Union 2015d). France participated heavily by deploying on average 1,600 troops – in contrast to Germany and the United Kingdom, whose troop contributions were almost non-existent (IISS 2009; 2010).

Nevertheless, further progress needed to be made since the interventions undertaken by the European Union still remained limited in scale and scope. Consequently, like his predecessor, Sarkozy intensified France's involvement with NATO while promoting the role of the European Union within the organisation. The Franco-American bilateral relationship rapidly shaped France's relationship with NATO and its participation in the interventions it undertook for humanitarian purposes. From the time of his election onwards, Sarkozy made it clear that the Franco-American friendship was a priority, and while he did not criticise the lack of participation by France in the 2003 Iraq War, he blamed his predecessor for letting the Franco-American friendship deteriorate (de Charette 2008, 11).

Sarkozy's will to renew the friendship became evident in his 2007 speech in front of the United States Congress. Even though he reminded the audience that France wanted to be "an independent ally, a free partner" (2007a), the speech was unequivocal in terms of the will to repair the relationship: "It is this ambitious and lucid France I have come to introduce to you today. A France that comes to the United States to renew this pact of friendship and alliance sealed in Yorktown between Washington and Lafayette" (2007a). This kind of declaration, combined with the appointment of the French Ambassador to the United States, Jean-David Levitte, as Sarkozy's advisor (Nouzille 2010, 758), the fact that the Sarkozys spent their first vacations in the United States instead of France (*L'Express* 2007) and the development of strong relationships with both Presidents George W. Bush and Obama rapidly led the President to be referred to as *Sarkozy l'Américain* (Nouzille 2010, 735).

In light of this strong Franco-American friendship, Sarkozy decided in April 2009 to fully reintegrate France into NATO (Sarkozy 2009a). It is important to emphasise that France was already part of most of NATO's civil and military committees. As Sarkozy explained,

> Since 1966, France has moved closer to NATO step by step, but most of the time without saying so. ... Since 1992, ... we have gone with NATO into Bosnia and then into Kosovo, after making Milosevic's Serbia give in, and finally into Afghanistan. We have become one of the leading troop contributors of the Alliance's operations. In 1992 we began renewing our attendance at the Military Committee, and we fully regained our place in 1996. Since the 1999 Strategic Concept, we have supported and participated in the transformation of the Alliance, which led in 2002 to important transformations. We participate in the Rapid Reaction Force of NATO. In 2004, breaking with the taboo of 1966, we began to insert French soldiers in the integrated structure ... . And we already have three French headquarters in Lille, Lyon and Toulon, certified for Allied operations. (2009b)

Nevertheless, while the actual implications of France's reintegration into NATO's structure were minimal,[13] it was very important from a symbolic point of view. It was seen as a contestation of the legacy of General Charles de Gaulle and an alignment with the United States.[14] Even though de Gaulle's political legacy created numerous debates, the idea that France was *alliée, mais pas alignée* (allied but not aligned) had been an important component of France's identity since the 1960s, and the decision thus received strong criticism. For instance, the former Prime Minister Lionel Jospin declared, "the decision taken by President Sarkozy ... was a major strategic mistake. It broke a consensus on the defence posture of France which had existed since General de Gaulle and was confirmed by François Mitterrand: solidarity with our allies, but non-alignment with the United States and autonomy of decision. This reintegration deprived France of an excellent position: to be politically united, militarily interoperable and strategically autonomous" (in Jauvert 2011; see also Védrine 2009, 311).

The shift was, however, undertaken by Sarkozy on the basis that France's lack of participation prevented it from occupying any important military role and contributing to the definition of NATO's military objectives and means (Sarkozy 2009b). As Sarkozy explained, "the time has come to end this situation because it is in the interest of France and it is in the interest of Europe. ... France will be stronger and more influential. Why? Because those who are absent are always wrong. Because France must co-lead rather than endure. Because we have to be where decisions and norms are being developed, rather than waiting outside to be notified" (2009b). He argued that it would also be beneficial for Europe since, as explained to the heads of states and governments of the Alliance, "the European Security and Defence Policy and the Atlantic Alliance are complementary and constitute two sides of the same policy" (2009c).

This key diplomatic shift was accompanied by a strong participation by France in NATO's operations undertaken for humanitarian purposes. In addition to participating heavily in Operation Unified Protector in Libya, France committed an average of 2,371 troops per month to ISAF in Afghanistan, and 1,551 troops to KFOR between 2005 and 2011 (IISS 2007; 2008; 2009; 2010; 2011; 2012). As illustrated by Graph 10, the majority of the troops deployed by France for humanitarian purposes were concentrated in NATO, and this contribution remained consistent. NATO's interventions had the advantage of having a strong mandate and extensive means, and consequently they allowed France to fulfil its perceived duty to protect without endangering its rank; in fact, they helped promote it.

*A worldwide commitment*

In terms of where France decided to intervene to protect, Graph 11 shows that the second half of the 2000s was marked by a renewal of the French presence. France was heavily involved in former Yugoslavia, Lebanon, Afghanistan, Libya, Côte d'Ivoire, the DRC, and the CAR and Chad.

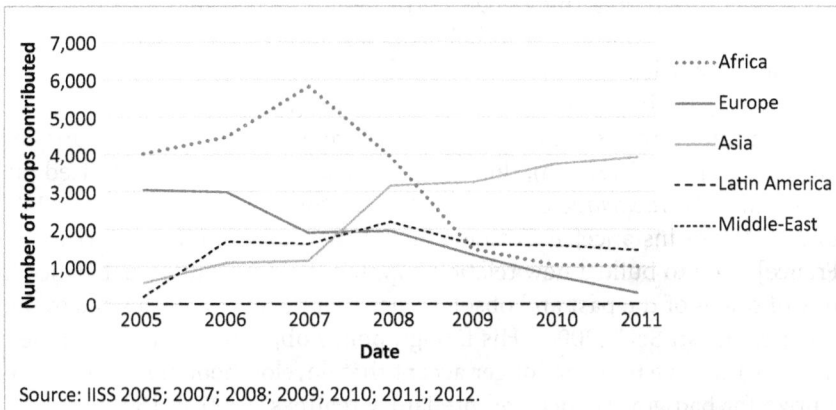

Source: IISS 2005; 2007; 2008; 2009; 2010; 2011; 2012.

Note: This graph does not take into account troops deployed outside France owing to security agreements or headquarters situated overseas (with the exception of the troops in Côte d'Ivoire from 2002 since they were used for *Opération Licorne*). With the exception of 2005 (August), it reflects the troop contribution in November of that year and therefore is not representative of the whole year. Additionally, it takes into account only troops on the ground and therefore is not representative of France's commitment to NATO's intervention in Libya in 2011, which was an air-strike-based intervention.

**Graph 11** France's troop contributions to interventions for humanitarian purposes by geographic area, 2005–11

As suggested previously, Europe was seen as a priority of Sarkozy's presidency in order to repair the damage caused by the 2005 referendum and to promote France's status worldwide. Additionally, as the previous chapters showed, France had been heavily involved in former Yugoslavia since the beginning of the conflicts. It is thus not surprising that its diplomatic support and military commitment to the conflict resolution in former Yugoslavia (in particular through KFOR) remained strong during the second half of the 2000s.

As also mentioned previously, Sarkozy's various executives remained involved in Lebanon, both diplomatically and militarily. As Sarkozy re-emphasised in 2007, "Lebanon has for centuries been dear to French hearts" (2007d). When tensions re-emerged in July 2006, the UN reinforced UNIFIL,[15] and in September 2006 France increased its troop contribution from 432 to 1,531. The French troop contribution then averaged 1,229 per month until December 2011 (UN 2005; 2006; 2007; 2008; 2009; 2010; 2011; 2012).

Sarkozy's executives also considerably increased France's contribution to ISAF in Afghanistan: the number of troops deployed was progressively augmented from 565 in 2005 to 3,932 in 2011 (IISS 2005; 2007; 2008; 2009; 2010; 2011; 2012). This increase reflected the new needs of the intervention; NATO explains that "as ISAF expanded into the east and south, its troops became increasingly engaged in fighting a growing insurgency in 2007 and 2008, while trying to help Afghanistan rebuild" (NATO 2015).

Last but not least, France was heavily involved in Africa. The election of Sarkozy gave hope to the opponents of *Françafrique*.[16] Even though he was committed to the idea that "Africa will remain an essential priority of our foreign policy" (2007d), the French President had also emphasised his criticism of *Françafrique* throughout the electoral campaign (Thiam 2008, 873–874). For instance, at Cotonou in 2006 he explained that "[Africa and France] need to build a new relationship, sanitised, uninhibited, balanced, free of traces of the past and obsolescence that persist on both sides of the Mediterranean Sea" (2006). His foreign policy objectives also emphasised the idea that "we must no longer accept that development aid can become a prize for bad governance and predatory regimes" (2007e, 152).

Additionally, when he was elected in 2007, Sarkozy appointed Jean-Marie Bockel as Secretary of State for Cooperation and *la Francophonie*, which was seen as a symbol of the will to rebuild Franco-African relations. Bockel was indeed a strong opponent of *Françafrique*, and in January 2008 he declared, "I want to sign its death certificate" (in Bernard 2008). Furthermore, Sarkozy rapidly proposed to create a "Union for the Mediterranean" that would be "a link between Europe and Africa" (Sarkozy 2007b) and would consequently increase the level of multilateralism in

Franco-African relations. The union was created in July 2008 during the French presidency of the European Union.

These hopes of reform rapidly suffered a blow, however, when the executive decided to continue its strong support for the Gabonese leader Omar Bongo. Despite his controversial records on democracy and human rights, he was received at the Elysée as early as May 2007, and Sarkozy also visited him in July 2007 (Gouëset 2010; Thiam 2008, 879). Additionally, the President made a highly controversial speech in Dakar on 26 July 2007 in which he appeared to defend colonialism and to give lessons to what he referred to as the "African man" (Thiam 2008, 879). He declared:

> The coloniser ... took but I also want to say with respect that he also gave. He built bridges, roads, hospitals, clinics, schools. He made virgin lands fertile, he provided his effort, his work, his knowledge. ... The tragedy of Africa is that the African man has not entered enough into history. ... In this universe where nature controls everything, man escapes the anguish of history that torments modern man, but man remains motionless in the middle of an immutable order where everything seems to be predetermined. Never does the man soar into the future. ... The sooner you take a good look at the reality of Africa and take it head on, the sooner the African Renaissance will begin. ... The reality of Africa is that of a great continent that has everything to succeed and that fails because it cannot free itself from its myths. (Sarkozy 2007c)

The hopes of reform brought by Sarkozy's election were also shaken up by Bockel's removal from the position of Secretary of State for Cooperation and *la Francophonie*, following the strong criticism of his declaration about the death of *Françafrique*.[17] He was 'moved' and became the Secretary of State for Defence and Veterans in June 2008.

Following these controversies, Sarkozy tried to shift his strategy. In December 2007 he attempted to renew dialogue with Rwandan President Paul Kagamé, and in January 2008 Kouchner recognised for the first time that France had made "a political mistake" in the way it handled the 1994 genocide (Gouëset 2010). Although this declaration was not an official apology for France's role, it constituted the first step towards the reconciliation of the two states and led to the re-establishment of France's diplomatic relations with Rwanda in December 2009 (Gouëset 2010).

Additionally, in February 2008 Sarkozy gave a key speech in Cape Town that aimed to correct the controversial Dakar speech (Thiam 2008, 883). After explaining the strong ties that linked France to Africa, the French President criticised the lack of representation of the African states in key international institutions such as the UN Security Council. He then announced the renegotiation and transparency of all the military agreements held with African states on the basis that "the Africa of 2008 is not the Africa of 1960". He also committed himself to promoting multilateralism by making "Europe a major partner of Africa" and to helping Africa "build its own collective security" since "France does not have a vocation to maintain armed forces in Africa indefinitely" (Sarkozy 2008).

In order to signal that the declarations were more than words and that France wanted to reduce its unilateral presence, the French headquarters in Abidjan and in Dakar were shut down in July 2008 and February 2010 respectively (Cumming 2013b, 109). Similar declarations continued to be made during the rest of Sarkozy's presidency. For instance, in 2011 he explained that stability would not be favoured over the promotion of human rights: "What is new, after decades during which the stability of regimes has prevailed ..., is France's will to assist with determining the movement of nations towards democracy" (2011a).

Some commentators have argued that this shift is visible only in such rhetoric and was not reflected in France's practice. For instance, in 2011 the slow reaction of the French executive in supporting the Tunisian Revolution raised concerns and led key commentators to suggest that France was still attached to stability in the region, in preference to the promotion of human rights (*Le Monde* 2011). France's involvement in Chad through *Opération Epervier* also raised questions regarding its involvement in the maintenance of dictators in power (Charbonneau 2008, 292).

Nevertheless, even though Sarkozy's strategy in Africa was tarnished by key mistakes and persistent grey areas, a commitment to intervene to promote human rights and to protect can still be seen. As Cumming explains, France "provid[ed] support to the four regional components of the African standby force, ... supported African peacekeeping, and ... oversaw the Europeanisation of its RECAMP initiative, which was renamed EUROCAMP in 2008 and placed under the European Council of Ministers (Cumming 2013b, 110). Furthermore, as Table 2 shows, in addition to intervening in Libya, France also intervened heavily for humanitarian purposes in Côte d'Ivoire, the DRC, and the CAR and Chad. With the exception of *Opération Licorne*, which had begun in 2002, these interventions occurred either through multilateral institutions such as the UN and the European Union/OSCE, or unilaterally to support multilateral forces.

As mentioned previously, France's military participation in the intervention in Libya was one of the strongest of the countries involved (Ministère de la Défense 2011b), and so was its participation in EUFOR DRC and EUFOR CAR/Chad (IISS 2009; 2010; Petiteville 2006, 94). In order to support EUFOR CAR/Chad, France also intervened unilaterally with *Opération Boali* in the CAR. *Boali* was undertaken as part of the RECAMP programme in order to prepare for the arrival of the Force Multinationale en Centrafrique (FOMUC, Multinational Force in the Central African

**Table 2** France's troop contributions to interventions for humanitarian purposes in Africa, 2005–11

| | Côte d'Ivoire | | Democratic Republic of the Congo | | | Ethiopia/ Eritrea | Liberia | Sudan | Western Sahara | Central African Republic/Chad | | | MICOPAX | Uganda | Total |
|---|---|---|---|---|---|---|---|---|---|---|---|---|---|---|---|
| | Licorne | UNOCI | MONUC | EUFOR DRC | MONUSCO | UNMEE | UNMIL | UNMIS/ UNAMID | MINURSO | Boali | MINURCAT | EUFOR CAR/ CHAD | MICOPAX | EUTM | Total |
| **2005** | 3,800 | 188 | 9 | | | 1 | 1 | | 25 | | | | | | 4,024 |
| **2006** | 3,800 | 187 | 6 | 461 | | 1 | 1 | | 17 | | | | | | 4,473 |
| **2007** | 3,800 | 185 | 6 | 12 | | 1 | 1 | 1 | 13 | 300 | 1 | | | | 5,820 |
| **2008** | 1,800 | 183 | 5 | | | | 2 | 2 | 18 | 230 | – | 1,500 | | | 3,951 |
| **2009** | 900 | 10 | 5 | | | | 1 | | 13 | 240 | 308 | 1,711 | | | 1,477 |
| **2010** | 772 | 7 | | | 5 | | 1 | | 13 | 240 | – | | | 25 | 1,063 |
| **2011** | 700 | 6 | | 14 | 5 | | 1 | | 13 | 240 | | | | 37 | 1,016 |

Note: This table does not take into account the troops deployed outside France owing to security agreements or headquarters situated overseas (with the exception of the troops in Côte d'Ivoire from 2002 since they were used for *Opération Licorne*). With the exception of 2005 (August), it reflects the troop contribution in November of each year and therefore is not representative of the whole year. Additionally, it takes into account only troops on the ground and therefore is not representative of France's commitment to NATO's intervention in Libya in 2011, which was an air-strike-based intervention.

EUTM     European Union Training Mission
MICOPAX     Mission de Consolidation de la Paix en Centrafique / Mission for the Consolidation of Peace in the Central African Republic
MONUSCO     United Nations Organization Stabilization Mission in the Democratic Republic of the Congo
UNAMID     United Nations–African Union Mission in Darfur
UNMIS     United Nations Mission in Somalia
Source: IISS 2005; 2007; 2008; 2009; 2010; 2011; 2012.

Republic) – the first African multinational force – and assist in the stabilisation of the country (Ministère de la Défense 2013).

Additionally, as mentioned in Chapter 4, French forces remained present in Côte d'Ivoire through *Opération Licorne* and UNOCI in order to help stabilise the country. In 2007, in light of the lack of progress in the political negotiations and the various delayed elections, "Security Council Resolution 1739 (2007) moved – at French insistence – to strengthen the position of prime minister as a counterbalance to the president" (Bellamy and Williams 2011, 831). The political negotiations restarted and eventually led to the 2007 Ouagadougou Agreement, which "established a transitional government of national unity with Soro appointed as prime minister, paved the way to national elections, created a process for resolving citizenship disputes, and called for the phased withdrawal of UNOCI and French forces concluding after the presidential election" (Bellamy and Williams 2011, 831–832).

However, the situation worsened in October 2010 with the holding of presidential elections following six delays (Hofnung 2011, 143). As Bellamy and Williams explain, "disputes about citizenship and ethnicity resurfaced; both sides used violence and intimidation, and dozens were killed in pre-election violence" (2011, 832). Following the second round of the presidential election in November, the two candidates Alassane Ouattara and Laurent Gbagbo both declared themselves President even though the UN had certified Ouattara's victory. This led to an increase of violence, and "the potential for mass atrocities appeared shortly thereafter" (Bellamy and Williams 2011, 833), thereby forcing France to temporarily intensify its presence between January and July 2011. France's troop contribution reached 1,600 in April before going back to 700 by the summer (Ministère de la Défense 2015).

The renewed violence also led France – and the UN – to adopt a less neutral position than it had in the past, even though both sides were responsible for committing atrocities. In particular, as Bellamy and Williams explain, "on 4 April, … UN helicopters as well as French attack helicopters assaulted military camps and destroyed heavy weapons and weapons stockpiles. This helped turn the tide of battle decisively in Ouattara's favour" (2011, 835). This shift was criticised by some for "blurr[ing] the lines between human protection and regime change" but was defended by Ban, who argued that the "sole purpose was to protect innocent people" (Bellamy and Williams 2011, 835, 836). Meanwhile, *Licorne* remained in Côte d'Ivoire until January 2015 to assist with the stabilisation of the country (Ministère de la Défense 2015).

Consequently, even though the growing international influence of R2P facilitated France's interventions by providing a favourable international normative context, the impact of the emerging norm on France was more one of constraint – by sometimes limiting where it could intervene to protect – than one of binding it to action. Thus, influenced by the domestic norm of human protection, the various executives continued to promote a broad understanding of human protection and to intervene to protect worldwide, mainly through NATO and the European Union, and unilaterally in order to fulfil France's perceived duty while also promoting its rank.

## Conclusion

After playing a limited role in the emergence of R2P, the various French executives became key advocates diplomatically and militarily from 2006. Sarkozy's executives, however, promoted a broad understanding of the international principle and more specifically of its origins, the measures that ought to be taken by the international community under pillar three and the cases it applies to: genocide, ethnic cleansing, war crimes and crimes against humanity. As suggested in Chapter 1, this specific understanding of R2P was not surprising given that variations often occur between the domestic and international definitions of an emerging norm during the localisation process, especially when a strong, distinct yet related domestic norm exists. However, this specific understanding of R2P ended up, at times, endangering the emerging norm while Sarkozy's executives were trying to implement it. This process is not uncommon during the subsidiarity process, but it showed how much impact France could have on R2P, even at a stage when it was gaining international traction.

In turn, R2P also began to impact France's conception of human protection, and in particular, it sometimes restricted how and when it could practise it. Nevertheless, in light of the strong domestic norm of human protection, this impact took time to occur and remained fairly limited beyond Myanmar/Burma. It thus constrained France rather than binding it to action, while in contrast, the domestic norm of human protection remained influential. In light of France's perceived duty to protect owing to its history, values and rank, the executives indeed continued to define human protection broadly and to intervene to protect, even when the international community did not refer to specific emergencies as falling under R2P. France was thus involved worldwide and used coercive force when it was deemed necessary. As in the 2000s, it mainly intervened via NATO and the European Union or even unilaterally to support multilateral interventions, while also strengthening its participation in some of the UN interventions undertaken for humanitarian purposes.

## Notes

1 As explained in the Introduction, this chapter mainly refers to R2P as a principle to reflect the fact that it was more than a concept after its endorsement

by the international community at the 2005 World Summit, yet it cannot be described as a norm until the 2011 intervention in Libya.

2  During this period the Secretary General also published two other key reports: "Early warning, assessment, and the responsibility to protect" (Ban 2010) and "The role of regional and sub-regional arrangements in implementing the responsibility to protect" (UN General Assembly 2011).

3  A referendum in 2000 reduced the length of the presidential mandate from seven to five years.

4  These resolutions were on Darfur (Resolution 1706), the protection of civilians (Resolution 1894) and Libya (Resolutions 1970, 1973, 2016 and 2040).

5  France supported the Tunisian Revolution quite late. This led to a key crisis in France and to the replacement of the Minister of Foreign Affairs, Alliot-Marie, by Juppé (*Le Monde* 2011; *Le Point* 2011b).

6  The ICISS report used the term 'responsibility to react' to avoid any confusion about the need to intervene militarily.

7  Even though it aimed to uphold the right of the victims to life and humanitarian assistance, the *devoir d'ingérence* still involved violating state sovereignty.

8  For instance, as discussed in the chapter, its support of the Gabon President Omar Bongo in 2007, the controversial Dakar speech made by the President in July 2007, Gaddafi's visit to the Elysée in December 2010 and France's late support of the Tunisian Revolution led to strong criticism (Bozo 2012 267–268; Cumming 2013a; Gouëset 2010).

9  The Libyan intervention is not included here because it consisted of air strikes, which are not taken into account in the data available.

10  It was however cancelled in 2009.

11  France contributed an average of 1,651 troops per month between 2005 and 2011, while the United Kingdom and the United States each contributed fewer than 350 troops (UN 2005; 2006; 2007; 2008; 2009; 2010; 2011; 2012).

12  By rapidly intervening in the conflict between Russia and Georgia, Sarkozy also showed that the European Union had the capacity to solve crises in its backyard (Bozo 2012, 262).

13  For instance, from a military point of view, it simply meant that 800 French military personnel were deployed in the *états-majors* of the organisation (Ambrosetti and Chesneau 2012).

14  President de Gaulle initiated France's withdrawal from the integrated structure of NATO in 1966 (de Gaulle 1966).

15  See Resolution 1701.

16  As mentioned in the Introduction, an expression that is often used in a pejorative way to criticise the 'neo-colonial' strategy of France in Africa.

17  Bockel's declarations had received strong criticism from Africa. For instance, Thiam argues that the Gabon authorities immediately reacted to the interview and criticised Bockel for delivering "a despising *cliché* that made African states into vulgar beggars who are endlessly asking for charity from France" (2008, 878).

# 6

# France and the responsibility to protect in a post-Libya era (2012–2017)

In May 2012, after a heated presidential campaign in which he promised to "carry high the voice and values of France to the world" (Hollande 2012b, 36), left-wing candidate François Hollande defeated right-wing President Nicolas Sarkozy. In the meantime, despite the stalemate in Syria, R2P continued to develop and remained an influential international norm. Some detractors argued, however, that the backlash faced after the regime change in Libya and the international community's incapacity to put an end to the atrocities being committed in Syria meant that R2P was dead (see for instance Rieff 2011).

Even though it is undeniable that the norm remained contested, it would, however, be mistaken to underestimate how far it had come. Between 2012 and 2017 the UN Security Council passed forty-seven resolutions referring to the international norm, thereby showing not only its importance, but also the international community's willingness to continue promoting it (Global Centre for the Responsibility to Protect 2019). Additionally, as mentioned in the Introduction, in the specific case of Syria, Glanville is right to argue that despite the international community's failure to put an end to the conflict, we can still detect the influence of the norm, for instance, in the fact that the international community argued that it had to react and tried to justify its failure to do more (2016, 185).

This chapter investigates France's relationship to R2P in the post-Libya era, and more specifically during Hollande's presidency (May 2012 – May 2017). It aims to determine France's position towards – and influence on – the international norm and the rationale behind it; and, in turn, the impact of R2P on France's domestic norm of human protection and its conception and practice of human protection more generally. The first section examines France's support for R2P and argues that Hollande and his various executives were strong promoters of the international norm normatively, diplomatically and militarily. However, it also explains that France's strong involvement was not always beneficial. The second section investigates the reasons behind this strong support. It argues that it can partly be explained by the fact that R2P was beginning to be internalised by France to a certain extent, but that this internalisation did not mean that the domestic norm became obsolete as it remained very influential during Hollande's presidency. Finally, the third section reflects on the shift in France's strategy to intervene for humanitarian purposes. It argues that despite a strong unilateral presence in Africa, it would be mistaken to argue that a return to *Françafrique* or a shift away from multilateralism was taking place.

## France, a strong promoter of R2P

From the beginning of his presidency in May 2012, President Hollande and his various executives were strong promoters of R2P normatively, diplomatically and militarily.

### A strong advocate normatively and diplomatically

The 2013 *livre blanc* on defence and national security showcased the importance of the norm and explained that its promotion was a priority. The 2008 *livre blanc* on defence and national security, written during Sarkozy's mandate, had already acknowledged France's will to fulfil its responsibilities, but the 2013 report went a step further by arguing that "the consensus on the responsibility to protect, as expressed at the UN World Summit in 2005, remains fragile, but France intends to make the consolidation of this principle a priority of its external action" (Guéhenno and Ministère de la Défense 2013, 24).

In light of this objective, France co-drafted more than two-thirds of the forty-seven UN Security Council Resolutions referring to R2P (Staunton 2018, 380): Resolutions 2085, 2100, 2227 and 2295 on Mali; 2093 on Somalia; 2095 on Libya; 2117 and 2220 on small arms and light weapons; 2121, 2127, 2134, 2149, 2196, 2217, 2262, 2301 and 2339 on the CAR; 2139, 2165 and 2258 on Syria; 2150, 2170, 2171, 2185 and 2250 on threats to international peace and security; 2155, 2187, 2206, 2223 and 2290 on South Sudan; 2211, 2277 and 2348 on the DRC; and 2286 on the protection of civilians. It also voted in favour of all of the resolutions which it did not co-draft.[1]

Throughout Hollande's presidency, the French permanent representatives to the UN also continued to emphasise the progress made by R2P over the years. In particular, in 2014 François Delattre declared,

> The General Assembly and the Security Council have made progress in the last few years in order to better implement their responsibility in the

prevention of conflicts and atrocities. We more often include the High Commissioner for Human Rights and the special Rapporteurs in our work. ... We
encourage more frequent participation by the civil society in our meetings.
The protection of civilians is now the priority of many peacekeeping operations. These are positive steps which allow us to be better informed and to
assist states to fulfil their responsibility to protect. (2014)

Nevertheless, there was a will to go further to "overcome the challenges to
R2P's implementation" (Delattre 2016). Gérard Araud argued that strong
cooperation between the various actors involved – such as "the Council of
Human Rights, regional organisations, the International Criminal Court,
humanitarian actors and civil society" – was needed to promote R2P. Similarly, all tools available had to be used (Araud 2012; see also Delattre 2014).

In addition to this broad commitment to better implement R2P, two
measures were made key priorities. The first was an increase in cooperation between the UN Security Council and the International Criminal
Court in order to fight impunity and help create a state of law. Delattre
argued in front of the General Assembly that "impunity de-structures
entire societies" (2015) and declared that "France supports the work of the
International Criminal Court; we thus promote the universality of the
Rome Statute in all the international platforms, in particular at the United
Nations Security Council, and also in our bilateral relations" (2015). He
used the example of the CAR and contended that "the fight against immunity is at the heart of the recovery of the state" (2015).

Second, in addition to promoting stronger cooperation between the UN
Security Council and the International Criminal Court, the various executives pressed for the permanent members of the UN Security Council, or
P5 (France, the United Kingdom, the United States, China and Russia) to
restrain the use of their veto power in mass atrocity situations (Staunton
2018, 380). While the idea had already been suggested by Hubert Védrine,
this proposal became a central goal of Hollande's executives. In September
2013 the French President personally defended the idea in front of the UN
General Assembly by explaining: "the UN has a responsibility to take
action. And whenever our organisation proves to be powerless, it is peace
that pays the price. That is why I am proposing that a code of good conduct
be defined by the permanent members of the Security Council, and that
in the event of a mass crime they can decide to collectively renounce their
veto powers" (Hollande 2013e). Similarly, using the example of Syria,
Delattre argued in front of the General Assembly that "we need to be able
to act. When mass atrocities are committed, the Council must not add the
failure to act to the failure to prevent" (2014).

A few weeks later, on 25 September 2014, the Minister of Foreign
Affairs, Laurent Fabius, co-chaired, with his Mexican counterpart José
Antonio Meade Kuribreña, a ministerial meeting which gathered together

UN member states, UN officials and representatives of international civil society in order to discuss a proposal on veto restraint and the conditions of its implementation (France Diplomatie 2015b). A year later, during the seventieth session of the UN General Assembly held in September 2015, France and Mexico put forward a "Political statement on the suspension of the veto in case of mass atrocities" that was open to signature by the members of the UN (France ONU 2015). The statement explains:

> We ... consider that the Security Council should not be prevented by the use of veto from taking action with the aim of preventing or bringing an end to situations involving the commission of mass atrocities. We underscore that the veto is not a privilege, but an international responsibility. In that respect, we welcome and support the initiative by France, jointly presented with Mexico, to propose a collective and voluntary agreement among the permanent members of the Security Council to the effect that the permanent members would refrain from using the veto in case of mass atrocities. (France ONU 2015)

As of August 2019, the initiative was supported by 102 member states (Permanent Mission of France to the United Nations 2019; see also Global Centre for the Responsibility to Protect 2017).

### A strong support militarily: Mali and the CAR

In addition to this normative and diplomatic support, Hollande's various executives played a key part in the deployment of military force to uphold R2P. France's involvement in Mali (*Opération Serval* and *Opération Barkhane*) and the CAR (*Opération Sangaris*) is particularly worth mentioning (Staunton 2018, 380).

In Mali in March 2012, part of the army led by Captain Amadou Haya Sanogo undertook a *coup d'état* against President Amadou Toumani Touré for failing to stop the spread of Islamist insurgents in the north of the country (which is roughly the size of France) (Tran 2013). As a result, the country became divided into two: the south was governed by an interim government, while the north was controlled by the National Movement for the Liberation of Azawad, which benefited from the support of – and at times, became sidelined by – terrorist factions such as Ansar Dine, the Mouvement pour l'Unicité et le Jihad en Afrique de l'Ouest and Al-Qaïda au Maghreb Islamique (Chafer 2014, 521).

Hollande had originally declared in November 2012 that France would not directly intervene but would simply provide logistical support to the UN intervention (in Soares 2012). However, after France co-drafted Resolution 2085 in December 2012, which "authorise[d] the deployment of an African-led International Support Mission in Mali ... to support the Malian authorities in their primary responsibility to protect the population" (UN Security Council 2012), the President announced a French intervention in January 2013 (Hollande 2013a). A few hours earlier, the French deployment began through *Opération Serval*.

This shift of position can be explained by three factors. First, UN troops would not be ready before September 2013 (Romano Prodi in Hirsch 2013). Second, the situation was deteriorating and the influence of Islamic groups was spreading. Last but not least, the President of Mali asked France for help. Therefore the French President argued that "the very existence of this friendly state, Mali, of the security of its population, and that of our nationals are at stake. ... I have therefore, on behalf of France, responded to the request for assistance from the President of Mali, which was supported by the West African countries" (Hollande 2013a). As Chafer argues, "with troops stationed in Senegal, Côte d'Ivoire and Chad, France [was] the major military power in the region. Faced with the threat of an Islamic takeover, the prospect of a humanitarian disaster and a request from the Malian government to intervene, it would have been extremely difficult for France to refuse" (2014, 524).

*Opération Serval* rapidly achieved its objectives: in September 2013 Araud declared in front of the UN General Assembly, "I welcome the swearing in of the new Malian President following a democratic process. This democratic process was made possible by the intervention of the ECOWAS forces and then the deployment of the UN mission MINUSMA [United Nations Multidimensional Integrated Stabilization Mission in Mali], with our support. The risks of sectarian violence have been addressed, the country has been unified, the state restored and the people protected" (2013). However, he warned the international community about the risks of not remaining involved: "Of course not all problems have been resolved. During this reconstruction phase the international community remains fully responsible for helping the authorities in their efforts to ensure national reconciliation, reform the security sector, promote development and the fight against impunity. This still remains essential in order to prevent past conflicts that have not been fully resolved from fuelling new violence" (Araud 2013). Consequently, *Opération Serval* did not end until August 2014 and was followed by *Opération Barkhane*, which mobilised an average of 1,600 troops per year in Mali (IISS 2015; 2016; 2017). It also aimed to help other African states – Burkina Faso, Mauritania, Niger and Chad – strengthen their development and security strategies (Ministère de la Défense 2017).

In December 2013, only a few months after the intervention in Mali, Hollande announced France's involvement in the CAR (Hollande 2013c).

As discussed in previous chapters, France had already been involved in this African state since October 2002 through *Opération Boali* in order to support the establishment of FOMUC and MICOPAX (Ministère de la Défense 2013). However, the events of 2013 forced the French executive to intensify France's commitment.

In March 2013, the rebel coalition Séléka took control of the majority of the CAR. The rebels argued that the President, François Bozizé, had not undertaken the reforms he had committed himself to in the Libreville Agreement.[2] Michel Djotodia, leader of the Séléka, proclaimed himself President and suspended the Constitution (ICRtoP 2013a). In light of the atrocities committed by the Séléka, this decision sparked much controversy. Self-defence militias known as anti-Balaka formed, and clashes with the Séléka soon occurred, causing large human rights abuses to be committed by both groups (ICRtoP 2013a). These tensions intensified when the anti-Balaka groups were seen as targeting Muslims, while the Séléka was believed to persecute Christians. As the International Coalition for the Responsibility to Protect (ICRtoP) explained, "the roots of the crisis stem[med] from socio-economic and political grievances and [were] not religious, [but] the freshly-made religious divisions add[ed] a dangerous new bent to the latest cycle of violence in CAR" (2013b).

Adama Dieng, Special Advisor to the Secretary General on the Prevention of Genocide, warned the Security Council in November 2013 that "urgent action is required now to stop the on-going serious and widespread violations of human rights that are being committed with impunity against the civilian population and the increase in sectarian attacks across the country" (2013). In January 2014 he went a step further by explaining that "the widespread, unchecked nature of attacks by ex-Séléka and anti-Balaka militia, as well as by armed civilians associated with them, against civilians on the basis of religion or ethnicity constitute crimes against humanity. If not halted, there is a risk of genocide in this country" (2014, 3). He then added, "we need to uphold our responsibility to protect Central Africans from the risk of genocide, war crimes and crimes against humanity yesterday" (2014, 4).

Through Resolution 2127, which was passed in December 2013, the UN Security Council established – among other things – a mandate for the African-led International Support Mission to the Central African Republic (MISCA) to protect civilians and stabilise the country (it was replaced in September 2014 by the United Nations Multidimensional Integrated Stabilization Mission in the Central African Republic, or MINUSCA). It also authorised French forces to be deployed "to take all necessary measures to support MISCA in the discharge of its mandate" (UN Security Council 2013).

Hollande had indeed offered to deploy troops and justified this deployment by arguing, "France will support this operation, it is her duty. Her duty of assistance and of solidarity towards a small country, the Central African Republic, far from here, a friend, the poorest country in the world, a country that calls us to help" (2013c). He received the support of key members of the international community for allowing such a large operation to take place promptly. In particular, Kofi Annan declared that "it was necessary to react and only France could react quickly. I'm glad François Hollande and France have accepted the responsibility entrusted to them by the UN resolution. ... We must acknowledge the work of France in Mali and Central African Republic. If everyone had the same moral impulse, the world would be very different" (2013).

The majority of the French involvement in the CAR took place under *Opération Sangaris*, which was deployed in December 2013 and originally consisted of 1,600 troops before reaching 2,000 in 2014. It had two objectives: to restore security and to prepare for – and support – the deployment of MISCA and MINUSCA (Ministère de la Défense 2016). While Hollande had argued that the intervention would be short (2013c), *Sangaris* was deployed until October 2016. Even though the majority of France's involvement was undertaken through *Opération Sangaris,* France also participated more modestly in EUFOR CAR from April 2014 (it deployed around 250 troops in 2014) and MINUSCA from September 2014 (with a contribution of eight troops in 2014) (IISS 2015; 2016; 2017).

*An active involvement that is not always beneficial: Syria*

France's support of R2P was, however, not always beneficial. Hollande's various executives were very vocal in their criticism of the atrocities being committed in Syria. For instance, Araud argued in front of the UN General Assembly in 2013 that the debate taking place on prevention was "surreal ... since at this very moment, while we're talking about prevention, the Syrian government is in the process of murdering its own people. More than 100,000 people have died. The Syrian government, while showing complete indifference, has used its air assets and then artillery against civilian neighbourhoods, in violation of international humanitarian law, and is now using chemical weapons" (2013; see also Delattre 2015).

However, France played a much more limited role than it had done in Libya, and in fact it can be argued that it contributed to a lack of international consensus on how to respond to the crisis. This can be explained by the fact that Hollande's executives argued that a political transition could not include the Syrian President (see for instance Hollande in *Les Echos* 2015). Aware of the backlash faced by the P3 after the intervention in Libya, Araud justified this position to the international community by arguing that "to request the removal of Bashar al Assad today does not equal to promoting regime change, it is recognising that those who perpetrate war and crimes against humanity towards thousands of individuals no longer have any legitimacy" (2012). Similarly, Hollande explained in 2017 that "if France was to say that there could be no talks in Geneva as long as Bashar [al-Assad] is still there, it would be inadmissible. But it has become necessary to assert that he has to leave at the end of the process" (in *France Info* 2017). However, as Ralph explains, "the insistence [of France, the United Kingdom and the United States] on regime change came at the expense of realizable ends ('ends in view') that were valuable if not ideal" (2018, 191); this leads him to support Jean-Marie Guéhenno's view that "for some countries, the fall of Assad would prove to be a much more important goal than a quick end of the war" (in Ralph 2018, 193).

Additionally, despite this lack of consensus – and the role played by France in this deadlock – Hollande and his executive became willing to intervene militarily in August 2013. They indeed actively prepared for a military intervention following the use of chemical weapons by the Assad regime. France had already recognised the national coalition as the legitimate representative of the Syrian nation in September 2012, and it provided humanitarian and material support to the opposition (Hollande 2013b), but the President declared that he was thinking about a military intervention: "the chemical massacre of Damascus cannot go unanswered. … France is ready to punish those who have taken the unspeakable decision to gas innocent people. … international law must evolve over time. It cannot be a pretext for allowing mass massacres to be perpetrated. That is why I recognise the principle of 'the responsibility to protect' civilian populations that the United Nations General Assembly voted for in 2005" (Hollande 2013b).

The French proposal to intervene militarily was rapidly taken off the table by the John Kerry–Sergei Lavrov disarmament accord, yet it remained a possibility throughout Hollande's presidency, even if the crisis took many twists and turns, not least the fact that the Islamic State of Iraq and the Levant (ISIL) became the main enemy. For instance, when President Donald Trump of the United States authorised air strikes in response to the chemical attack undertaken by Assad's regime in April 2017, Hollande declared that the Americans "were made to understand that the strike was approved, and that if they had asked, we would have considered the possibility of a joint operation" (in *France Info* 2017). This approach was again criticised for having the potential to divide the international community even further and promoting an option that would worsen the humanitarian situation in the country since even if the strikes were mainly targeted at strategic sites, the Assad regime would probably retaliate (see for instance *Guardian* 2017).

Consequently, throughout Hollande's presidency, France was a strong supporter of R2P diplomatically, normatively and militarily. The various executives' willingness to restrain the use of the veto power in mass atrocity situations and the rapid authorisation of key interventions in Mali and the CAR were particularly noteworthy. However, France's robust understanding of R2P was not always beneficial, as illustrated by France's approach to the Syrian conflict.

### The end of France's domestic norm of human protection?

France's commitment to human protection – and R2P more specifically – having been explored, it is interesting to analyse the reasons driving its commitment. The sections "The growing influence of R2P" and "The ongoing influence of France's domestic norm of human protection" below focus on the extent of the role played by both R2P and France's domestic norm of human protection, but first it is important to emphasise that France's active role can again not be fully understood without taking into account the changing domestic and international contexts. First, it can be argued that promoting France as a key actor of human protection became a necessity for Hollande because France's central role in the field of human protection was one of the few policies that seemed to increase his low approval rates. Even though the latter had been dropping since his election, they did indeed begin to increase for the first time after the intervention in Mali (Leclerc 2013).

Second, France's key role in human protection had for decades allowed the various executives to promote the idea that France is the 'homeland of human rights' and 'more than a middle sized power', which are both central components of its identity and directly impact its international status. During Hollande's presidency, promoting this representation of France seemed more important than ever when France lost some of its leadership in Europe and the UN Security Council. In particular, Angela Merkel led the discussions on the refugee 'crisis' in Europe and the stalemate on the UN Security Council on Syria meant that France had little room to act. It could thus not afford to be stigmatised in other areas of human protection (Staunton 2018, 387).

Third and finally, as the section "A return to *Françafrique*?" explains in more depth, France had to face key budgetary constraints because of the financial crisis. In spite of this, as Fabius argued, the executive at the time was determined to show that France would "guarantee its independence and its action capacity in a new world and despite the fact that we are limited by strong budgetary constraints. We will thus be able to remain a 'power of influence' whose voice is expected, heard and respected" (2012). In light of the clarity of the domestic and international contexts, the chapter now turns to the specific role played by the two norms.

## The growing influence of R2P

The development of R2P and France's extensive support of the international norm during Hollande's presidency suggest that R2P had a growing influence on France (Staunton 2018, 380–381). This influence can be seen in the more conventional way in which Hollande's executives defined the international norm. It is indeed interesting to note that in contrast to their predecessors, Hollande's various executives avoided commenting on the origins of R2P, thereby contradicting the claim that R2P's origins lay in France's diplomatic efforts in the 1980s (see, for instance, Guéhenno and Ministère de la Défense 2013, 24).

This shift can partly be explained by a will to avoid endangering France's rank by making sure that France would be seen as a key actor of human protection, rather than being criticised for its controversial position. Promoting a broad – and controversial – understanding of R2P would indeed have isolated France and endangered the potential support of the international community for some of its key proposals, such as the restraint of the P5's veto power.

However, it also suggests that the internalisation of R2P had begun to take place. As explained in the Introduction, studying the internalisation of a norm is challenging: "because they are not controversial, ... these norms are often not the centrepiece of political debate" (Finnemore and Sikkink 1998, 904). However, this argument is supported by the fact that, as mentioned previously, R2P was endorsed in key domestic policies such as the 2013 *livre blanc* (Guéhenno and Ministère de la Défense 2013, 24). Additionally, Hollande's executives continued to promote a better and stronger implementation of the norm, for instance by developing, for the first time, a concrete proposal to restrain the veto power to address the crimes R2P aims to prevent.

Moreover, France's new interventions for humanitarian purposes during that period were mainly limited to cases specifically defined as falling under R2P. Additionally, crises such as those in Syria demonstrated that Hollande felt obliged to act in light of R2P: for instance, as mentioned earlier, following the chemical attacks in August 2013, he justified the promotion of retaliatory air strikes by declaring, "I recognise the principle of 'the responsibility to protect' civilian populations that the United Nations General Assembly voted for in 2005" (Hollande 2013b). Yet his reluctance to intervene unilaterally despite his will to respond to the attacks and oust Assad showed that he felt constrained in what he could and could not do. As mentioned in Chapter 1, this growing influence was not surprising, for while the international norm can have a limited impact on a state like France during the early stages of its development (especially if the state has a related – yet distinct – domestic norm of human protection), its influence is expected to strengthen as it develops, as was the case with R2P during Hollande's presidency.

*The ongoing influence of France's domestic norm of human protection*

The beginning of the internalisation of R2P in France, however, did not mean that France's domestic norm became irrelevant or obsolete. Like their predecessors, Hollande's various executives partly justified France's commitment to human protection and involvement in key interventions by arguing that it was France's duty in light of its history, values and rank. For instance, in 2013, Hollande explained:

> France must give itself one objective and one objective only: at all times, ensure its security, meet the expectations of its partners and its allies and preserve peace in the world. This is France's vocation there because it is a permanent member of the United Nations Security Council, it has this responsibility. It is France's vocation because it is a founding country of the European Union, it carries an ideal of peace between nations. It is France's vocation because it holds, in light of its history, a military and diplomatic capacity, which it puts at the service of its own interests ... and of international law. ... "The great countries are great for having wanted to be", said General de Gaulle. France always wants to be a great nation. Not for herself, no! To carry the values of the Republic. (2013e)

This influence was facilitated by the strength of the domestic norm, but also by the fact that while R2P gained strength during Hollande's presidency, it remained contested.

Therefore in Mali, Hollande argued that "France will always be there when it comes not to its fundamental interests, but to the rights of a population, that of Mali, who want to live freely and in democracy" (2013a). Likewise in the CAR, the President justified France's involvement by arguing that it was "France's duty. ... France is expected there in order to prevent a humanitarian catastrophe. It will be there" (Hollande 2013c).

The ongoing influence of France's domestic norm of human protection also led Hollande's various executives to sustain a broad understanding of the scope of R2P. First, even though the World Summit Outcome Document did not refer to R2P as containing three responsibilities – to prevent, to react and to rebuild – as the original ICISS report did, Hollande and his executives continued to embrace this approach. The 2008 *livre blanc* on European and foreign policy had already argued that R2P "entails a triple dimension: responsibility to prevent, responsibility to intervene, if need be with armed forces, and the responsibility to reconstruct" (Juppé and Schweitzer 2008, 48). Similarly, in 2012 the French Permanent Representative to the UN reminded the General Assembly that "besides the responsibility to act, ... R2P includes, with the same obligation, the responsibility to prevent and to rebuild" (Araud 2012; see also Araud 2013).

Additionally, as in Sarkozy's presidency, while the importance of prevention continued to be emphasised, the necessity to use force in certain cases was also underlined. For instance, in 2012 Araud mentioned that France had named an R2P focal point for the promotion of prevention and suggested that the next UN Secretary General's report should be on prevention. However, he warned the General Assembly that "the idea of a sequencing between the three pillars and the use of peaceful means, and the definition of pre-established criteria before action, would be simple excuses for inaction" (2012). Similarly, he argued, "we shouldn't forget that prevention may involve the use of force" and used the intervention in Mali as an example (Araud 2013). This robust approach to R2P was visible in the interventions undertaken by Hollande's various executives in Mali and the CAR, and also in their approach to the Syrian conflict.

Last but not least, France continued to promote a broad understanding of the four crimes. In particular, it aimed to promote a wide understanding of what constitutes a war crime in order to include the protection of cultural heritage under R2P. Referring to the destruction by ISIL of key archaeological sites such as Nimrud, Hatra, Nineveh and Mosul in Iraq, Hollande's various executives argued that it amounted to "cultural cleansing, which could constitute a war crime" (France Diplomatie 2015a). Consequently, on 2–3 December 2016 it co-organised with the United Arab Emirates a conference in Abu Dhabi on the protection of cultural heritage which led to a pledge to create an international fund dedicated to finance the protection of endangered cultural heritage and to establish a network that could temporarily welcome endangered heritage (France Diplomatie 2016). Additionally, after co-sponsoring Resolution 2199 in 2015,[3] it co-drafted with Italy what became Resolution 2347 on the "destruction and trafficking of cultural heritage by terrorist groups and in situations of armed conflict" in March 2017 (UN Security Council 2017a). UNESCO's Director-General Irina Bokova argued that the resolution was "historic" (in UN Security Council 2017b, 3). This norm entrepreneurship reflects the influence of the domestic norm in terms of the wide understanding of the scope of R2P, but also shows how in light of the domestic norm,

France felt compelled to influence the evolution and development of the international norm.

## The evolution of France's practice of human protection in perspective

Having clarified the reasons for France's involvement, it is important to reflect on how France implemented human protection during Hollande's presidency. Its heavy commitment in Mali and the CAR may indeed suggest some key changes in the way Hollande and his various executives decided to intervene to protect in comparison to their predecessors, but these changes need to be put into perspective.

*A return to* Françafrique?

In terms of the area chosen for interventions for humanitarian purposes, Graph 12 suggests a strong preference for Africa. In contrast to Sarkozy's presidency, when an average of 3,118 troops per month were deployed in Africa, 2,417 in Asia, 1,755 in Europe, 1,474 in the Middle East and 2 in Latin America (IISS 2005; 2007; 2008; 2009; 2010; 2011; 2012), Hollande and his executives deployed 4,176 troops per year in Africa, 571 in Asia, 149 in Europe, 974 in the Middle East and 1 in Latin America (IISS 2013; 2014; 2015; 2016; 2017).[4]

On the basis of these observations, it could be argued that there was a return to *Françafrique*. However, this would be mistaken. On his first visit to Africa in October 2012, in the emblematic city of Dakar where Sarkozy had pronounced his very controversial speech in 2007, Hollande explained that "the time of *Françafrique* has passed: there is France and there is Africa. There is the partnership between France and Africa, with relations based on respect, clarity and solidarity" (2012a).[5] Following this speech, which clearly aimed to distance his African policy from Sarkozy's, the French President initially declared that France would not intervene in Mali but would instead provide logistical support (Hollande in Soares 2012). However, as explained previously, the deterioration of the situation (in particular the growing influence of the terrorists), the delays in the deployment of the UN operation and the request of the President of Mali left the French President little room not to act. As Hollande argued, "we were the only state which had the military capacity to act immediately next to our African friends" (Hollande 2013d). Similar circumstances led France to intervene in the CAR.

In order not to be accused of neo-colonialism or being promoters of *Françafrique,* Hollande's executives continued to emphasise that France

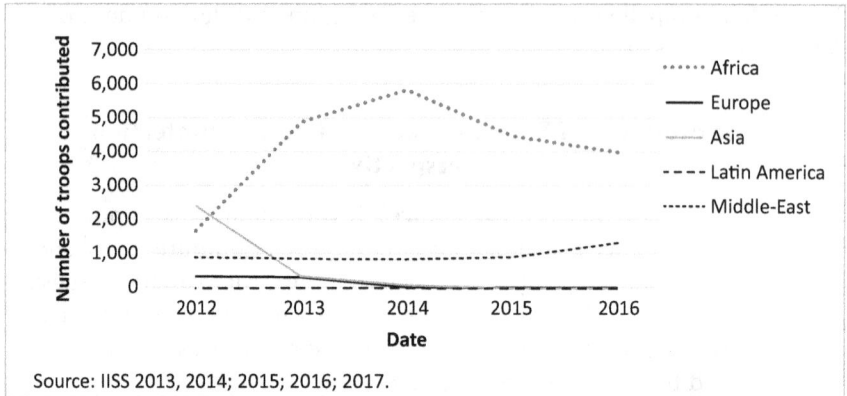

Source: IISS 2013, 2014; 2015; 2016; 2017.

Note: This graph does not take into account troops deployed outside France owing to security agreements or headquarters situated overseas. It reflects the troop contribution in November of each year and therefore is not representative of the whole year. Additionally, it takes into account only troops on the ground.

**Graph 12** France's troop contributions to interventions for humanitarian purposes by geographic area, 2012–16

was acting with the support of the international community and was not replacing Africans, but was acting with them (see for instance Hollande 2013b; 2013d). Therefore once the core objectives of *Opération Serval* had been achieved in Mali, it was replaced by *Opération Barkhane* in August 2014. *Barkhane* aimed to help "the partner states acquire the capacity to ensure their security autonomously. It is based on a global approach (political, security and development)" (Ministère de la Défense 2017). It was thus extended to Mauritania, Niger, Chad and Burkina Faso, which had created the G5 Sahel with Mali in February 2014 to boost cooperation on development and regional security (Ministère de la Défence 2017). In 2016 the operation amounted to "3,500 troops organised around two battlegroups based in Gao, in Mali, and N'Djamena, in Chad, with a network of forward-operating bases and combat outposts" (IISS 2017, 79). Additionally, when allegations that some French soldiers from *Opération Santargis* had been involved in sexual abuse, the French executive turned to the UN to investigate these accusations. President Hollande argued that if they were true, it would be "the honour of France that would be questioned" and that "exemplary sanctions would be imposed because there cannot be impunity" (in *L'Express* 2016).

Similarly, when reflecting on France's reduced commitment elsewhere, it is important to take into account the international and domestic context at the time. As mentioned previously, R2P was beginning to impact when and where France did or did not intervene. Additionally, from a domestic point of view, France was facing two key challenges that impacted its capacity to intervene abroad for humanitarian purposes. The first was the financial crisis, which put considerable pressure on the French defence budget. In order to reduce the public spending deficit, Hollande had announced strong austerity measures – which included cuts within the defence budget – in order to save €50 billion (IISS 2015, 64). Additionally, the various terrorist attacks that took place in France from January 2015 onwards meant that up to 13,000 troops had to be deployed within France to support the *Plan Vigipirate*, its national security alert system, and *Opération Sentinelle*, the anti-terrorist operation undertaken on French territory, and consequently these troops were not available for deployment overseas (IISS 2017, 78). Hollande's executives could thus no longer commit troops worldwide, especially when a large number were deployed in the CAR and Mali, and others were taking part in the international coalition fighting ISIL in Iraq from 2014.

As a consequence, as in the past, France remained committed to playing an important role in human protection via other means. For instance, in addition to promoting the training of peacekeeping forces in Africa, it promoted a peaceful resolution of the Israeli-Palestinian conflict. In fact, this was one of the few points of foreign policy that was mentioned in Hollande's campaign manifesto (Hollande 2012b, 37). At a peace conference organised in Paris in January 2017, the French President criticised President-elect Trump's proposal to recognise Jerusalem as Israel's capital (*La Croix* 2017) and reaffirmed his will to see the international community work towards the creation of two independent states: "the solution of two states is not the dream of yesterday's system, it is still, it is always the future goal of the international community in all its diversity" (Hollande 2017).

*A shift away from multilateralism?*

In terms of the institutional framework chosen to undertake interventions for humanitarian purposes, there was a strong preference for unilateral interventions. The new *livre blanc* on defence and national security published in 2013 hinted that this type of operation would be necessary:

> The evolution of the strategic context could lead our country to have to take the initiative in operations, or to assume, more often than in the past, a substantial role in the responsibilities involved in the conduct of the military action. France therefore makes the principle of strategic autonomy the basis of its strategy in relation to intervention abroad. It will develop the critical capacities that allow initiative and autonomous action, and also the capacity to take along its allies and partners. (Guéhenno and Ministère de la Défense 2013, 83)

Sarkozy had also carried out this type of intervention during his mandate: an average of 2,117 troops per year were deployed unilaterally between 2005 and 2011 (IISS 2005; 2007; 2008; 2009; 2010; 2011; 2012). However, as illustrated in Chapter 5, France also actively intervened through NATO, the UN and the European Union during Sarkozy's presidency, whereas it did not do so during Hollande's.

This apparent preference for unilateral interventions nevertheless needs to be challenged. First, the interventions in Mali and the CAR took place because the UN would not be able to deploy troops for several months and France had been asked for help by both states. Additionally, Hollande and his executives made sure that France's interventions were endorsed by the UN Security Council or, at the very least, were supported by the majority of the international community. These interventions also involved the participation of other countries where possible. For instance, in Mali, "during *Opération Serval*'s main operational phase, France was dependent on European, Canadian and US support assets for some key tasks, mainly strategic lift, air-to-air refuelling, logistics and intelligence" (IISS 2014, 66). Similarly in the CAR, French troops worked closely with MISCA and MINUSCA.

Additionally, while Graph 13 might seem to suggest that France considerably reduced its commitment to NATO and the European Union/OSCE to favour unilateral interventions, this idea needs to be put into

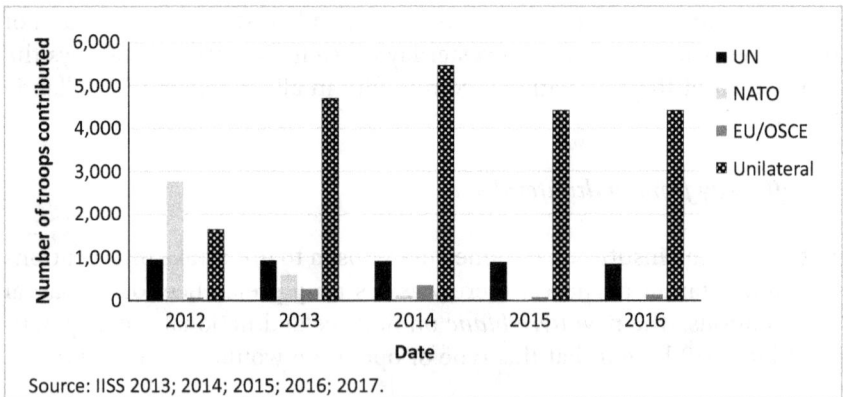

Source: IISS 2013; 2014; 2015; 2016; 2017.

Note: This graph does not take into account troops deployed outside France owing to security agreements or headquarters situated overseas. It reflects the troop contribution in November of each year and therefore is not representative of the whole year. Additionally, it takes into account only troops on the ground.

**Graph 13** France's troop contributions to interventions for humanitarian purposes by institutional framework, 2012–16

perspective: rather than showing a withdrawal by France, it reflects the fact that these organisations did not undertake major interventions for humanitarian purposes during that time because they were focusing on prevention or fighting terrorism instead. Given that the graph shows only France's participation in interventions that were undertaken for humanitarian purposes, it does not reflect its overall involvement with these organisations.

France was indeed committed to continually building the capacities of NATO, the UN and the European Union to efficiently prevent and respond to humanitarian crises. Hollande and his executives reaffirmed France's commitment to NATO (see for instance Fabius 2012; Hollande 2016) and emphasised their determination to develop the organisation's capacity to "face different types of conflicts, ranging from collective defence to the undertaking of stabilisation operations" (Guéhenno and Ministère de la Défense 2013, 62–63). France also remained committed to supporting the interventions that the organisation was undertaking for humanitarian purposes. For instance, even though Hollande promised the withdrawal of French troops from Afghanistan by December 2012 (2012b, 37),[6] France remained involved until the end of the operation: "1,200 troops remained in Afghanistan in 2013 to help train the Afghan army, and if they [were] required by the US for combat duty, [were] available. Four hundred French troops [remained] alongside their allies until the final withdrawal date of December 2014" (IISS 2013, 98).

However, Hollande argued during a visit from Jens Stoltenberg, NATO's Secretary General, that the Alliance's primary role was Article 5 of the Treaty, which guarantees that an attack against one member of the Alliance is equivalent to an attack against all its members. He thus explained that "NATO must also remain a forum where the Allies talk about all security issues, but intervening everywhere is out of the question; it is not its function, it is not its mandate and it is not its interest. Yes, we must address what is happening in the Middle East, in Africa, terrorist threats, but it is not NATO's … vocation to intervene, even if on a case-by-case basis there is support that can be provided to countries which might request it" (2016).

Therefore, as mentioned previously, Hollande's executives promoted restraint of the use of the veto power by the P5 so that the UN Security Council would no longer be limited in its capacity to address mass atrocity situations. Similarly, in addition to contributing to the European Union's limited interventions (for instance, France played a central role in EUFOR CAR), they worked towards the development of a European defence and foreign policy. Fabius had argued in 2012 that it was necessary: "the Libyan crisis has shown that Europeans can play their part in the successful management of a conflict. We handled most of the risks, responsibilities and military contributions. But this crisis has also shown that we still need the support of the United States" (2012). Likewise, the 2013 *livre blanc* encouraged the European Union to promote prevention and joint interventions abroad by explaining that "security in the countries from the Sahel area to equatorial Africa, the fight against any form of terrorism, the peace process in the Middle East, assistance for the success of political transition in some Arab countries, the ending of the conflicts in the Caucasus, the consolidation of peace in the Balkans and notably in Kosovo are all subjects requiring the European Union to develop its actions" (Guéhenno and Ministère de la Défense 2013, 65–66).

While acknowledging the European Union's growing capacity and experience in addressing key crises and maintaining peace, the *livre blanc* deplored the fact that the regional institution's operations remained too small or too short, or were undertaken only in support of other interventions. It argued that a lack of political will, an inefficient use of the means available to the European Union Commission and member states and a lack of coordination between civil and military means were preventing the European Union from going further (Guéhenno and Ministère de la Défense 2013, 66). It thus explained that France would do everything in its power to remedy these issues, starting with bilateral cooperation with other key member states such as the United Kingdom and Germany, the pooling and sharing of resources between member states and the development of a clear European Union strategy (Guéhenno and Ministère de la Défense 2013, 66–67). These objectives were reaffirmed throughout Hollande's presidency. For instance, at the European Union Summit in Bratislava in 2016, Hollande (and Merkel) promoted key initiatives such as the easier funding of European Union operations abroad, the pooling of resources between members and the establishment of a European Union military headquarters (IISS 2017, 80).

Additionally, in order to facilitate the European Union's capacity to intervene, Hollande's executives, like their predecessors, promoted a stronger cooperation between NATO and the European Union. As the 2013 *livre blanc* argued, "NATO and the European Union are not competing with one another. These two organisations are complementary, whether we are talking about interventions abroad or initiatives such as mutualisation and capacity sharing (pooling and sharing and small defence)" (Guéhenno and Ministère de la Défense 2013, 63). Similarly, in 2016, during a visit from Stoltenberg, Hollande argued that "the alliance, and it is also a constant position of France, must continue to develop its relationship with the European Union. I am in favour of a European defence, and

I want the defence of Europe to first be assured by the Europeans in the framework of the Alliance, so the relationship between NATO and the European Union is essential" (2016).

## Conclusion

During the post-Libya era, Hollande and his various executives played a central role in the promotion of R2P normatively, diplomatically and militarily. Their proposals to restrain the use of the veto power by the P5 and promote a responsibility to protect cultural heritage, and France's rapid interventions in Mali and the CAR, were particularly noteworthy, even though France's involvement was not always beneficial, as is illustrated by its position on Syria. In terms of France's practice of human protection, its efforts were particularly focused on Africa because of the domestic and international contexts and the fact that France had been directly asked for help. Additionally, France did not hesitate to intervene unilaterally, while the UN gathered troops, and continued to promote the European Union's capacity to intervene to protect after reminding NATO that it could not aim to intervene "everywhere".

While France strongly supported the norm during Hollande's presidency and consequently contributed to its strengthening, it is interesting to note that R2P's influence on France was also growing. As explained earlier in this chapter, France was indeed beginning to internalise the international norm. This was to be expected since, as mentioned in Chapter 1, while an international norm can have a limited impact on a state like France during the early stages of its development, especially since France has a related domestic norm of human protection, its influence is expected to strengthen as it develops. However, the fact that this process of internalisation had begun did not mean that France's domestic norm was replaced by the international one. The domestic norm indeed remained very influential and contributed to France's support of R2P, its wide understanding of the scope of the international norm and its will to influence its development. The ongoing influence of the domestic norm was facilitated by its strength, but also by the fact that while R2P was strengthened during Hollande's presidency, it remained contested.

## Notes

1  Resolutions 2109, 2228, 2241, 2252, 2296, 2304, 2327 and 2340 on Sudan and South Sudan; 2317 on Somalia; 2254 and 2332 on Syria; and 2237 and 2288 on Liberia were not co-drafted by France.

2 The Libreville Agreement was signed in January 2013 after the Séléka overthrew President Bozizé for not doing enough in the north-east of the country to fight instability and promote accountability (ICRtoP 2013a).
3 Resolution 2199 "condemn[ed] the destruction of cultural heritage in Iraq and Syria" and "decide[d] that all Member States shall take appropriate steps to prevent the trade in Iraqi and Syrian cultural property" (UN Security Council 2015).
4 This data takes into account only troops on the ground.
5 Hollande had already made this commitment during the presidential campaign (2012b, 37).
6 France had been actively involved in ISAF which aimed "to assist the Afghan Interim Authority in the maintenance of security in Kabul and its surrounding areas, so that the Afghan Interim Authority as well as the personnel of the United Nations can operate in a secure environment" (UN Security Council 2001).

# Conclusion

This book has argued that in order to fully understand the development of international principles and norms of human protection such as humanitarian intervention and R2P, we have to analyse France's conception of, and contribution to, human protection since the 1980s. To do so, the book has explained that we need to analyse a tale of two norms: France's domestic norm of human protection on the one hand, and the dominant international principle or norm of human protection at the time on the other. In order to fulfil this goal, it has developed a theoretical framework in which to analyse their historical interaction as the principles and norms evolved. By doing this, the book has brought together human protection, France's foreign policy and International Relations theory and has made key contributions to each field. This Conclusion provides an overview of these contributions while summarising the core findings of the book.

## Human protection

As mentioned in the Introduction, France's role in human protection has been overlooked by the existing literature even though France is one of the five permanent members of the UN Security Council and a key European power, and has made important contributions to human protection since the 1980s. This shortfall has prevented us from fully understanding how key principles and norms of human protection have emerged and developed, and more specifically the impact – both positive and negative – that individual states like France can have – and have had – throughout their development. It has also stopped us from analysing the growing influence of these international principles and norms on states like France as they developed. By providing the first comprehensive account of France's relationship to human protection since the 1980s by investigating the impact that the interconnected yet distinct domestic and international norms of human protection have had on each other over time, the book has begun to correct this shortfall and suggests that we must expand the focus of the literature to other non-Anglo-Saxon states which are supportive of human protection if we are to ever gain a full understanding of human protection.[1]

Before discussing the growing influence of international norms such as R2P on France, it is important to reflect on what the book has taught us in terms of France's influence on human protection. It has argued that France has played a central role in human protection since the 1980s. France's role has at times been beneficial to the development of human protection principles and norms and the practice of human protection, but not always.

More specifically, the book has explained that during the late 1980s and early 1990s, France played a role as norm entrepreneur in the emergence of humanitarian intervention by promoting key resolutions to the UN General Assembly and Security Council and actively intervening world-wide for humanitarian purposes. As Gareth Evans argues, France's conception of human protection "had real resonance in the new circumstances of the post-cold war world" (2008a, 32). Additionally, throughout the 1990s France, under the leadership of François Mitterrand (1981–95) and then Jacques Chirac (1995–2007), helped shape the way the international community practised human protection through its military contribution to international interventions undertaken for humanitarian purposes.

However, during Chirac's presidency, even though France remained committed to intervening for humanitarian purposes, its normative contribution was more limited than in the late 1980s and early 1990s. During the second half of the 1990s, while assuming that the right to intervene already existed and was here to stay, France did not stop the norm contestation faced by humanitarian intervention and indeed even contributed to it, for instance by undertaking the controversial *Opération Turquoise* in Rwanda, and supporting coercive interventions in former Yugoslavia. Similarly, because, as Evans argues in clear and unambiguous terms, "the French were part of the problem" (2013b) by the end of the 1990s, France was excluded from the ICISS and therefore played no role in the emergence of R2P. In the early 2000s, however, France demonstrated that its voice still mattered despite its lack of norm entrepreneurship of R2P, in particular by making sure that the Iraq War did not receive the authorisation of the Security Council. It also intervened heavily for humanitarian purposes.

From 2006, Nicolas Sarkozy's various executives (2007–12), began to actively support R2P both diplomatically and militarily. This active support was not always beneficial to the development of the international norm. As the cases of Myanmar/Burma and Libya showed, France indeed ended up endangering its development – at times – by promoting a broad under-standing of R2P. In view of the influence of France's domestic norm of human protection since the 1980s and its will to promote its status, and in light of the broad definition of R2P in 2005, the promotion by France of a broad understanding of R2P was not surprising. It demonstrated, however, the impact a state like France could have during the development of the international norm, even if it was not involved in its emergence.

After Libya, François Hollande (2012–17) and his executives became – to a certain extent – a more traditional promoter of the international norm since they no longer argued that R2P had French roots. France's support of R2P during that period was diplomatic and military, but also normative thanks to its key proposals such as the restraint of the veto power. Hollande's various executives, however, also continued to promote a wide understanding of the scope of the norm in order to ensure that it was implemented comprehensively and robustly.

## France's foreign policy

The next key contribution of this book lies in the fact that it reshapes our understanding of France's foreign policy and allows us not only to better comprehend its past and contemporary foreign policy, but also to antici-pate its future one. By shedding light on the importance of France's domes-tic norm of human protection over the years on the one hand and investigating the growing impact of international norms such as R2P on France's conception and practice of human protection on the other, it provides a new lens through which to understand and analyse France's foreign policy. As explained in more depth in the next section, "Inter-national Relations theory," R2P began to restrict where and how France could respond to mass atrocities during Sarkozy's presidency, and its influ-ence progressively strengthened throughout Hollande's mandate.

Additionally, analysing the influence of France's domestic norm, which emerged in the 1980s, helps us to better understand France's commitment to protect, the various executives' broad understanding of human protec-tion, and the fact that France only promoted the creation of a right to intervene in the domestic affairs of a state in order to fulfil its perceived duty to protect.

The book has also provided a better understanding of the relationship between various aspects of France's identity and its foreign policy. The various executives' obsession with being seen as 'the homeland of human rights', as well as with France's rank, has indeed contributed to France being actively involved in human protection. But as illustrated throughout the book, the executives' obsession with France's rank also influenced how they intervened for humanitarian purposes. One could argue that states will always endeavour to design their foreign policy in a way that promotes their image and status internationally, but as Grosser argues, "for [France], prestige constitutes an end in itself" (1995, 64). As a consequence, France's practice of human protection evolved over time in terms of the breadth of its interventions, the institutional framework chosen to intervene and the strategy used in the field in order to prevent situations where promoting human protection and promoting France's rank constituted conflicting goals. In other words, while its commitment to human rights has partly explained why France wanted to play a central role in human protection, the obsession with its status has explicated not only its active role, but also how it has implemented human protection.

This leads us to another contribution when it comes to France's foreign policy. By analysing France's military interventions for humanitarian purposes – which represent the majority of the interventions it has undertaken abroad – the book has revealed broader lessons in terms of France's priorities and its relations with global institutions, particularly the UN, the European Union and NATO. It has shown France's military commitment to NATO in light of the means available to the organisation and the strong mandate of the operations it undertakes for humanitarian purposes. Similarly, it has demonstrated France's will to promote the European Union's foreign policy and its capacity to intervene for humanitarian purposes over time. Furthermore, it has showed that even though France avoided intervening through the UN for humanitarian purposes from the mid-1990s onwards because of the lack of means and the weaker mandates its interventions faced, it has considered it to be the central platform for discussing international issues. It has also been willing to support its interventions, either by providing limited troop contributions or via more substantial unilateral operations which support UN missions without being restrained by their narrow mandates.

The book has also demonstrated both variation and continuity in terms of where France has intervened for humanitarian purposes over the years. At the beginning of the 1990s, Mitterrand and his various executives favoured intervening worldwide. In the second half of the 1990s, in light of the change of domestic and international contexts and in order to fulfil France's perceived duty to intervene to protect without endangering its rank, Chirac's executives focused on Europe. The 2000s witnessed some continuity with the second half of the 1990s, with a strong focus on Europe, but the executives also began renewing their interventions in the Middle East and Africa. Hollande's presidency was more unusual since France mainly intervened militarily for humanitarian purposes in Africa, mainly because of domestic and international constraints, rather than because of a will to resume *Françafrique* practices.

## International Relations theory

The book also makes a contribution to the literature on norm diffusion. It has emphasised the importance of taking into account the interplay between related yet distinct domestic and international principles and norms and has shown how this can be achieved by putting forward an innovative theoretical framework which builds on, yet overcomes some of the weaknesses of, the norm life cycle and the norm circulation models respectively put forward by Finnemore and Sikkink (1998) and Acharya (2015).[2] It has argued that four key phases can be identified in the relationship between two specific domestic and international norms: entrepreneurship, localisation, subsidiarity and internalisation. Because norms are not static but rather are in constant evolution, these stages should not be seen as a unidirectional representation of the development of norms; instead each stage should be seen as one segment of their development that will be repeated as the international context evolves and/or new forms of contestation emerge. Even though this framework was designed specifically to study France's relationship to human protection over time, it can be used to study the interplay of other domestic and international norms and therefore makes a broader contribution to the literature on norm diffusion and IR theory more generally.

With regard to the focus of this book, the framework allowed us to better understand the emergence and development of key international principles and norms such as humanitarian intervention and R2P, since it allowed us to take into account the role played by specific states like France. It also helped us understand the way France has been influenced by these international normative developments as they strengthen. Following the discussion of the influence of France on humanitarian intervention and R2P in the section "Human protection", this section discusses the impact that these international principles and norms have had on France's conception and practice of human protection.

During the 1990s and early 2000s, while France's domestic norm of human protection was very influential on the various executives, the same cannot be said about humanitarian intervention and R2P. This lack of influence on France is not surprising since the impact of an international principle or norm on a state like France is only expected to be proportional to its strength, especially when a related domestic norm exists and is influential. Yet, as explained in the book, humanitarian intervention was a relatively weak international principle in the 1990s and R2P was only a concept in the early 2000s.

Things began to change, however, when R2P started gaining international traction during Sarkozy's presidency and was consolidated during Hollande's. During Sarkozy's presidency, R2P began to restrict where France could intervene, while during Hollande's, it began to be internalised to a certain extent and thus influenced not only where France was involved but also why it was involved. Once again, this was to be expected since, as explained in more depth in Chapter 1, while a state like France can play a strong role in the emergence and development of an international norm like R2P, its influence progressively reduces as the international norm becomes stronger. In contrast, while an international norm can have a limited impact on a state like France during the early stages of its development – especially if that state has a related domestic norm – its influence will strengthen as it develops.

The beginning of the internalisation of R2P, however, did not signal the death of the domestic norm. The norm remained influential during both Sarkozy's and Hollande's presidencies: it influenced why France promoted a broad understanding of the international norm's scope, and why it was involved in human protection – including why it wanted to play a central role in the development and evolution of R2P. The ongoing influence of the domestic norm was facilitated by its strength and also by the fact that while R2P gained traction during Hollande's mandate, it remained contested.

The extent of the book's theoretical contribution also lies in the fact that it has examined a case in which an international principle or norm (humanitarian intervention and R2P) interacts with a state (France) that is positively disposed to it, but still has its own interpretation of what it should entail and how it ought to be understood by the rest of the international community in light of the influence of its own related yet distinct domestic norm (France's domestic norm of human protection). In this respect, it contrasts with the contributions by Amitav Acharya and others, who have tended to focus on cases in which states are resistant to or wary of the international principle or norm, and has thus provided a different and valuable view of how norms develop and interact.

## The way forward

These contributions can help us to better anticipate the future. Given the strong impact of France's domestic norm of human protection on the various executives over time and also the growing influence of R2P, it can be assumed that France will remain committed to human protection in the future. When it decides to intervene militarily, it is likely to do so in a way that will help promote – or at the very least, not endanger – its rank, for instance, by collaborating with organisations such as NATO or by intervening unilaterally in support of multilateral operations, and by relying on strong mandates. It will also probably continue to promote the European Union's capacity to respond to atrocity situations.

In terms of France's specific relationship with R2P, it is likely that France's domestic norm of human protection will continue to exist in parallel with the international norm and that the two norms will – at times, although less often – clash with one another. The internalisation of the international norm suggests that France will keep promoting the international norm and will increasingly be influenced in terms of when and where it can intervene to protect.

However, in view of the ongoing influence of the domestic norm and France's practice of human protection over the last few decades, France will probably always try to promote a robust understanding of R2P where the use of force under pillar three is still seen as a possible option that must be used if other measures fail and a positive outcome is likely to occur. Similarly, it will continue to promote a broad understanding of the scope of R2P in order to include situations such as the destruction of cultural heritage. In light of the status of the international norm, this process will require reliance on extensive collaborations with other members of the international community, but it will likely be perceived as necessary for the executive to promote France's conception of human protection, and to fulfil the role it has to play in human protection.

As in the past, it can be expected that France's efforts will sometimes lead to the strengthening of the international norm, but they may also endanger it at times, though, theoretically speaking, to a lesser extent than in the past. Therefore anyone interested in human protection, France's foreign policy or norm diffusion should monitor France's current and future commitment to human protection and, more specifically, its relationship to R2P.

## Notes

1 As mentioned in the Introduction, the literature has investigated the role played by Anglo-Saxon states and states which are wary of the principles and norms, such as the BRICS.
2 These limitations were discussed in Chapter 1.

# Appendix: France's presidents, prime ministers and ministers of foreign affairs (1981–2017)

| President | Prime Minister | Minister of Foreign Affairs |
|---|---|---|
| François Mitterrand (May 1981 – May 1995) | Pierre Mauroy (May 1981 – July 1984) | Claude Cheysson (May 1981 – December 1984) |
| | Laurent Fabius (July 1984 – March 1986) | Roland Dumas (December 1984 – March 1986) |
| | Jacques Chirac (March 1986 – May 1988): first *cohabitation* | Jean-Bernard Raimond (March 1986 – May 1988) |
| | Michel Rocard (March 1986 – May 1991) | Roland Dumas (May 1988 – March 1993) |
| | Edith Cresson (May 1991 – April 1992) | Alain Juppé (March 1993 – May 1995) |
| | Pierre Bérégovoy (April 1992 – March 1993) | |
| | Edouard Balladur (March 1993 – May 1995): second *cohabitation* | |
| Jacques Chirac (May 1995 – May 2007) | Alain Juppé (May 1995 – June 1997) | Hervé de Charette (May 1995 – June 1997) |
| | Lionel Jospin (June 1997 – May 2002): third *cohabitation* | Hubert Védrine (June 1997 – May 2002) |
| | Jean-Pierre Raffarin (May 2002 – May 2005) | Dominique de Villepin (May 2002 – March 2004) |
| | Dominique de Villepin (May 2005 – May 2007) | Michel Barnier (March 2004 – May 2005) |
| | | Philippe Douste-Blazy (June 2005 – May 2007) |

| President | Prime Minister | Minister of Foreign Affairs |
| --- | --- | --- |
| Nicolas Sarkozy (May 2007 – May 2012) | François Fillon (May 2007 – May 2012) | Bernard Kouchner (May 2007 – November 2010)<br>Michèle Alliot-Marie (November 2010 – February 2011)<br>Alain Juppé (February 2011 – May 2012) |
| François Hollande (May 2012 – May 2017) | François Fillon (May 2012 – December 2016)<br>Bernard Cazeneuve (December 2016 – May 2017) | Laurent Fabius (May 2012 – February 2016)<br>Jean-Marc Ayrault (February 2016 – May 2017) |

# References

Acharya, Amitav. 2004. "How ideas spread: whose norms matter? Norm localization and institutional change in Asian regionalism." *International Organization* 58 (2): 239–275.

Acharya, Amitav. 2011. "Norm subsidiarity and regional orders: sovereignty, regionalism, and rule-making in the Third World." *International Studies Quarterly* 55 (1): 95–123.

Acharya, Amitav. 2013. "The R2P and norm diffusion: towards a framework of norm circulation." *Global Responsibility to Protect* 5 (4): 466–479.

Acharya, Amitav. 2015. "The responsibility to protect and a theory of norm circulation." In *Theorising the Responsibility to Protect*, edited by Ramesh Thakur and William Maley. Cambridge: Cambridge University Press.

Adelman, Howard. 2000. "Rwanda revisited: in search for lessons." *Journal of Genocide Research* 2 (3): 431–444.

Adelman, Howard, and Astri Suhrke. 2004. "Rwanda." In *The UN Security Council: From the Cold War to the 21st Century*, edited by D. M. Malone. Boulder: Lynne Rienner.

Adler, Emanuel. 1997. "Seizing the middle ground: constructivism in world politics." *European Journal of International Relations* 3 (3): 319–363.

African Union. 2011. "Report of the chairperson of the commission on the activities of the AU high level ad hoc committee on the situation in Libya." Accessed 16 June 2015. www.au.int/en/sites/default/files/275 – Report on Libya _Eng _ %283%29.pdf.

Allaire, Marie-Bénédicte, and Philippe Goulliard. 2002. *L'incroyable septennat: Jacques Chirac à l'Élysée (1995–2002)*. Paris: Fayard.

Allen, Tim, and David Styan. 2000. "A right to interfere? Bernard Kouchner and the new humanitarianism." *Journal of International Development* 12 (6): 825–842.

Amalric, Jacques. 2008. "Ellipses." *Libération*, 16 December. Accessed 14 June 2012. www.liberation.fr/evenement/0101262701-ellipses.

Ambassade de France au Liban. 2019. "La France et la FINUL." Accessed 20 February 2019. https://lb.ambafrance.org/La-France-et-la-FINULna.

Ambrosetti, David, and Sébastien Chesneau. 2012. "France." Accessed 4 July 2019. www.operationspaix.net/64-fiche-d-information-de-l-etat-france.html.

Annan, Kofi. 2000. *We the Peoples: The Role of the United Nations in the 21st Century*. Millennium Report of the Secretary-General. Accessed 4 July 2019. https://www.un.org/en/events/pastevents/we_the_peoples.shtml.

Annan, Kofi. 2005. *In Larger Freedom: Report of the Secretary-General of the United Nations for Decision by Heads of State and Government in September 2005*. Accessed 4 July 2019. https://www.un.org/en/events/pastevents/in_larger_freedom.shtml.

Annan, Kofi. 2013. "Kofi Annan: 'Seule la France pouvait agir vite en Centrafrique.'" Accessed 4 July 2019. www.lejdd.fr/International/Kofi-Annan-Seule-la-France-pouvait-agir-vite-en-Centrafrique-643873.

APR2P. 2008. "Cyclone Nargis and the responsibility to protect: Myanmar/Burma briefing No. 2." Asia Pacific Centre for the Responsibility to Protect. Accessed 4 July 2019. www.r2pasiapacific.org/documents/Burma_Brief2.pdf.

Araud, Gérard. 2012. "Déclaration de la France au débat interactif informel sur la responsabilité de protéger (5 septembre 2012)." Accessed 25 March 2015. http://responsibilitytoprotect.org/France(5).pdf.

Araud, Gérard. 2013. "Statement by Mr Gérard Araud, Permanent Representative of France to the United Nations." Accessed 14 August 2015. https://onu.delegfrance.org/11-September-2013-General-Assembly. www.globalr2p.org/media/files/france-in-french.pdf.

Assemblée Nationale. 1994. "Compte rendu intégral de la séance du mardi 12 Avril 1994." Accessed 4 July 2019. http://archives.assemblee-nationale.fr/10/cri/1993–1994-ordinaire2/008.pdf.

Bakong, Patrice Emery. 2012. *La politique militaire Africaine de la France: forces sociales et changements récents*. Paris: Éditions L'Harmattan.

Balleix, Corinne. 2011. "La politique française de coopération au développement." *Afrique contemporaine* 236 (4): 95–107.

Ban, Ki-Moon. 2009. "A/63/677: report of the Secretary General: implementing the responsibility to protect." United Nations. Accessed 11 February 2013. www.un.org/ga/search/view_doc.asp?symbol=A/63/677.

Ban, Ki-Moon. 2010. "A/64/864: early warning, assessment, and the responsibility to protect." United Nations. Accessed 11 February 2013. www.globalr2p.org/publications/37.

Ban, Ki-Moon. 2011. "Human protection and the 21st century United Nations." Accessed 20 March 2019. https://www.un.org/sg/en/content/sg/speeches/2011–02–02/cyril-foster-lecture-oxford-university-human-protection-and-21st.

Banégas, Richard, and Roland Marchal. 2013. "La politique africaine: stratégie d'impuissance, ou impasse d'une politique d'indécision." In *La politique étrangère de Jacques Chirac*, edited by Christian Lequesne and Maurice Vaisse. Paris: Éditions Riveneuve.

Barber, Rebecca. 2009. "The responsibility to protect the survivors of natural disaster: Cyclone Nargis, a case study." *Journal of Conflict & Security Law* 14 (1): 3–34.

Barnett, Michael. 2005. "Humanitarianism transformed." *Perspectives on Politics* 3 (4): 723–740.

Barnett, Michael N. 2010. *The International Humanitarian Order*. New York: Routledge.

Barnett, Michael N. 2011. *The Empire of Humanity: A History of Humanitarianism*. Ithaca: Cornell University Press.

Barnett, Michael N., and Thomas George Weiss. 2008. *Humanitarianism in Question: Politics, Power, Ethics*. Ithaca: Cornell University Press.

Bellamy, Alex. 2002. *Kosovo and International Society*. New York: Palgrave.

Bellamy, Alex. 2004. "Motives, outcomes, intent and the legitimacy of humanitarian intervention." *Journal of Military Ethics* 3 (3): 216–232.

Bellamy, Alex. 2009a. *Responsibility to Protect: The Global Effort to End Mass Atrocities*. Malden, MA: Polity Press.

Bellamy, Alex. 2009b. "When is it right to fight? International law and *jus ad bellum*." *Journal of Military Ethics* 8 (3): 231–245.

Bellamy, Alex. 2010. "Kosovo and the advent of sovereignty as responsibility." In *Kosovo, Intervention, and Statebuilding: The International Community and the Transition to Independence*, edited by Aidan Hehir. Abingdon: Routledge.

Bellamy, Alex. 2011. *Global Politics and the Responsibility to Protect: From Words to Deeds*. Abingdon: Routledge.

Bellamy, Alex. 2012. *Massacres and Morality: Mass Atrocities in an Age of Civilian Immunity*. Oxford: Oxford University Press.

Bellamy, Alex. 2016. "The humanisation of security? Towards an international human protection regime." *European Journal of International Security* 1 (1): 112–133.

Bellamy, Alex, and Nicholas J. Wheeler. 2011. "Humanitarian intervention in world politics." In *The Globalisation of World Politics: An Introduction to International Relations*, edited by J. Baylis, S. Smith and P. Owens. New York: Oxford University Press.

Bellamy, Alex, and Paul Williams. 2011. "The new politics of protection? Côte d'Ivoire, Libya and the responsibility to protect." *International Affairs* 87 (4): 825–850.

Bellamy, Alex, Paul Williams, and Stuart Griffin. 2004. *Understanding Peacekeeping*. Malden, MA: Polity Press.

Benoit, Jean-Paul. 2004. "Un certain désangement français militaire direct." In *La politique de securité de la France en Afrique*, edited by Pierre Pascallon. Paris: L'Harmattan.

Berman, Paul. 2005. *Power and the Idealists: Or, the Passion of Joschka Fischer, and its Aftermath*. Brooklyn, NY: Soft Skull Press.

Bernard, Philippe. 2008. "Entretien avec Jean-Marie Bockel: 'Je veux signer l'acte de décès de la "Françafrique"'." Accessed 4 July 2019. https://www.lemonde.fr/afrique/article/2008/01/15/jean-marie-bockel-je-veux-signer-l-acte-de-deces-d e-la-francafrique_999524_3212.html.

Bettati, Mario. 1987. "Un droit d'ingérence humanitaire?" In *Le devoir d'ingérence: peut-on les laisser mourir?*, edited by Mario Bettati and Bernard Kouchner. Paris: Denoël.

Bettati, Mario. 1993. "L'ONU et l'action humanitaire." *Politique étrangère* 58 (3): 641–658.

Bettati, Mario. 1995. "L'ONU, promoteur de l'assistance humanitaire." In *La France et l'ONU depuis 1945*, edited by A. Lewin. Condé-sur-Noireau: Arléa-Corlet.

Bettati, Mario. 2014. Interview with the author. 26 January.

Bettati, Mario, and Bernard Kouchner. 1987. *Le devoir d'ingérence: peut-on les laisser mourir?* Paris: Denoël.

Betts, Alexander, and Phil Orchard. 2014. *Implementation and World Politics: How International Norms Change Practice.* Oxford: Oxford University Press.

Biscop, Sven, and Jo Coelmont. 2012. *Europe, Strategy and Armed Forces: The Making of a Distinctive Power.* London: Routledge.

Boniface, Pascal. 2008. "Les opérations militaires extérieures." *Pouvoirs* 125 (2): 55–67.

Borgis, Claude. 2004. "De nouvelles modalités d'aide militaire française indirecte: vers une 'Africanisation' de la Sécurité." In *La politique de sécurité de la France en Afrique*, edited by Pierre Pascallon. Paris: L'Harmattan.

Bossuat, Gérard. 2012. *La France et la construction de l'unité européenne: de 1919 à nos jours.* Paris: Armand-Colin.

Bovcon, Maja. 2009. "France's conflict resolution strategy in Côte d'Ivoire and its ethical implications." *African Studies Quarterly* 11 (1): 1–24.

Bozo, Frédéric. 2012. *La politique étrangère de la France depuis 1945.* Paris: Flammarion.

Bryant, Janet. 2000. "France and NATO from 1966 to Kosovo: coming full circle?" *European Security* 9 (3): 21–37.

Buffotot, Patrice. 2005. *Europe des armées, ou, Europe désarmée?* Paris: Michalon.

Bush, George, and Tony Blair. 2003. "Joint statement on Iraq." 8 April. Accessed 10 October 2018. https://2001-2009.state.gov/p/eur/rls/rm/2003/19406.htm.

Caballero-Anthony, Mely, and Belinda Chng. 2009. "Cyclones and humanitarian crises: pushing the limits of R2P in Southeast Asia." *Global Responsibility to Protect* 1 (2): 135–155.

Chafer, Tony. 2014. "Hollande and Africa policy." *Modern & Contemporary France* 22 (4): 513–531.

Charbonneau, Bruno. 2008. "Dreams of empire: France, Europe, and the new interventionism in Africa." *Modern & Contemporary France* 16 (3): 279–295.

Charillon, Frédéric. 2002. "Peut-il encore y avoir une politique étrangère française?" *Politique étrangère* 67 (4): 915–929.

Charillon, Frédéric. 2007. "La politique étrangère de la France: l'heure des choix." *Politique étrangère* 1: 139–150.

Chirac, Jacques. 1987. "Morale humanitaire et action politique." In *Le devoir d'ingérence: peut-on les laisser mourir?*, edited by Mario Bettati and Bernard Kouchner. Paris: Denoël.

Chirac, Jacques. 1995a. "Interview accordée par M. Jacques Chirac, Président de la République, au 'Time Magazine'." Accessed 6 July 2014. www.jacqueschirac-asso.fr/archives-elysee.fr/elysee/elysee.fr/f...cles_de_presse_et_interventions_televisees/1995/decembre/fi003751.html.

Chirac, Jacques. 1995b. "Message de M. Jacques Chirac, Président de la République, adressé aux armées." Accessed 6 July 2014. http://discours.vie-publique.fr/notices/967000800.html.

Chirac, Jacques. 1995c. "Voeux aux Français (31 décembre)." Présidence de la République. Accessed 6 July 2014. www.jacqueschirac-asso.fr/archives-elysee.fr/elysee/elysee.fr/francais/interventions/interviews_articles_de_presse_et_interventions_televisees/1995/decembre/voeux_aux_francais_du_president_de_la_republique.261.html.

Chirac, Jacques. 1996. "Discours de M. Jacques Chirac, Président de la République, sur les relations franco-américaines, le règlement du conflit yougoslave, la réforme de l'OTAN, l'arrêt définitif des essais nucléaires français et l'aide au développement, Washington le 1er février 1996." Vie Publique. Accessed 7 January 2014. http://discours.vie-publique.fr/notices/967001900.html.

Chirac, Jacques. 1998. "Interview accordée par M. Jacques Chirac, Président de la République, à la chaine américaine PBS." Vie Publique. Accessed 7 January 2014. www.jacqueschirac-asso.fr/archives-elysee.fr/elysee/elysee.fr/francais/interventions/interviews_articles_de_presse_et_interventions_televisees/1998/juin/fi003208.html.

Chirac, Jacques. 1999a. "Interview radiotélévisée de M. Jacques Chirac, Président de la République, sur la situation au Kosovo (29 mars)." Accessed 7 January 2014. www.jacqueschirac-asso.fr/archives-elysee.fr/elysee/elysee.fr/francais/interventions/interviews_articles_de_presse_et_interventions_televisees/1999/mars/fi002973.html.

Chirac, Jacques. 1999b. "Interview télévisée de M. Jacques Chirac, Président de la République, sur l'évolution de la situation au Kosovo (6 avril)." Vie Publique. Accessed 7 January 2014. www.jacqueschirac-asso.fr/archives-elysee.fr/elysee/elysee.fr/francais/interventions/interviews_articles_de_presse_et_interventions_televisees/1999/avril/fi002969.html.

Chirac, Jacques. 1999c. "Interview télévisée de M. Jacques Chirac, Président de la République, sur l'évolution de la situation au Kosovo (12 avril)." Vie Publique. Accessed 7 January 2014. www.jacqueschirac-asso.fr/archives-elysee.fr/elysee/elysee.fr/francais/interventions/interviews_articles_de_presse_et_interventions_televisees/1999/avril/fi002965.html.

Chirac, Jacques. 1999d. "Interview radiotélévisée de M. Jacques Chirac, Président de la République, sur l'évolution de la situation au Kosovo (27 mai)." Vie Publique. Accessed 7 January 2014. www.jacqueschirac-asso.fr/archives-elysee.fr/elysee/elysee.fr/francais/interventions/interviews_articles_de_presse_et_interventions_televisees/1999/mai/fi002932.html.

Chirac, Jacques. 1999e. "La France dans un monde multipolaire." *Politique étrangère* 4: 803–812.

Chirac, Jacques. 2002. "Discours prononcé par M. Jacques Chirac, Président de la République, à l'occasion de la reception des ambassadeurs." Accessed 2 March 2015. www.jacqueschirac-asso.fr/archives-elysee.fr/elysee/elysee.fr/francais/interventions/discours_et_declarations/2002/aout/conference_des_ambassadeurs.40394.html.

Chirac, Jacques. 2003. "La réaction de Jacques Chirac". RFI. Accessed 10 February 2016. www1.rfi.fr/actufr/articles/039/article_20691.asp.

Chirac, Jacques. 2007. *Mon combat pour la paix*. Paris: Odile Jacob.

Chirac, Jacques. 2011. *Le temps présidentiel: memoires 2*. Paris: NiL Éditions.

Chivvis, Christopher S. 2012. "Libya and the future of liberal intervention." *Survival* 54 (6): 69–92.

Clark, Wesley. 2001. *Waging Modern War: Bosnia, Kosovo, and the Future of Combat*. Oxford: Public Affairs.

Claude, Gérard. 2007. "Chirac 'l'Africain': dix ans de politique africaine de la France 1996–2006." *Politique étrangère* 4 (Hiver): 905–918.

Cohen, Roberta, and Francis M. Deng. 2016. "Sovereignty as responsibility: building block for R2P." In *The Oxford Handbook of the Responsibility to Protect*, edited by Alex Bellamy and Tim Dunne. Oxford: Oxford University Press.

Colombani, Jean Marie, and Jacques François Simon. 1991. "Un entretien avec M. Bernard Kouchner: 'Nous entrons dans une époque où il ne sera plus possible d'assassiner massivement à l'ombre des frontières' nous déclare le secrétaire d'État à l'action humanitaire." *Le Monde*, 30 April. Accessed 28 May 2012. http://abonnes.lemonde.fr/cgi-bin/ACHATS/acheter.cgi?offre=ARCHIVES& type_item=ART_ARCH_30J&objet_id=674851&xtmc=un_entretien_avec_m_ bernard_kouchner_nous_entrons_dans_une_epoque_ou_il_ne_sera_plus_ possible_d_assassiner_massivement_a_l_ombre_des_frontieres_nous_declare_ le_secretaire_d_etat_a_l_action_humanitaire&xtcr=1.

*Courrier International*. 2004. "La France au banc des accusés: dans ces pays-là, un génocide n'est pas trop important." Accessed 26 February 2019. https:// www.courrierinternational.com/article/2004/04/08/dans-ces-pays-la-un- genocide-n-est-pas-trop-important.

Cumming, Gordon. 1995. "French development assistance to Africa: towards a new agenda?" *African Affairs* 94 (376): 383–398.

Cumming, Gordon D. 2013a. "Nicolas Sarkozy's Africa policy: change, continuity or confusion?" *French Politics* 11 (1): 24–47.

Cumming, Gordon D. 2013b. "'A piecemeal approach with no vision': French policy towards Africa under Nicolas Sarkozy." In *The Sarkozy Presidency: Breaking the Mould*, edited by Gino Raymond. New York: Palgrave Macmillan.

Dalloz, Jacques. 2002. *La France et le monde depuis 1945*. Paris: Armand Collin.

Davey, Eleanor. 2012. "Beyond the 'French doctors', the evolution and interpretation of humanitarian action in France." Humanitarian Policy Group working paper. Accessed 4 July 2019. https://www.odi.org/sites/odi.org.uk/files/odi-assets/ publications-opinion-files/7874.pdf.

Davey, Eleanor. 2015. *Idealism beyond Borders: The French Revolutionary Left and the Rise of Humanitarianism, 1954–1988*: Cambridge: Cambridge University Press.

Davidson, Jason W. 2011. *America's Allies and War: Kosovo, Afghanistan, and Iraq*. New York: Palgrave Macmillan.

de Charette, Hervé. 2008. "Nicolas Sarkozy et la politique étrangère de la France: entre changement et continuité." *Revue internationale et stratégique* 70 (2): 7–12.

de Gaulle, Charles. 1966. "Lettre de Charles de Gaulle à Lyndon B. Johnson." Accessed 7 January 2014. www.cvce.eu/obj/lettre_de_charles_de_gaulle_a_lyndon_b_johnson_7_mars_1966-fr-d97bf195–34e1–4862-b5e7–87577a8c1632.html.

de Russé, Anne-Henry. 2010. "La France dans l'OTAN: la culture militaire française et l'identité stratégique en question." Accessed 4 July 2019. https://www.ifri.org/sites/default/files/atoms/files/fs22derusse.pdf.

de Villepin, Dominique. 2003a. "Conférence de presse à New York le 20 Janvier 2003." Accessed 16 February 2016. https://dominiquedevillepin.fr/tag/irak/.

de Villepin, Dominique. 2003b. "Le discours de Villepin sur l'Irak à l'ONU." Accessed 9 February 2015. www.lefigaro.fr/politique/le-scan/2014/04/08/25001–20140408ARTFIG00066-le-discours-de-villepin-sur-l-irak-a-l-onu.php.

de Villepin, Dominique. 2005. "Speech in front of the United Nations General Assembly during the 2005 World Summit." Accessed 18 April 2015. www.un.org/webcast/summit2005/statements14.html.

Delattre, François. 2014. "Intervention durant le dialogue interactif informel à l'Assemblée Générale." Accessed 15 August 2015. http://statements.unmeetings.org/media2/4493820/france.pdf.

Delattre, François. 2015. "Intervention durant le dialogue interactif informel à l'Assemblée Générale." Accessed 24 May 2017. www.globalr2p.org/media/files/france-french-1.pdf.

Delattre, François. 2016. "Statement delivered by France at the Informal Interactive Dialogue on R2P." Accessed 24 May 2017. www.globalr2p.org/media/files/france-eng.pdf.

Dieng, Adama. 2013. "The statement of Under Secretary-General/Special Adviser on the Prevention of Genocide, Mr. Adama Dieng, on the human rights and humanitarian situation in the Central African Republic." Accessed 25 May 2017. www.un.org/en/preventgenocide/adviser/pdf/Statement by Mr. Adama Dieng, United Nations Special Adviser on the Prevention of Genocide, at the Arria Formula Meeting of.pdf.

Dieng, Adama. 2014. "The statement of Under Secretary-General/Special Adviser on the Prevention of Genocide Mr. Adama Dieng on the human rights and humanitarian dimensions of the crisis in the Central African Republic." Accessed 25 May 2017. www.un.org/en/preventgenocide/adviser/pdf/SAPG Statement at UNSC on the situation in CAR- 22 Jan 2014.pdf.

Diop, Doudou Salla. 2004. "La nouvelle coopération France–Afrique en matière de sécurité." In *La politique de sécurité de la France en Afrique*, edited by Pierre Pascallon. Paris: L'Harmattan.

Domergue, Danièle. 1998. "Coopération et interventions militaires en Afrique: la fin d'une aventure ambiguë?" *Guerres mondiales et conflits contemporains* 191: 117–134.

Domergue-Cloarec, Danièle. 2005. *La crise ivoirienne de novembre–décembre 2005*. Montpellier: Université Paul-Valéry.

Dumas, Roland. 1991. "La France et le droit d'ingérence humanitaire." *Relations internationales et stratégiques* 3: 57.

Dumas, Roland. 2011. *Coups et blessures: 50 ans de secrets partagés avec François Mitterrand*. Paris: Broché.

Dunne, Tim, and Eglantine Staunton. 2016. "The genocide convention and Cold War humanitarian intervention." In *The Oxford Handbook of the Responsibility to Protect*, edited by Alex Bellamy and Tim Dunne. Oxford: Oxford University Press.

EEAS. 2017. *EU Battlegroups*. European External Action Service. Accessed 1 March 2019. https://eeas.europa.eu/headquarters/headquarters-homepage_en/33557/EU%20Battlegroups.

EEAS. 2019. *EUFOR Operation ALTHEA European Union Military Operation Bosnia and Herzegovina (BiH)*. European External Action Service. Accessed 2 July 2019. www.euforbih.org/eufor/images/pdfs/Mission_Factsheet_1906.pdf.

El Moustaoui, Fatima. 2011. *Mitterrand et le Moyen-Orient*. Paris: L'Harmattan.

Eurocorps. 2013. "History." Accessed 14 December 2013. www.eurocorps.org/.

European Institute. 2009. "European defence timeline." Accessed 10 December 2014. www.europeaninstitute.org/index.php/eu-facts/897-european-defence-timeline.

European Union. 1992. *Treaty of Maastricht on European Union*. Brussels: European Union.

European Union. 2001. "EU programme for the prevention of violent conflict." Accessed 26 February 2015. www.eplo.org/eu-documents.

European Union. 2003. "A secure Europe in a better world: European security strategy." Accessed 26 February 2015. http://europa.eu/legislation_summaries/justice_freedom_security/fight_against_organised_crime/r00004_en.htm.

European Union. 2006a. "Military Committee of the European Union (EUMC)." Accessed 4 July 2019. http://europa.eu/legislation_summaries/foreign_and_security_policy/cfsp_and_esdp_implementation/r00007_en.htm.

European Union. 2006b. "Military Staff of the European Union (EUMS)." Accessed 4 July 2019. http://europa.eu/legislation_summaries/foreign_and_security_policy/cfsp_and_esdp_implementation/r00006_en.htm.

European Union. 2011. "Political and Security Committee (PSC)." Accessed 4 July 2019. http://europa.eu/legislation_summaries/foreign_and_security_policy/cfsp_and_esdp_implementation/r00005_en.htm.

European Union. 2015a. "ALTHEA/BiH." Accessed 2 March 2015. www.eeas.europa.eu/csdp/missions-and-operations/althea-bih/index_en.htm.

European Union. 2015b. "ARTEMIS/DRC." Accessed 2 March 2015. www.eeas.europa.eu/csdp/missions-and-operations/artemis-drc/index_en.htm.

European Union. 2015c. "CONCORDIA/FYROM." Accessed 2 March 2015. www.eeas.europa.eu/csdp/missions-and-operations/concordia/mission-description/index_en.htm.

European Union. 2015d. "EUFOR/CHAD/RCA." Accessed 4 July 2019. www.eeas.europa.eu/csdp/missions-and-operations/eufor-tchad-rca/mission-description/index_en.htm.

Evans, Gareth J. 2008a. *The Responsibility to Protect: Ending Mass Atrocity Crimes Once and For All*. Washington, DC: Brookings Institution Press.

Evans, Gareth J. 2008b. "Time for an aid invasion?" Accessed 2 April 2015. www.theage.com.au/news/opinion/time-for-an-aid-invasion/2008/05/18/1211049061508.html.

Evans, Gareth. 2013a. "When is it right to fight? War, peace and mass atrocity crimes." Accessed 3 November 2013. www.gevans.org/speeches/speech536. html.

Evans, Gareth J. 2013b. Interview with the author. 6 November.

Fabius, Laurent. 2012. "La France et l'OTAN – tribune de Laurent Fabius (*International Herald Tribune* – 5 décembre 2012)." Accessed 4 July 2019. https://otan.delegfrance.org/La-France-et-l-OTAN-Tribune-de.

Fall, Abdou. 2004. "Les demandes de révision de la politique militaire de la France en Afrique à partir de 1990." In *La politique de sécurité de la France en Afrique*, edited by Pierre Pascallon. Paris: L'Harmattan.

Filiu, Jean-Pierre. 2013. "Relance de la politique arabe et relations privilégiées au Maghreb et au Moyen-Orient." In *La politique étrangère de Jacques Chirac*, edited by Christian Lequesne and Maurice Vaisse. Paris: Éditions Riveneuve.

Findlay, Trevor. 2002. *The Use of Force in UN Peace Operations*. Oxford: Oxford University Press.

Finnemore, Martha. 1996a. "Constructing norms of humanitarian intervention." In *The Culture of National Security: Norms and Identity in World Politics*, edited by P. J. Katzenstein. New York: Columbia University Press.

Finnemore, Martha. 1996b. *National Interests in International Society*. Ithaca: Cornell University Press.

Finnemore, Martha, and Kathryn Sikkink. 1998. "International norm dynamics and political change." *International Organization* 52 (4): 887–917.

Finnemore, Martha, and Kathryn Sikkink. 2001. "Taking stock: the constructivist research program in international relations and comparative politics." *Annual Review of Political Science* 4: 391–416.

Fleitz, Frederick H. 2002. *Peacekeeping Fiascoes of the 1990s: Causes, Solutions, and U.S. Interests*. Westport, CT: Praeger.

Foreign and Commonwealth Office of the United Kindgom. 1998. "Franco-British St Malo Declaration." Accessed 2 November 2015. www.cvce.eu/obj/franco_british_st_malo_declaration_4_december_1998-en-f3cd16fb-fc37-4d52-936f-c8e9bc80f24f.html.

Forsythe, David P. 1991. "Human rights in a post-Cold War world." *Fletcher Forum of World Affairs* 15 (2): 55–69.

France Diplomatie. 2010. "France and Bosnia-Herzegovina." Accessed 16 November 2015. www.diplomatie.gouv.fr/en/country-files/bosnia-herzegovina/france-and-bosnia-herzegovina/.

France Diplomatie. 2015a. "Iraq – further destruction of cultural heritage (March 6, 2015)." Accessed 4 July 2019. https://www.diplomatie.gouv.fr/en/country-files/iraq/events/article/iraq-further-destruction-of.

France Diplomatie. 2015b. "Why France wishes to regulate use of the veto in the United Nations Security Council." Accessed 4 July 2019. www.diplomatie.gouv.fr/en/french-foreign-policy/united-nations/france-and-the-united-nations/article/why-france-wishes-to-regulate-use.

France Diplomatie. 2016. "Conférence internationale sur la protection du patrimoine en péril – déclaration d'Abou Dhabi (3 décembre 2016)." Accessed 4

July 2019. https://www.diplomatie.gouv.fr/fr/politique-etrangere-de-la-france/
diplomatie-culturelle/les-actualites-et-evenements-de-la-diplomatie-culturelle-
en-2016/conference-internationale-sur-la-protection-du-patrimoine-en-peril-
abou-dabi-2/article/conference-in.

*France Info*. 2017. "Syrie: pour François Hollande, Bachar Al-Assad 'porte
désormais l'étiquette de massacreur chimique." Accessed 25 May 2017.
www.francetvinfo.fr/monde/revolte-en-syrie/attaque-chimique-en-syrie/
syrie-pour-francois-hollande-bachar-al-assad-porte-desormais-l-etiquette-
de-massacreur-chimique_2142112.html.

France ONU. 2015. "Political statement on the suspension of the veto in case of
mass atrocities." Représentation Permanente de la France auprès des Nations
Unies à New York. Accessed 26 November 2015. www.franceonu.org/IMG/
pdf/2015_08_07_veto_political_declaration_en.pdf.

Francia, Roberto, and Miguel Angel Medina Abellan. 2006. "Striving for a common
foreign policy: a brief history." In *European Foreign Policy: From Rhetoric to
Reality?*, edited by Alicia Ambos Dieter Mahncke and Christopher Reynolds.
Brussels: College of Europe Studies.

Freeman, Colin. 2011. Libya crisis: Benghazi fights for its life as Gaddafi attacks.
*The Telegraph*. Accessed 1 March 2019. https://www.telegraph.co.uk/news/
worldnews/africaandindianocean/liby...8/Libya-crisis-Benghazi-fights-for-its-
life-as-Gaddafi-attacks.html.

Gallagher, Adrian. 2014. "What constitutes a 'manifest failing'? Ambiguous and
inconsistent terminology and the Responsibility to Protect." *International Relations* 28 (4): 428–444.

Gelie, Philippe. 2011. "La France a parachuté des armes aux rebelles libyens."
Accessed 16 June 2015. www.lefigaro.fr/international/2011/06/28/01003-
-20110628ARTFIG00704-la-france-a-parachute-des-armes-aux-rebelles-
libyens.php.

Gierycz, Dorota. 2010. "From humanitarian intervention (HI) to responsibility to
protect (R2P)." *Criminal Justice Ethics* 29 (2): 110–128.

Glanville, Luke. 2010. "The antecedents of 'sovereignty as responsibility." *European
Journal of International Relations* 17 (2): 233–255.

Glanville, Luke. 2012. "The responsibility to protect beyond borders." *Human
Rights Law Review* 12 (1): 1–32.

Glanville, Luke. 2016. "Does R2P matter? Interpreting the impact of a norm."
*Cooperation and Conflict* 51 (2): 184–199.

Global Centre for the Responsibility to Protect. 2017. "UN Security Council
Code of Conduct." Accessed 17 April 2017. www.globalr2p.org/our_work/
un_security_council_code_of_conduct.

Global Centre for the Responsibility to Protect. 2019. "UN Security Council Resolutions and Presidential Statements Referencing R2P." Accessed 4 July 2019.
www.globalr2p.org/resources/335.

Gouëset, Catherine. 2010. "La Françafrique de Nicolas Sarkozy, changement ...
et continuité." Accessed 4 July 2019. www.lexpress.fr/actualite/monde/afrique/
la-francafrique-de-nicolas-sarkozy-changement-et-continuite_851223.html.

Gounin, Yves. 2009. "La crise du complexe." In *La France en Afrique: le combat des Anciens et des Modernes*, edited by Yves Gounin and Jean-Christophe Rufin. Brussels: De Boeck.

Graff, James, and Bruce Crumley. 2003. "France is not a pacifist country." Accessed 4 July 2019. http://content.time.com/time/magazine/article/0,9171,423466,00.html.

Grégoire, Joseph Philippe, 2002. "The bases of French peace operations doctrine: problematical scope of France's military engagements within the UN or NATO framework." Strategic Studies Institute. Acccessed 4 July 2019. https://ssi.armywarcollege.edu/pubs/display.cfm?pubID=127.

Gregory, Shaun. 2000a. "France and missions de paix." *The RUSI Journal* 145 (4): 58–63.

Gregory, Shaun. 2000b. "The French Military in Africa: past and present." *African Affairs* 99 (396): 435–448.

Grosser, Alfred. 1995. "Le rôle et le rang." In *La France et l'ONU depuis 1945*, edited by A. Lewin. Condé-sur-Noireau: Arléa-Corlet.

*Guardian*. 2017. "US military strikes on Syria: what we know so far." Accessed 1 March 2019. https://www.theguardian.com/world/2017/apr/07/us-airstrikes-on-syria-donald-trump-what-we-know-so-far.

Guéhenno, Jean, and Ministère de la Défense. 2013. "Livre blanc 2013: défense et sécurité nationale." Accessed 13 August 2015. www.defense.gouv.fr/actualites/memoire-et-culture/livre-blanc-2013.

Guillot, Philippe. 1994. "France, peacekeeping and humanitarian intervention." *International Peacekeeping* 1 (1): 30–43.

Hansen, Andrew. 2008. "The French military in Africa." Council on Foreign Relations. Accessed 7 June 2012. www.cfr.org/france/french-military-africa/p12578.

Hehir, Aidan. 2013. "Introduction: Libya and the responsibility to protect." In *Libya, the Responsibility to Protect and the Future of Humanitarian Intervention*, edited by Robert Murray and Aidan Hehir. New York: Palgrave Macmillan.

Hirsch, Afua. 2013. "French troops arrive in Mali to stem rebel advance." *The Guardian*. Accessed 25 May 2017. https://www.theguardian.com/world/2013/jan/11/france-intervene-mali-conflict.

Hofnung, Thomas. 2011. *La crise ivoirienne: de Félix Houphouët-Boigny à la chute de Laurent Gbagbo*. Paris: La Découverte.

Hollande, François. 2012a. "Discours de Dakar." Accessed 26 May 2017. https://www.scribd.com/document/109835017/Le-discours-de-Francois-Hollande-devant-l-Assemblee-nationale-du-Senegal-a-Dakar-le-12-octobre-2012.

Hollande, François. 2012b. "Le changement, c'est maintenant: mes 60 engagements pour la France." Accessed 4 July 2019. https://archive.org/details/EL245_P_2012_077.

Hollande, François. 2013a. "Annonce par François Hollande de l'intervention française au Mali." Accessed 15 August 2015. www.voltairenet.org/article177141.html.

Hollande, François. 2013b. "Discours de Monsieur le Président de la République à la Conférence des Ambassadeurs." Accessed 13 August 2015. www.diplomatie.gouv.fr/fr/IMG/pdf/27–08_Conference_des_Ambassadeurs_cle8421e4.pdf.

Hollande, François. 2013c. "Discours du Président de la République annonçant le déploiment de troupes Françaises en Centrafrique." Accessed 4 July 2019. www.defense.gouv.fr/operations/centrafrique/dossier-de-presentation-de-l-operation-sangaris/operation-sangaris.

Hollande, François. 2013d. "Intervention de F. Hollande sur la politique de défense à l'IHEDN." Accessed 17 July 2019. https://www.voltairenet.org/article178650.html.

Hollande, François. 2013e. "Speech by François Hollande, President of the French Republic at the 68th United Nations General Assembly." Accessed 13 August 2015. www.ambafrance-us.org/spip.php?article4925.

Hollande, François. 2016. "Déclaration de M. François Hollande, Président de la République, sur l'OTAN, à Paris le 3 juin 2016." Accessed 26 May 2017. http://discours.vie-publique.fr/notices/167001690.html.

Hollande, François. 2017. "Allocution du Président de la République à l'occasion de la conférence pour la paix au Proche-Orient." Accessed 29 May 2017. www.diplomatie.gouv.fr/fr/dossiers-pays/israel-territoires-palestiniens/processus-de-paix/initiative-pour-la-paix-au-proche-orient/article/conference-de-paris-pour-la-paix-au-proche-orient-la-journee-en-direct.

Holzgrefe, J. L. 2003. "The humanitarian intervention debate." In *Humanitarian Intervention: Ethic, Legal, and Political Dilemmas*, edited by J. L. Holzgrefe and Robert O. Keohane. Cambridge: Cambridge University Press.

Hopf, Ted. 1998. "The promise of constructivism in International Relations theory." *International Security* 23 (1): 171–200.

ICISS. 2001. *The Responsibility to Protect: Report of the International Commission on Intervention and State Sovereignty*. Ottawa: International Development Research Centre.

ICRtoP. 2008. "France suggested invoking responsibility to protect." International Coalition for the Responsibility to Protect. Accessed 30 May 2017. www.responsibilitytoprotect.org/index.php/crises/128-the-crisis-in-burma/1628-france-suggests-helping-myanmar-without-government-backing.

ICRtoP. 2013a. "Crisis in the Central African Republic." International Coalition for the Responsibility to Protect. Accessed 25 May 2017. www.responsibilitytoprotect.org/index.php/crises/crisis-in-the-central-african-republic.

ICRtoP. 2013b. "Q&A: The responsibility to protect (RtoP) and the Central African Republic." International Coalition for the Responsibility to Protect. Accessed 25 May 2017. responsibilitytoprotect.org/FINAL CAR Q and A.pdf.

IICK. 2000. *The Kosovo Report by the Independent International Commission on Kosovo: Conflict, International Response, Lessons Learned*. Oxford: Oxford University Press.

IISS. 1993. "NATO." *The Military Balance* 93 (1): 30–65.

IISS. 1994. "NATO." *The Military Balance* 94 (1): 34–72.

IISS. 1995. "NATO." *The Military Balance* 95 (1): 33–67.

IISS. 1996. "NATO and non-NATO Europe." *The Military Balance* 96 (1): 32–48.

IISS. 1997. "Europe." *The Military Balance* 97 (1): 28–100.

IISS. 1998. "NATO and non-NATO Europe." *The Military Balance* 98 (1): 30–100.
IISS. 1999. "NATO and non-NATO Europe." *The Military Balance* 99 (1): 30–103.
IISS. 2000. "NATO and non-NATO Europe." *The Military Balance* 100 (1): 35–108.
IISS. 2001. "NATO and non-NATO Europe." *The Military Balance* 101 (1): 29–104.
IISS. 2002. "NATO and non-NATO Europe." *The Military Balance* 102 (1): 27–84.
IISS. 2003. "Europe." *The Military Balance* 103 (1): 29–84.
IISS. 2004. "NATO Europe." *The Military Balance* 104 (1): 35–76.
IISS. 2005. "Europe." *The Military Balance* 105 (1): 45–106.
IISS. 2007. "Europe." *The Military Balance* 107 (1): 93–186.
IISS. 2008. "Europe." *The Military Balance* 108 (1): 101–204.
IISS. 2009. "Chapter Three: Europe." *The Military Balance* 109 (1): 99–206.
IISS. 2010. "Chapter Three: Europe." *The Military Balance* 110 (1): 103–210.
IISS. 2011. "Chapter Four: Europe." *The Military Balance* 111 (1): 73–172.
IISS. 2012. "Chapter Four: Europe." *The Military Balance* 112 (1): 71–182.
IISS. 2013. "Chapter Four: Europe." *The Military Balance* 113 (1): 89–198.
IISS. 2014. "Chapter Four: Europe." *The Military Balance* 114 (1): 59–160.
IISS. 2015. "Chapter Four: Europe." *The Military Balance* 115 (1): 57–158.
IISS. 2016. "Chapter Four: Europe." *The Military Balance* 116 (1): 55–162.
IISS. 2017. "Chapter Four: Europe." *The Military Balance* 117 (1): 63–182.
Jauvert, Vincent. 2011. "Jospin: 'L'Afghanistan, ce n'était pas notre guerre." Accessed 4 July 2019. http://globe.blogs.nouvelobs.com/archive/2011/09/07/jospin-l-afghanistan-ce-n-etait-pas-notre-guerre.html.
Jeangène Vilmer, Jean-Baptiste. 2012. "De la mythologie française du droit d'ingérence à la responsabilité de protéger: une clarification terminologique." *Annuaire français de relations internationales* 13: 81–100.
Jones, Bruce D. 2007. "Rwanda." In *United Nations Interventionism 1991–2004*, edited by Mats Berdal and Spyros Economides. Cambridge: Cambridge University Press.
Jospin, Lionel. 1997a. "Déclaration de M. Lionel Jospin, Premier ministre, sur la politique de défense de la France, Paris le 4 septembre 1997". Vie Publique. Accessed 4 July 2019. http://discours.vie-publique.fr/notices/973145084.html.
Jospin, Lionel. 1997b. "Déclaration de M. Lionel Jospin, Premier ministre, sur la valeur universelle des droits fondamentaux de la personne humaine, la commémoration de la Déclaration Universelle des Droits de l'homme et le projet de loi du Gouvernement, créant une instance chargée de veiller à la déontologie des services de sécurité, Paris le 10 décembre 1997." Accessed 4 July 2019. http://discours.vie-publique.fr/notices/973145659.html.
Juppé, Alain. 2001. "Évènements de Srebrenica: audition de M. Alain Juppé." Mission d'Information Commune, Assemblée Nationale. Accessed 4 July 2019. www.assemblee-nationale.fr/11/dossiers/srebrenica/audition5.asp.
Juppé, Alain. 2011. "Remise du prix des droits de l'Homme de la République française." Accessed 4 July 2019. https://onu-geneve.delegfrance.org/Remise-du-prix-des-droits-de-l.
Juppé, Alain, and Louis Schweitzer. 2008. "La France et l'Europe dans le monde: livre blanc sur la politique étrangère et européenne de la France (2008

– 2020)." Accessed 25 March 2015. www.ladocumentationfrancaise.fr/rapports-publics/084000459/.

Kouchner, Bernard. 1987. "Le devoir d'ingérence." In *Le devoir d'ingérence: peut-on les laisser mourir?*, edited by Mario Bettati and Bernard Kouchner. Paris: Denoël.

Kouchner, Bernard. 1991a. "Devoir d'assistance." *Le Monde*, 20 September. Accessed 28 May 2012. http://abonnes.lemonde.fr/cgi-bin/ACHATS/acheter. cgi?offre=ARCHIVES&type_item=ART_ARCH_30J&objet_id=540498&xtmc= devoir_d_assistance&xtcr=4.

Kouchner, Bernard. 1991b. *Le malheur des autres*. Paris: Odile Jacob.

Kouchner, Bernard. 2002. "La responsabilité de protéger." *Le Monde*, 8 June. Accessed 28 May 2012. http://abonnes.lemonde.fr/cgi-bin/ACHATS/acheter. cgi?offre=ARCHIVES&type_item=ART_ARCH_30J&objet_id=759698&xtmc= la_responsabilite_de_proteger&xtcr=5.

Kouchner, Bernard. 2010. "France's statement at the opening of the 65th session of the United Nations General Assembly." Accessed 25 March 2015. http://gadebate.un.org/Portals/1/statements/634211896746875000FR_fr. pdf.

Kouchner, Bernard. 2014. Interview with the author. 11 February.

Krasner, Stephen D. 1995. "Sovereignty, regimes, and human rights." In *Regime Theory and International Relations*, edited by Volker Rittberger. Oxford: Clarendon Press.

Krasner, Stephen D. 2001. "Abiding sovereignty." *International Political Science Review / Revue internationale de science politique* 22 (3): 229–251.

Kroslak, Daniela. 2007. *The Role of France in the Rwandan Genocide*. London: Hurst & Co.

*La Croix*. 2017. "Conflit israélopalestinien: François Hollande plaide pour 'deux États'." Accessed 21 February 2019. https://www.la-croix.com/Monde/Moyen-Orient/Francois-Hollande-plaide-pour-deux-Etats-israelien-palestinien-2017-01-15-1200817354.

Ladsous, Hervé. 1994. "S/1994/933: letter dated 4 August 1994 from the Chargé d'Affaires A.I. of the Permanent Mission of France to the United Nations addressed to the Secretary General." United Nations Security Council. Accessed 4 July 2019. http://documents-dds-ny.un.org/doc/UNDOC/GEN/N94/318/41/img/N9431841.pdf?OpenElement.

*Le Figaro*. 2007. "Droits de l'homme: couac entre Kadhafi et Sarkozy". Accessed 15 June 2016. www.lefigaro.fr/international/2007/12/11/01003–20071211ARTFIG00420–kadhafi-suscite-des-remous-a-lassemblee-nationale. php.

Le Guilledoux, Dominique. 1998. "La visite de M. Mitterrand à Sarajevo: six heures dans la capitale bosniaque." *Le Monde*, 30 June. Accessed 26 October 2012. http://abonnes.lemonde.fr/cgi-bin/ACHATS/ARCHIVES/archives.cgi?ID= 2197ffc66e63dcdf87c8f06ea71e22e47608ffa74affb3d3.

*Le Monde*. 2011. "Tunisie: les propos 'effrayants' d'Alliot-Marie suscitent la polémique." Accessed 1 March 2019. https://www.lemonde.fr/afrique/article/

2011/01/13/tunisie-les-propos-effrayants-d-alliot-marie-suscitent-la-polemique_
    1465278_3212.html.

*Le Point.* 2011a. "La France reconnaît l'opposition comme 'représentant légitime
    du peuple libyen." Accessed 4 July 2019. www.lepoint.fr/monde/la-france-
    reconnait-l-opposition-comme-representant-legitime-du-peuple-libyen-
    10–03–2011–1304764_24.php.

*Le Point.* 2011b. "Michèle Alliot-Marie quitte le gouvernement." Accessed 1
    March 2019. https://www.lepoint.fr/politique/michele-alliot-marie-quitte-le-
    gouvernement-27-02-2011-1300259_20.php.

Leclerc, Raphael. 2013. "L'intervention au Mali sera positive pour la popular-
    ité de Hollande." *L'Express.* Accessed 15 January 2013. www.lexpress.fr/
    actualite/politique/l-intervention-au-mali-sera-positive-pour-la-popularite-de-
    hollande_1209888.html.

Léotard, François. 1995. "Les casques bleus français au service de la paix." In
    *La France et l'ONU depuis 1945*, edited by André Lewin. Condé-sur-Noreau:
    Arléa-Corlet.

*Les Echos.* 2015. "Syrie: Hollande insiste sur le départ de Bachar al-Assad."
    Accessed 25 May 2017. https://www.lesechos.fr/01/10/2015/lesechos.fr/
    021371497327_syrie–hollande-insiste-sur-le-depart-de-bachar-al-assad.htm
    – 47U5qQU0dli7DOkz.99.

*L'Express.* 2005. "La Bosnie, Mitterrand et moi." Accessed 15 January 2015. https://
    www.lexpress.fr/culture/livre/la-bosnie-mitterrand-et-moi_487407.html.

*L'Express.* 2007. "Sarkozy en vacances, répond aux journalistes." Accessed 4
    July 2019. www.lexpress.fr/actualite/politique/sarkozy-en-vacances-repond-
    aux-journalistes_465904.html.

*L'Express.* 2016. "Abus sexuels en Centrafrique: pour Hollande, 'l'honneur de la
    France serait engagé'." Accessed 15 March 2017. www.lexpress.fr/actualite/
    societe/abus-sexuels-en-centrafrique-pour-hollande-l-honneur-de-la-
    france-serait-engage_1778832.html.

Leymarie, Philippe. 2002. "L'éternel retour des militaires français en Afrique."
    Accessed 4 July 2019. www.monde-diplomatique.fr/2002/11/LEYMARIE/17052.

*Libération.* 2011. "Lundi sanglant en Libye: Sarkozy condamne 'l'usage inacceptable
    de la force'." Accessed 16 June 2015. www.liberation.fr/monde/2011/02/21/lundi-
    sanglant-en-libye-sarkozy-condamne-l-usage-inacceptable-de-la-force_716424.

Lombart, Laurent. 2007a. "François Mitterrand et le droit international: un tropisme
    personnel conjugué à une nécessité géopolitique." Institut François Mitterrand.
    Accessed 4 July 2019. www.mitterrand.org/Francois-Mitterrand-et-le-droit.html
    – nb51.

Lombart, Laurent. 2007b. "La politique extérieure du Président Jacques Chirac dans
    un monde américano-centré." Accessed 10 November 2014. www.afri-ct.org/
    La-politique-exterieure-du?lang=fr.

Long, Marceau. 1994. *Livre blanc sur la Défense*, edited by Ministère de la Défense.
    Paris: Ministère de la Défense.

Macleod, Alex. 1997. "French policy toward the war in the Former Yugoslavia: a
    bid for international leadership." *International Journal* 52 (2): 243–264.

Macleod, Alex. 2004. "Just defending national interests? Understanding French policy towards Iraq since the end of the Gulf War." *Journal of International Relations and Development* 7 (4): 356–387.

Macleod, Alex, and Catherine Voyer-Léger. 2004. "La France: d'une puissance moyenne à l'autre." *Études internationales* 35 (1): 73–96.

Madelin, Philippe. 2002. *Jacques Chirac: une biographie*: Paris: Flammarion.

Mallet, Jean-Claude, and Ministère de la Défense. 2008. "Défense et sécurité nationale: le livre blanc." Accessed 25 March 2015. www.ladocumentationfrancaise.fr/rapports-publics/084000341/.

Malone, David. 2006. *The International Struggle over Iraq: Politics in the UN Security Council 1980-2005*. Oxford: Oxford University Press.

McGreal, Chris. 2007. "France's shame?" *The Guardian*, 11 January. Accessed 16 June 2012. www.guardian.co.uk/world/2007/jan/11/rwanda.insideafrica/print.

McNulty, Mel. 2000. "French arms, war and genocide in Rwanda." *Crime, Law & Social Change* 33: 105–129.

McQueen, Carol. 2005. *Humanitarian Intervention and Safety Zones: Iraq, Bosnia, and Rwanda*. New York: Palgrave Macmillan.

Mearsheimer, John J. 1994. "The false promise of international institutions." *International Security* 19 (3): 5–49.

Melandri, Pierre. 2013. "La guerre d'Irak et la brouille franco-americaine." In *La politique étrangère de Jacques Chirac*, edited by Christian Lequesne and Maurice Vaisse. Paris: Éditions Riveneuve.

Mérimée, Jean-Bernard. 1994. "S/1994/734: letter dated 20 June 1994 from the Permanent Representative of France to the United Nations addressed to the Secretary-General." United Nations Security Council. Accessed 4 July 2019. www.undemocracy.com/S-1994–734.pdf.

Miller, Barbara. 2011. "Defiant Gaddafi issues chilling threat." Accessed 16 June 2015. www.abc.net.au/worldtoday/content/2011/s3146582.htm.

Ministère de la Défense. 2011a. "L'opération Harmattan." Accessed 15 June 2015. www.defense.gouv.fr/actualites/operations/l-operation-harmattan.

Ministère de la Défense. 2011b. "Le dispositif Harmattan en un coup d'oeil." Accessed 16 June 2015. www.defense.gouv.fr/air/dossiers/les-temps-forts-de-l-operation-harmattan-en-libye.

Ministère de la Défense. 2012. "Côte d'Ivoire: chronologie et repères historiques." Accessed 18 February 2015. www.defense.gouv.fr/operations/autres-operations/operations-achevees/operation-licorne-2002–2015/dossier-de-presentation-de-l-operation-licorne/cote-d-ivoire-chronologie-et-reperes-historiques.

Ministère de la Défense. 2013. "L'opération Boali." Accessed 20 November 2015. www.defense.gouv.fr/operations/autres-operations/operations-achevees/operation-boali-2002–2013/l-operation-boali.

Ministère de la Défense. 2014. "Les forces françaises en Côte d'Ivoire." Accessed 4 July 2019. www.defense.gouv.fr/operations/autres-operations/operations-achevees/operation-licorne-2002–2015/dossier-de-presentation-de-l-operation-licorne/les-forces-francaises-en-cote-d-ivoire.

Ministère de la Défense. 2015. "Dossier de presse: fin de l'opération Licorne, 22 septembre 2002 – 21 janvier 2015." Accessed 4 July 2019. www.defense. gouv.fr/operations/autres-operations/operations-achevees/operation-licorne-2002–2015/dossier-de-presentation-de-l-operation-licorne/dossier-de-presentation-de-l-operation-licorne-aux-forces-francaises-en-cote-d-ivoire.

Ministère de la Défense. 2016. "Dossier de presse: opération Sangaris." Accessed 4 July 2019. https://www.defense.gouv.fr/.../20160713+DP+Sangaris+VF.pdf.

Ministère de la Défense. 2017. "Opération Barkhane." Accessed 15 August 2015. www.defense.gouv.fr/operations/sahel/dossier-de-presentation-de-l-operation-barkhane/operation-barkhane.

Mitterrand, François. 1981. "Discours de M. François Mitterrand, Président de la République, devant le monument de la Révolution à Mexico, mardi 20 octobre 1981 (discours dit de Cancun)." Vie Publique. Accessed 4 July 2019. http://discours.vie-publique.fr/notices/817144500.html.

Mitterrand, François. 1987. "Il n'y peut y avoir de repos … ." In Le devoir d'ingérence: peut-on les laisser mourir?, edited by Mario Bettati and Bernard Kouchner. Paris: Denoël.

Mitterrand, François. 1988. "Discours de M. François Mitterrand, Président de la République, devant l'Assemblée générale des Nations Unies." Accessed 6 October 2015. http://discours.vie-publique.fr/notices/887022600.html.

Mitterrand, François. 1990. "Discours de La Baule." Accessed 4 July 2019. www1. rfi.fr/actufr/articles/037/article_20103.asp.

Mitterrand, François. 1992. "Conférence de presse de M. François Mitterrand, Président de la République, sur l'application des sanctions et l'aide humanitaire à la Yougoslavie, l'éventualité d'une intervention militaire, le siège des institutions communautaires, et la ratification du Traité de Maastricht, Lisbonne le 27 juin 1992." Vie Publique. Accessed 4 July 2019. http://discours.vie-publique.fr/notices/927009000.html.

Mitterrand, François. 1995. "Un role essential, un lieu unique." In La France et l'ONU depuis 1945, edited by A. Lewin. Condé-sur-Noireau: Arléa-Corlet.

Morgenthau, Hans Joachim, and Kenneth W. Thompson. 1985. Politics Among Nations: The Struggle for Power and Peace. New York: Knopf.

Morillon, Philippe. 1998. "The military aspects of field operations." In United Nations Peace-Keeping Operations: A Guide to French Policies, edited by Brigitte Stern. Tokyo: United Nations University Press.

Mucyo, Jean de Dieu, Jérôme Ngendahimana, Géraldine Bakashyaka, Alice Rugira, José Kagabo, Jean-Paul Kimonyo, and Jean-Damascène Bizimana. 2008. Rapport de la Commission Nationale indépendante chargée de rassembler les preuves montrant l'implication de l'état français dans le génocide perpetré au Rwanda en 1994. Commission Nationale Indépendante, République du Rwanda. Accessed 4 July 2019. http://mucyoreport.rw/.

Muehlenbeck, Philip E. 2012. Betting on the Africans: John F. Kennedy's Courting of African Nationalist Leaders. Oxford: Oxford University Press.

Nardin, Terry, and Melissa Williams. 2006. Humanitarian Intervention. New York: New York University Press.

NATO. 2014. "Peace support operations in Bosnia and Herzegovina." North Atlantic Treaty Organization. Accessed 25 February 2015. www.nato.int/cps/en/natolive/topics_52122.htm.

NATO. 2015. "ISAF's mission in Afghanistan (2001–2014)." North Atlantic Treaty Organization. Accessed 20 November 2015. www.nato.int/cps/en/natohq/topics_69366.htm.

NATO. 2018. "NATO's role in Kosovo." North Atlantic Treaty Organization. Accessed 19 February 2019. https://www.nato.int/cps/en/natolive/topics_48818.htm.

Nougayrède, Natalie, Philippe Bolopion and Thomas Ferenczi. 2008. "Birmanie: vif débat sur la 'responsabilité de protéger.'" Accessed 28 May 2012. http://abonnes.lemonde.fr/cgi-bin/ACHATS/ARCHIVES/archives.cgi?ID=d42e9943ca36afde010671b4d7b11e94c7bd10975fc4896e&print=1.

Nouzille, Vincent. 2010. *Les dossiers de la CIA sur la France*. Paris: Fayard.

Obama, Barack, David Cameron and Nicolas Sarkozy. 2011. "Libya's pathway to peace." Accessed 16 June 2015. www.nytimes.com/2011/04/15/opinion/15iht-edlibya15.html?_r=0.

Pape, Robert. 2012. "When duty calls: a pragmatic standard of humanitarian intervention." *International Security* 37 (1): 41–80.

Permanent Mission of France to the United Nations. 2019. "France and the UN Reform." Accessed 10 September 2019. https://onu.delegfrance.org/France-and-the-UN-reform-8615.

Petiteville, Franck. 2006. *La politique internationale de l'Union européenne*: Paris: Presses de Sciences Po.

Ploton, Frédéric. 2003. *Chronique d'une guerre annoncée: Irak: 20 mars – 9 Avril 2003*. Paris: France-Loisirs.

Priest, Dana. 1999. "France played skeptic on Kosovo attacks." *Washington Post*. Accessed 2 January 2014. www.washingtonpost.com/wp-srv/national/daily/sept99/airwar20.htm.

Prunier, Gérard. 1997. *The Rwanda Crisis: History of a Genocide*. London: Hurst & Company.

Quilès, Paul. 1998. *Rapport d'information sur les opérations militaires menées par la France, d'autres pays et l'ONU au Rwanda entre 1990 et 1994*, La Mission d'Information de la Commission de la Défense Nationale et des Forces Armées et de la Commission des Affaires Étrangères, Assemblée Nationale. Accessed 4 July 2019. www.assemblee-nationale.fr/11/rap-info/i2022.asp.

Quilès, Paul, and François Lamy. 1999. "Rapport d'information sur le conflit au Kosovo". Assemblée Nationale. Accessed 17 July 2019. www.assemblee-nationale.fr/rap-info/i2022.asp.

Ralph, Jason. 2018. "Pragmatic constructivist ethics and the responsibility to protect". *International Organization* 72: 173–203.

Ramsbotham, Olivier, and Tom Woodhouse. 1999. *Encyclopedia of International Peacekeeping Operations*. Santa Barbara: ABC-CLIO.

Renou, Xavier. 2002. "A new French policy for Africa?" *Journal of Contemporary African Studies* 20 (1): 5–28.

Revel, Jean-François. 1979. "Le devoir d'ingérence." *L'Express*, 16 June.

Rieff, David. 2011. "R2P, R.I.P." *New York Times*. Accessed 30 August 2016. www. nytimes.com/2011/11/08/opinion/r2p-rip.html?mcubz=1.

Risse, Thomas, and Kathryn Sikkink. 1999. "The socialisation of international human rights norms into domestic practices." In Thomas Risse, Stephen C. Ropp, and Kathryn Sikkink, *The Power of Human Rights: International Norms and Domestic Change*. Cambridge: Cambridge University Press.

Rollet, Cédric. 2006. *De la FORPRONU a l'IFOR: la France en Bosnie 1992–1996*. Centre de Doctrine d'Emploi des Forces. Accessed 4 July 2019. www.cdef. terre.defense.gouv.fr.

Saint-Exupéry, Patrick. 1998. "France-Rwanda: le syndrome de Fachoda." *Le Figaro*, 13 January. Accessed 28 August 2012. http://recherche.lefigaro.fr/recherche/access/lefigaro_fr.php?archive=BszTm8dCk78Jk8uwiNq9T8CoS9GECSHiM-Dcwz5%2B7uJk4cgD1FYoCGuvD0%2BbxJetQ0yiEsbJZVduZy6BaSOXVcw%3D%3D.

Sarkozy, Nicolas. 2006. "Déclaration de M. Nicolas Sarkozy, ministre de l'intérieur et de l'aménagement du territoire, sur la démocratie au Bénin et sur l'établissement de nouvelles relations entre la France et l'Afrique, Cotonou le 19 mai 2006." Accessed 4 July 2019. http://discours.vie-publique.fr/notices/063001811.html.

Sarkozy, Nicolas. 2007a. "Discours de Nicolas Sarkozy devant le Congrès des États-Unis." Accessed 4 July 2019. www.voltairenet.org/article152875.html.

Sarkozy, Nicolas. 2007b. "Discours de victoire de Nicolas Sarkozy le dimanche 6 mai 2007." Accessed 4 July 2019. www.lepoint.fr/politique/election-presidentielle-2012/election-presidentielle-2007-le-discours-de-victoire-de-nicolas-sarkozy-21–04–2011–1322298_324.php.

Sarkozy, Nicolas. 2007c. "Le discours de Dakar de Nicolas Sarkozy." Accessed 4 July 2019. www.lemonde.fr/afrique/article/2007/11/09/le-discours-de-dakar_976786_3212.html – AvXx09DL3WOgYzMX.99.

Sarkozy, Nicolas. 2007d. "Le discours de politique étrangère de Nicolas Sarkozy." Accessed 20 May 2015. www.lemonde.fr/societe/article/2007/08/27/le-discours-de-politique-etrangere-de-m-sarkozy-integralite_947776_3224.html – ZOoDVZtQ2TmIdYp7.99.

Sarkozy, Nicolas. 2007e. "Mes objectifs en matière de politique internationale." *Politique africaine* 1 (105): 149–152.

Sarkozy, Nicolas. 2007f. "Mon projet: ensemble, tout devient possible." Accessed 27 October 2014. http://perso.limsi.fr/pointal/_media/divers:monprojet.pdf.

Sarkozy, Nicolas. 2007g. "Nicolas Sarkozy, discours à Bercy (29/04/07)." Accessed 4 July 2019. https://www.singulier.eu/textes/reference/texte/pdf/NS-Bercy.pdf.

Sarkozy, Nicolas. 2008. "Discours de M. le Président de la République devant le Parlement Sud-Africain, Le Cap, jeudi 28 février 2008." Accessed 4 July 2019. www.diplomatie.gouv.fr/fr/IMG/pdf/PARLEMENT_AS.pdf.

Sarkozy, Nicolas. 2009a. "Allocution de M. Nicolas Sarkozy, Conseil de l'Atlantique Nord, Strasbourg, samedi 4 avril 2009." Accessed 4 July 2019. 04.04_Allocution_du_PR_OTAN.pdf.

Sarkozy, Nicolas. 2009b. "'Codiriger plutôt que subir': extraits du discours prononcé par Nicolas Sarkozy le 11 mars devant la Fondation pour la recherche stratégique, officialisant le retour de la France dans le commandement intégré de l'Alliance." Accessed 4 June 2015. www.lemonde.fr/politique/article/2009/03/12/le-discours-de-nicolas-sarkozy-sur-l-otan_1166786_823448.html – RbIhEF1cbUX4VGUW.99.

Sarkozy, Nicolas. 2009c. "Lettre de M. Nicolas Sarkozy, Président de la République, adressée aux chefs d'état et de gouvernement de l'Alliance atlantique, sur le retour de la France dans le commandement intégré de l'OTAN, le 19 mars 2009." Accessed 4 July 2019. http://discours.vie-publique.fr/notices/097000901.html.

Sarkozy, Nicolas. 2011a. "Conférence des Ambassadeurs: discours de M. Sarkozy (31 août 2011)." Accessed 4 July 2019. www.rpfrance-otan.org/Conference-des-Ambassadeurs.

Sarkozy, Nicolas. 2011b. "Réunion sur la Libye à l'ONU: Discours du Président de la République." Accessed 11 May 2015. www.rpfrance-otan.org/reunion-sur-la-Libye-a-l-ONU.

Sarkozy, Nicolas. 2011c. "Verbatim – Sarkozy justifie l'intervention militaire en Libye." Accessed 15 June 2015. www.lepoint.fr/monde/verbatim-sarkozy-justifie-l-intervention-militaire-en-libye-19–03–2011–1308723_24.php.

Saul, Samir. 1995. "La France et la crise du Golfe 1990–1991: analyse politico-économique d'un virage." Études internationales 26 (1): 83–111.

Schmidt, Elizabeth. 2013. Foreign Intervention in Africa: From the Cold War to the War on Terror. Cambridge: Cambridge University Press.

Schmitz, Hans Peter, and Kathryn Sikkink. 2002. "International human rights." In Handbook of International Relations, edited by Walter Carlsnaes, Thomas Risse-Kappen and Beth A. Simmons. Thousand Oaks, CA, and London: SAGE.

Segaunes, Natalie, and Henri Vernet. 2007. "Rama Yade: 'La France n'est pas un paillasson.'" Accessed 4 July 2019. www.leparisien.fr/une/rama-yade-la-france-n-est-pas-un-paillasson-10–12–2007–3291409068.php.

Sicurelli, Daniela. 2010. The European Union's Africa Policies: Norms, Interests, and Impact. Farnham, Surrey: Ashgate Publishing Ltd.

Sikkink, Kathryn. 1993. "The power of principled ideas: human rights policies in the United States and Western Europe." In Ideas and Foreign Policy: Beliefs, Institutions, and Political Change, edited by Judith Goldstein and Robert O. Keohane. Ithaca: Cornell University Press.

Sikkink, Kathryn. 1998. "Transnational politics, International Relations theory, and human rights." PS: Political Science and Politics 31 (3): 517–523.

Smouts, Marie Claude. 1997. "Les aspects politiques des opérations de maintien de la paix." In La vision française des opérations de maintien de la paix, edited by Yves Daudet, Philippe Morillon and M.-C. Smouts. Paris: Monchrestien.

Smouts, Marie Claude. 1998. "Political aspects of peace-keeping operations." In United Nations Peace-Keeping Operations: A Guide to French Policies, edited by Brigitte Stern. Tokyo: United Nations University Press.

Soares, Ursula. 2012. "Opération militaire au Mali: la France n'interviendra pas 'elle-même.'" RFI Afrique. Accessed 25 May 2017. www.rfi.fr/afrique/20121113-operation-militaire-mali-france-interviendra-pas-elle-meme-union-africaine-addis-abeba-conseil-securite.

Soulet, Jean-Francois. 2012. "France en Bosnie (1992–1995): il y a vingt ans … l'exceptionnelle implication de la France dans le conflit bosniaque." Accessed 4 July 2019. www.diploweb.com/spip.php?page=imprimer&id_article=964.

Stark, Hans. 2002. "Paris, Berlin et Londres vers l'émergence d'un directoire européen?" *Politique étrangère* 67 (4): 967–982.

Staunton, Eglantine. 2016. "Two decades later: understanding the French response to the Rwandan genocide." *Modern & Contemporary France* 24 (3): 299–315.

Staunton, Eglantine. 2018. "France and the responsibility to protect: a tale of two norms". *International Relations* 32 (3): 366–387.

Steans, Jill. 2010. *An Introduction to International Relations Theory: Perspectives and Themes*. New York: Longman.

Subtil, Marie Pierre. 1994. "Dans l'attente d'une décision des Nations unies: le projet d'intervention française au Rwanda suscite de plus en plus de critiques." Accessed 28 February 2019. https://www.lemonde.fr/archives/article/1994/06/23/dans-l-attente-…on_francaise_au_rwanda_suscite_de_plus_en_plus_de_critiques&xtcr=2.

Sutton, Michael. 2007. *France and the Construction of Europe, 1944–2007: The Geopolitical Imperative*. New York: Berghahn Books.

Tardy, Thierry. 1999. *La France et la gestion des conflits yougoslaves (1991–1995): enjeux et leçons d'une opération de maintien de la paix de l'ONU*. Paris: Bruylant.

Tardy, Thierry. 2002. "La France et l'ONU, entre singularité et ambivalence." *Politique étrangère* 67 (4): 931–947.

Tardy, Thierry. 2003. "France and the US: the inevitable clash?" *International Journal* 59 (1): 105–126.

Tesón, Fernando R. 2005. "Ending Tyranny in Iraq." *Ethics & International Affairs* 19 (2): 1–20.

Thiam, Assane. 2008. "La politique africaine de Nicolas Sarkozy: rupture ou continuité?" *Politique étrangère* 4 (Hiver): 873–884.

Tiersky, Ronald. 2008. *France Returns to Center Stage*. Philadelphia: Current History, Inc.

Tisdall, Simon. 2013. "France in the Central African Republic is latest use of 'Hollande doctrine'." Accessed 4 July 2019. www.theguardian.com/commentisfree/2013/dec/05/france-central-african-republic-hollande-doctrine.

Torrelli, Maurice. 1992. "De l'assistance à l'ingérence humanitaires?" *International Review of the Red Cross* 74 (795): 238–258.

Tourard, Hélène. 2000. "La France dans la crise du Kosovo: cohabitation et processus décisionnel." *Annuaire français de relations internationales* 1: 197–205.

Tran, Mark. 2013. "Mali: a guide to the conflict." Accessed 25 May 2017. https://www.theguardian.com/world/2013/jan/16/mali-guide-to-the-conflict.

Treacher, Adrian. 2000. "A case of reinvention: France and military intervention in the 1990s." *International Peacekeeping* 7 (2): 23–40.

UN. 1945. "Charter of the United Nations." United Nations. Accessed 17 March 2014. https://www.un.org/en/documents/charter/.

UN. 1990. "Summary of contributions to peacekeeping operations by countries."
United Nations. Accessed 4 July 2019. https://peacekeeping.un.org/en/troop-
and-police-contributors.

UN. 1991. "Summary of contributions to peacekeeping operations by countries." United Nations. Accessed 4 July 2019. https://peacekeeping.un.org/en/
troop-and-police-contributors.

UN. 1992. "Summary of contributions to peacekeeping operations by countries." United Nations. Accessed 4 July 2019. https://peacekeeping.un.org/en/
troop-and-police-contributors.

UN. 1993. "Summary of contributions to peacekeeping operations by countries." United Nations. Accessed 4 July 2019. https://peacekeeping.un.org/en/
troop-and-police-contributors.

UN. 1994. "Summary of contributions to peacekeeping operations by countries." United Nations. Accessed 4 July 2019. https://peacekeeping.un.org/en/
troop-and-police-contributors.

UN. 1995. "Summary of contributions to peacekeeping operations by countries." United Nations. Accessed 4 July 2019. https://peacekeeping.un.org/en/
troop-and-police-contributors.

UN. 1996a. "Somalia – UNOSOM II." United Nations. Accessed 4 July 2019.
www.un.org/Depts/DPKO/Missions/unosom2p.htm.

UN. 1996b. "Summary of contributions to peacekeeping operations by countries." United Nations. Accessed 4 July 2019. https://peacekeeping.un.org/en/
troop-and-police-contributors.

UN. 1997. "Summary of contributions to peacekeeping operations by countries." United Nations. Accessed 4 July 2019. https://peacekeeping.un.org/en/
troop-and-police-contributors.

UN. 1998. "Summary of contributions to peacekeeping operations by countries." United Nations. Accessed 4 July 2019. https://peacekeeping.un.org/en/
troop-and-police-contributors.

UN. 1999. "Summary of contributions to peacekeeping operations by countries." United Nations. Accessed 4 July 2019. https://peacekeeping.un.org/en/
troop-and-police-contributors.

UN. 2000. "Summary of contributions to peacekeeping operations by countries." United Nations. Accessed 4 July 2019. https://peacekeeping.un.org/en/
troop-and-police-contributors.

UN. 2001. "Summary of contributions to peacekeeping operations by countries." United Nations. Accessed 4 July 2019. https://peacekeeping.un.org/en/
troop-and-police-contributors.

UN. 2002. "Summary of contributions to peacekeeping operations by countries." United Nations. Accessed 4 July 2019. https://peacekeeping.un.org/en/
troop-and-police-contributors.

UN. 2003. "Summary of contributions to peacekeeping operations by countries." United Nations. Accessed 4 July 2019. https://peacekeeping.un.org/en/
troop-and-police-contributors.

UN. 2004. "Summary of contributions to peacekeeping operations by countries." United Nations. Accessed 4 July 2019. https://peacekeeping.un.org/en/troop-and-police-contributors.

UN. 2005. "Summary of contributions to peacekeeping operations by countries." United Nations. Accessed 4 July 2019. https://peacekeeping.un.org/en/troop-and-police-contributors.

UN. 2006. "Summary of contributions to peacekeeping operations by countries." United Nations. Accessed 4 July 2019. https://peacekeeping.un.org/en/troop-and-police-contributors.

UN. 2007. "Summary of contributions to peacekeeping operations by countries." United Nations. Accessed 4 July 2019. https://peacekeeping.un.org/en/troop-and-police-contributors.

UN. 2008. "Summary of contributions to peacekeeping operations by countries." United Nations. Accessed 4 July 2019. https://peacekeeping.un.org/en/troop-and-police-contributors.

UN. 2009. "Summary of contributions to peacekeeping operations by countries." Accessed 4 July 2019. https://peacekeeping.un.org/en/troop-and-police-contributors.

UN. 2010. "Summary of contributions to peacekeeping operations by countries." United Nations. Accessed 4 July 2019. https://peacekeeping.un.org/en/troop-and-police-contributors.

UN. 2011. "Summary of contributions to peacekeeping operations by countries." Accessed 4 July 2019. https://peacekeeping.un.org/en/troop-and-police-contributors.

UN. 2012. "Summary of contributions to peacekeeping operations by countries." United Nations. Accessed 4 July 2019. https://peacekeeping.un.org/en/troop-and-police-contributors.

UN General Assembly. 1988. "A/RES/43/131: humanitarian assistance to victims of natural disasters and similar emergency situations." United Nations. Accessed 4 July 2019. www.un.org/documents/ga/res/43/a43r131.htm.

UN General Assembly. 1990. "A/RES/45/100: humanitarian assistance to victims of natural disasters and similar emergency situations." United Nations. Accessed 4 July 2019. http://documents.un.org/basic_E.html.

UN General Assembly. 1991. "A/RES/46/182: strengthening of the coordination of humanitarian emergency assistance of the United Nations." United Nations. Accessed 7 October 2013. www.un.org/documents/ga/res/46/a46r182.htm.

UN General Assembly. 2004. "A more secure world: our shared responsibility. Report of the Secretary-General's High-Level Panel on Threats, Challenges and Change." United Nations. Accessed 4 July 2019. https://documents-dds-ny.un.org/doc/UNDOC/GEN/N04/602/31/PDF/N0460231.pdf?OpenElement.

UN General Assembly. 2005. "A/60/L.1: 2005 World Summit outcome." United Nations. Accessed 4 July 2019. hwww.un.org/en/documents/index.html.

UN General Assembly. 2009. "A/63/PV.97: sixty-third session, 97th plenary meeting." United Nations. Accessed 25 March 2015. http://documents.un.org/welcome.asp?language=E.

UN General Assembly 2011. "A/65/877–S/2011/393: the role of regional and sub-regional arrangements in implementing the responsibility to protect." United Nations. Accessed 4 July 2019. https://undocs.org/A/65/877.

UN Security Council. 1991a. "S/22442: letter dated 4 April 1991 from the Chargé d'Affaires of the Permanent Mission of France to the United Nations addressed to the President of the Security Council." United Nations Security Council. Accessed 4 July 2019. http://documents.un.org/basic_E.html.

UN Security Council. 1991b. "S/PV.2982: 2982th Meeting of the United Nations Security Council." United Nations Security Council. Accessed 4 July 2019. http://documents.un.org/basic_E.html.

UN Security Council. 1991c. "S/RES/688: Resolution 688." United Nations Security Council. Accessed 4 July 2019. www.un.org/Docs/scres/1991/scres91.htm.

UN Security Council. 1992a. "S/PV.3069: 3069th meeting of the United Nations Security Council." United Nations Security Council. Accessed 15 June 2012. http://documents.un.org/basic_E.html.

UN Security Council. 1992b. "S/PV.3082: 3082nd meeting of the United Nations Security Council." United Nations Security Council. Accessed 15 June 2012. http://documents.un.org/basic_E.html.

UN Security Council. 1992c. "S/RES/794: Resolution 794." Accessed 15 June 2012. http://documents.un.org/basic_E.html.

UN Security Council. 1993a. "S/PV.3135: 3135th meeting of the United Nations Security Council." United Nations Security Council. Accessed 15 June 2012. http://documents.un.org/basic_E.html.

UN Security Council. 1993b. "S/PV.3163: 3163rd meeting of the United Nations Security Council." United Nations Security Council. Accessed 15 June 2012. http://documents.un.org/basic_E.html.

UN Security Council. 1993c. "S/PV.3175: 3175th meeting of the United Nations Security Council." United Nations Security Council. Accessed 15 June 2012. http://documents.un.org/basic_E.html.

UN Security Council. 1993d. "S/PV.3191: 3191st meeting of the United Nations Security Council." United Nations Security Council. Accessed 15 June 2012. http://documents.un.org/basic_E.html.

UN Security Council. 1993e. "S/PV.3200: 3200th meeting of the United Nations Security Council." United Nations Security Council. Accessed 15 June 2012. http://documents.un.org/basic_E.html.

UN Security Council. 1993f. "S/PV.3217: 3217th meeting of the United Nations Security Council." United Nations Security Council. Accessed 15 June 2012. http://documents.un.org/basic_E.html.

UN Security Council. 1993g. "S/PV.3228: 3228th meeting of the United Nations Security Council." United Nations Security Council. Accessed 15 June 2012. http://documents.un.org/basic_E.html.

UN Security Council. 1993h. "S/PV.3234: 3234th meeting of the United Nations Security Council." United Nations Security Council. Accessed 15 June 2012. http://documents.un.org/basic_E.html.

UN Security Council. 1993i. "S/RES/819: Resolution 819." United Nations Security Council. Accessed 15 June 2012. http://documents.un.org/basic_E.html.

UN Security Council. 1993j. "S/RES/824: Resolution 824." United Nations Security Council. Accessed 15 June 2012. http://documents.un.org/basic_E.html.

UN Security Council. 1993k. "S/RES/860: Resolution 860." United Nations Security Council. Accessed 15 June 2012. http://documents.un.org/basic_E.html.

UN Security Council. 1993l. "S/RES/872: Resolution 872." United Nations Security Council. Accessed 15 June 2012. http://documents.un.org/basic_E.html.

UN Security Council. 1994a. "S/PV.3392: 3392nd meeting of the United Nations Security Council." United Nations Security Council. Accessed 4 July 2019. http://documents.un.org/basic_E.html.

UN Security Council. 1994b. "S/RES/929: Resolution 929." United Nations Security Council. Accessed 4 July 2019. www.un.org/Docs/scres/1994/scres94.htm.

UN Security Council. 1995. "S/RES/998: Resolution 998." United Nations Security Council. Accessed 15 June 2012. http://documents.un.org/basic_E.html.

UN Security Council. 1999. "S/PV.4011: 4011st meeting of the United Nations Security Council." United Nations Security Council. Accessed 4 July 2019. http://documents.un.org/basic_E.html.

UN Security Council. 2001. "S/RES/1386: Resolution 1386." United Nations Security Council. Accessed 25 February 2015. www.un.org/Docs/scres/2001/sc2001.htm.

UN Security Council. 2003. "S/RES/1464: Resolution 1464." United Nations Security Council. Accessed 20 February 2015. www.un.org/Docs/scres/2003/sc2003.htm.

UN Security Council. 2004a. "S/RES/1528: Resolution 1528." United Nations Security Council. Accessed 4 July 2019. www.un.org/en/sc/documents/resolutions/2004.shtml.

UN Security Council. 2004b. "S/RES/1559: Resolution 1559." United Nations Security Council. Accessed 4 July 2019. www.un.org/en/sc/documents/resolutions/2004.shtml.

UN Security Council. 2004c. "S/RES/1572: Resolution 1572." United Nations Security Council. Accessed 4 July 2019. www.un.org/en/sc/documents/resolutions/2004.shtml.

UN Security Council. 2004d. "S/PV.5100: 5100th meeting." United Nations Security Council. Accessed 4 July 2019. https://www.securitycouncilreport.org/wp-content/uploads/POC%20SPV5100.pdf.

UN Security Council. 2009. "S/PV.6216: 6216th meeting of the United Nations Security Council." United Nations Security Council. Accessed 23 March 2015. http://documents.un.org/basic_E.html.

UN Security Council. 2011a. "S/PV.6498: 6498th meeting of the United Nations Security Council." United Nations Security Council. Accessed 24 March 2015. http://documents.un.org/basic_E.html.

UN Security Council. 2011b. "S/PV.6621: 6621st meeting of the United Nations Security Council." United Nations Security Council. Accessed 24 March 2015. http://documents.un.org/basic_E.html.

UN Security Council. 2011c. "S/RES/1970: Resolution 1970." United Nations Security Council. Accessed 23 March 2015. http://documents.un.org/basic_E.html.

UN Security Council. 2011d. "S/RES/1973: Resolution 1973." United Nations Security Council. Accessed 24 March 2015. http://documents.un.org/basic_E.html.

UN Security Council. 2012. "Resolution 2085." United Nations Security Council. Accessed 13 August 2015. www.un.org/en/ga/search/view_doc.asp?symbol=S/RES/2085(2012).

UN Security Council. 2013. "S/RES/2127: Resolution 2127." United Nations Security Council. Accessed 24 March 2015. http://documents.un.org/basic_E.html.

UN Security Council. 2015. "Resolution 2199." United Nations Security Council. Accessed 4 July 2019. https://documents-dds-ny.un.org/doc/UNDOC/GEN/N15/040/28/pdf/N1504028.pdf?OpenElement.

UN Security Council. 2017a. "Resolution 2347." United Nations Security Council. Accessed 4 July 2019. http://documents.un.org/basic_E.html.

UN Security Council. 2017b. "S.Pv/7907: 7907th Meeting of the UN Security Council." United Nations Security Council. Accessed 4 July 2019. https://documents-dds-ny.un.org/doc/UNDOC/PRO/N17/078/34/pdf/N1707834.pdf?OpenElement.

Utley, Rachel. 2000. *The French Defence Debate: Consensus and Continuity in the Mitterrand Era*. London: Macmillan Press.

Vaïsse, Justin. 2003. "Making sense of French foreign policy." Accessed 30 January 2019. https://www.brookings.edu/opinions/making-sense-of-french-foreign-policy/.

Vaughn, Jocelyn, and Tim Dunne. 2015. "Leading from the front: America, Libya and the localisation of R2P." *Cooperation and Conflict* 50 (1): 29–49.

Védrine, Hubert. 1996. *Les mondes de François Mitterrand: à l'Élysée 1981–1995*. Paris: Fayard.

Védrine, Hubert. 2000. "Droit d'ingérence, démocratie, sanctions: refonder la politique étrangère française." Accessed 10 January 2014. www.monde-diplomatique.fr/2000/12/VEDRINEs/14576.

Védrine, Hubert. 2002. "Cohabitation, Europe: comment se fabrique la politique étrangère?" *Politique étrangère* 67 (4): 863–877.

Védrine, Hubert. 2009. *Le temps des chimères: articles, préfaces et conférences (2003–2009)*. Paris: Fayard.

Vie Publique. 2011. "La politique de défense: chronologie." Accessed 2 November 2012. www.vie-publique.fr/politiques-publiques/politique-defense/chronologie/.

Waltz, Kenneth N. 1979. *Theory of International Politics*. New York: McGraw-Hill.

Weber, Henri. 1999. "Retour sur la guerre du Kosovo: entretien avec Hubert Védrine." *La revue socialiste* 2: 22–43.

Weiss, Thomas G. 2012a. *Humanitarian Intervention*. 2nd edn. Cambridge: Polity Press.

Weiss, Thomas G. 2012b. "Humanitarian intervention." In *An Introduction to International Relations*, edited by Richard Devetak, Anthony Burke and Jim George. Cambridge: Cambridge University Press.

Weldes, Jutta. 1996. "Constructing national interests." *European Journal of International Relations* 2 (3): 275–318.

Western European Union. 1992. "Petersberg ministerial declaration." Accessed 4 July 2019. http://eeas.europa.eu/csdp/about-csdp/petersberg/index_en.htm.

Wheeler, Nicholas J. 2000. *Saving Strangers: Humanitarian Intervention in International Society.* Oxford: Oxford University Press.

Wheeler, Nicholas J. 2003. "The humanitarian responsibilities of sovereignty: explaining the development of a new norm of military intervention for humanitarian purpose in international society." In *Humanitarian Intervention and International Relations*, edited by Jennifer Welsh. New York: Oxford University Press.

Wiener, Antje. 2014. *A Theory of Contestation.* New York: Springer.

Wilton, Robert. 2008. "The beginning and the end of humanitarian intervention: Kosovo 1999." *Defense & Security Analysis* 24 (4): 363–380.

Zic, Zoran. 2000. "French foreign policy elites and the crises in the former Yugoslavia." *Perspectives on Political Science* 29 (1): 17–22.

Ziegler, Charles E. 2016. "Special issue: critical perspectives on the responsibility to protect: BRICS and beyond." *International Relations* 30 (3): 262–277.

Zuqian, Zhang. 2002. "La politique étrangère de la France entre continuité et ajustements post-guerre froide." *Revue internationale et stratégique* 45 (1): 113–120.

# Index

EU authorised representative for GPSR:
Easy Access System Europe, Mustamäe tee 50,
10621 Tallinn, Estonia
gpsr.requests@easproject.com

www.ingramcontent.com/pod-product-compliance
Lightning Source LLC
Chambersburg PA
CBHW070844300326
41935CB00039B/1440